MY FATHER'S
DAUGHTER

As we walk through the reading corridors of her life, we are delighted as she strikes match stick after match stick to illuminate extremely touching accounts of failings and risings, struggles and achievements, scandals and honour as well as survival strategies that resonate for a lot of people. Another thing that stands out in the book is Onyeka's imaginative and recollection abilities. She tells her story and the reader is deeply immersed in her experiences and reality.

In "My Father's Daughter", we also read about starvation and death, opportunities and hope, gratitude and ingratitude, excess joy and deep-rooted pain, life and death, wealth and squandered riches, family and extended relationship ties and numerous adventures.

Ifeoma Chibogwu
http://www.ifeomaspeakstv.com/

Now, I am confused. Which is better? Is it Onyeka the singer or Onyeka the writer? To me the One Love crooner is as good a writer as she is a singer. Or better still, her prose is as melodious and captivating as her music. I am impressed by her audacity and frankness in telling it all, not just her personal history, but capturing the Nigerian narrative as witnessed by a 14 year old watching her country ravaged by civil war.

Onyeka writes like a journalist with a good news sense. Everywhere you touch there is news. News about Onyeka's encounter with historical figures from Chief MKO Abiola to Gen. Sani Abacha to Fela Anikulapo-Kuti to an impressive list of front page newsmakers.

Mike Awoyinfa
Nigerian journalist and writer.

Onyeka Onwenu was born in Port Harcourt in 1952. After her education in Nigeria and the United States, she returned to her country of birth with a bang, making waves as a frontline actress, broadcaster, singer-songwriter, public servant and politician.

My Father's Daughter is a riveting story that tells all without being a kiss-and-tell. It opens a window of revelation on the hitherto untold story of Onyeka's marriage and family life. It is at once a personal story and a contemporary history of Nigeria that critically analyses the Nigerian civil war, the hopes that propelled Biafra, and how the flame of the new republic was extinguished

This autobiography, the like of which has never before been written by a Nigerian, details personal tragedy and glorious triumphs, national political chicanery and their adverse consequences on the entity. It is a mirror on the country's entertainment industry, its successes and scandals, as well as the dubious role of the media in it all.

My Father's Daughter blazes a new trail in the art of the memoir that is guaranteed to command countless adherents.

Chuks Iloegbunam
Veteran Journalist and Publisher.

My Fathers Daughter is a riveting narration of Onyeka Onwenus enthralling journey through life. We are held captive as she takes us into her world – from the heart-warming affection of her father to living through the anguish of the Nigeria-Biafra war, from remarkable mothers love to family intrigues, from feminism to a career that has put her in the limelight for decades. Her reflections and reviews are expressive and stroke our senses; nothing is left out.

This book is deeply personal and emotional; it is about strength of purpose in the face of adversity, the struggle to overcome seething obstacles and the tenacity in surviving the odds. Interesting and vibrant, Onyekas story is laced with wit and the underlying humour is infectious.

Provocative and audacious, Onyeka Onwenu gives gripping details of her trials and triumphs- and everything in between – as she shares diverse experiences from her childhood, the travails of being a performing artiste, personal encounters with eminent personalities, and the lessons learned that have shaped her life. We are taken through the agony of her dark moments, the thrill of her successes, and her unwavering awe-inspiring trust in God.

In descriptive and pulsating detail, she talks about being a wife, a mother and breadwinner, of being a woman with a vision and purpose. She tells us about her relationship with her father, the qualities she inherited from him and the strength of character of her mother. It is a story about life, love and living.

Onyeka Onwenu's passion for her country, Nigeria, goes beyond patriotism. In this book, we read how she challenged and defied the status quo through her work in government, her career as a journalist and as one of the country's foremost musicians. It was daunting and thought-provoking, yet with a clear message of hope.

My Fathers Daughter is a compelling story of strength, determination and integrity. This is Onyeka Onwenu's story, and she tells it well. This is her truth.

She is, indeed, her father's daughter and her mother's legacy.

Ngozi Osu,
Book Editor & Literary Consultant

MY FATHER'S
DAUGHTER

ONYEKA ONWENU

origami

Parrésia Publishers Ltd.
82, Allen Avenue, Ikeja, Lagos, Nigeria.
+2348154582178, +2348062392145
origami@parresia.com.ng
www.parresia.com.ng

ISBN: 978-978-53425-8-1

Printed in Nigeria by Parrésia Press

Dedication

I dedicate this book to the memories of four young people who positively impacted my life and whose untimely passing had a near devastating effect on my family and me. The death of a loved one, in and of itself, is exceedingly painful, but more so when it is that of a young person whose promising life is no more. In 2004, I watched my 85-year-old mother bury her brilliant and beautiful daughter Zoe-Dibugwu. She had been ill for some time; her death was not entirely unexpected. But when it came, it was stinging. It is particularly traumatic for parents to bury their children because it quite simply goes against the natural order of things. As the hearse bearing Zoe's body from the mortuary to the Onwenu compound in Obinetiti made its way up the driveway, my mum walked out to receive her daughter home. She did so with calls of 'Nne o! Nne o!' My heart broke into tiny pieces. 'Nne' is what you called your mother. When an older person or parent addresses a younger person as such, it is entirely endearing. In death, it is deeply moving. It was in that moment that I glimpsed the depth of such loss and a mother's sorrow at having to bury a child she had borne and raised.

MICHAEL IZUCHUKWU EGBUNA, son of Chinelo Egbuna (2015): I was in a management meeting on a Monday morning, when I got the news that Michael had died, just hours earlier. I remember seeing my phone fly out of my hand, landing two feet away, as if my spirit did not want to have anything to do with the instrument that delivered such terrible news. Michael and my son, Tijani became friends in JSS 2 (Junior Secondary School). So close were they that their friendship enveloped our two families, from parents and grandparents to aunts and uncles. I literally watched Michael and his sister, Michelle, grow up. Michael and Tijani had been apart for many years as both attended college on two different continents. But death came two months before they were to be reunited in Nigeria.

Michael was 27 years old when we lost him. Even in his short lifespan, he inspired so many friends and relatives, enriching our lives with kindness and love. He was very special to all who had the privilege of knowing him.

ORADILIM ORAKWUSI 'Orao' (2017): Orao was the illustrious son of my friend, Margaret Onyema Orakwusi, whose tribute appears in the 'Encounters' section of this book. Even though I never met him, I knew Orao through his mum and siblings. He was, quite simply, a brilliant all-rounder; talented and compassionate. A soon-to-be medical student, he was also an artist, a saxophonist and a writer. Orao was noted for philanthropy in school and in church. He used his talents and funds to bring people together and solve problems in the community.

I call him the man who saw God before he died. For a 24-year-old, this young man was focused and purposeful beyond his age. Orao, in his writings and utterances constantly pondered on issues that were philosophical and deep. He would meditate on the enormity of the love of God, which we are privileged to experience. Writing and drawing himself into God's presence just before he passed, I reckon that his abrupt departure was well known to God.

'Only the good die young,' I have heard it said. This is true of Orao and the other young people to whom I have dedicated this book.

UCHEOMA OTIGBUO (10 December 2018): Ucheoma was the daughter of my sister Dr Ijeoma Onwenu-Otigbuo. She was also a daughter to me, more than she was a niece. She was beautiful and intelligent, a big sister to her four siblings, and a loving cousin to my sons. Ucheoma was a lawyer and a mother of four beautiful children. There are only three people whom my mother would defer to in the family - my sister Zoe, Ucheoma and myself. You could say that she was loath to look for our trouble. Once, without knowing that Ucheoma was around the corner, her visiting grandma carried on with complaints about her not eating *garri* but preferring only pounded yam with her soup. Grandma had volunteered to make the yam meal, but was soon advising my sister not to give in to Ucheoma's demand for this special treatment. Ijeoma, who was aware of her daughter's presence, egged my mother on until Ucheoma was well within view. Without saying a word, my mother's usual 'I-am-in-control' attitude gave way to profuse apologies. 'My dear, I did not say anything,' my mother lamely offered. However, the damage had been done. Grandma spent the remaining part of her visit trying to make amends.

Ucheoma's death at 37 hit my family very hard. We huddled together for months trying to make sense of it all. I was worried for my sons who were very close to her, particularly the younger one, Abraham, with whom she shared a special bond. I was also angry that she died on December 10, the same date that my father died and my sister, Zoe, narrowly missed dying on. I wondered why December 10, until it struck me that it may have been my father's way of saying, 'I've got them - they are with me in heaven.'

OLAWALE ONIGBANJO (2019): My friend, Maureen Amanechi-Onigbanjo of the House of Maufechi, has been my designer since

1986. I knew her before she got married and before her son Olawale was born. He was her pride and joy, his siblings as well.

In 1989, I received a photo invitation to Olawale's first birthday. I had forgotten about it until his passing at 31. I unexpectedly found it on top of a pile of photos while looking for something else entirely. This was a week before his burial and just days after visiting my grief-stricken friend, his mother. What were the chances that such a small invitation that I had forgotten about would be resting on top of a carton of photographs I had been looking at for months? I took it as a message for Wale's mum that he was at peace, and I told her so. It turned out that I confirmed an earlier message from someone else. Glory be to God.

These four young people were extraordinary and on an upward trajectory before their untimely deaths. Why does God take the best, sometimes before they fully unfold? I do not know. I am not God, and so cannot provide any answers. However, I can draw lessons from the lives of these wonderful young people. Yes, the old can learn from the young.

I can certainly reflect on the inspiring impact they made in their short and purposeful lives. May their beautiful souls rest in peace. May God comfort the families and friends they left behind.

I also use this dedication as a contact point to all parents, especially mothers, who have had to bury their children. You have a special place in God's heart. He sees you. He knows it all. He will beautify you.

Contents

Preface

A Story Is Like A Child

Astory is born the same way a child is born. It grows. It evolves. It has progression. First, it stays away from the world, as it grows hidden inside its mother's womb. Though it is unseen, it is alive as the mother feels movements within her. I have carried this story around for a long time. Like a pregnancy, I have felt the pulse of each recollection and the heartbeat of each memory. Like childbearing, bringing forth this story has been painful because I had to look back at things that time had put away. In my looking back, I unearthed some of the pain that had been buried and tucked away in the void of time. Yet, this story had to be told.

In 1978, I took a writing course at The New School for Social Research in New York as part of my Masters degree in Media Studies. One of my teachers, an author, gave me a book. In it, she wrote: 'Onyeka, I look forward to your words. Your style is uniquely anecdotal; you have a voice, and I look forward to reading from you.'

At that time, I did not think I had much to write, but unknown to me; I was pregnant. If you are reading this book, you can see that the baby has been born, 42 years after my teacher's encouraging words. This newborn baby is a product of being surrounded by adults who shared stories and Igbo folklore with me as a child.

Writing this book has afforded me a panoramic view of my life and a vantage point of self-reflection that would never have been possible. It has also served as a quintessential moment of stocktaking. I have had to review life's many twists and turns, highs and lows, triumphs and failures, mistakes and regrets, all of which have in one way or the other defined my existence. I have had to pause on this journey ever so often to recount with nostalgia the various permutations of fate, and the place of divinity and humanity in how my life is evolving.

In this book, I have been extremely open as never before. I have talked about people who have enriched my life, either by design or default. I have taken stock of my achievements and my mistakes, as well as lessons learned. *My Father's Daughter* is a story of love, a father's love. Love found, lost, and then found again. This book is for those who wish to learn from the missteps and accomplishments of others. It is also for those who may find a kindred spirit in a woman who has lived through diverse challenges, yet triumphs still in the knowledge that she is truly, her father's daughter.

Love in this book occurs and manifests in many ways. My father's love shaped my early years; it taught me about God's love. If a human father could love me as much as my dad did, then I could only imagine how awesome, total and all-encompassing the love of my heavenly father is. But through my experiences with other people - family and friends - I have also come to appreciate that love is a complicated thing. I have asked myself at different times: How can human beings genuinely love when love can be so hard?

I have written this book for my children to know that with faith in God, one can do any good thing. It is a testimony of God's goodness in my life. I have also written it for the younger generations who are starting out in this thing called life. I hope that they can learn from my mistakes, be strengthened and encouraged by my sense of purpose.

This book is for every young person who has lost a parent or parents. The heavenly father stepped in when my earthly father was no more. He showed me that if I could keep my eyes on Him and remain committed to reaching my goals, I would stand out from the crowd.

Prologue

Onyekachi, Papa And The Ear Of Corn

'Vroom!' was the deep sound of Papa's car, a white Chevrolet Impala. He stopped the car a few feet away from the fence and I immediately left what I was doing and went into hiding. Papa had earlier purchased an ear of corn at a church bazaar, for a guinea - a pound and a shilling. This was a lot of money at the time. Items at church bazaars were bought for much more than they were worth as a way of raising money for projects.

I wanted to eat the ear of corn, so I asked Papa, but he was too busy preparing for his outing. He did not respond. I assumed that his silence was permission to eat the corn, so I took it to an older cousin who helped me to roast it. We both ate it. Between the roasting and the eating, however, it dawned on me that Papa had not given his express permission. I became worried: I had taken something without consent. With Papa's return, worry turned into shame, and shame into fear. So, I hid.

'*Nwunye nnia, Nnenne,*' Papa called in excitement as he opened the door to the house. He called me, not by my name, but by the affectionate appellations which only he used, and which had since replaced my birth names. He met silence. On any other occasion, I would have left whatever I was doing to run straight into his open arms at the sound of his voice. He would carry me high in the air and ask how I was doing and if I had eaten. We would then both sit down to eat his meal.

'*Nwunye nnia,*' he called again, darting frantically around the house looking for me, as though in search of a lost gold coin. I heard him but did not respond, as I did not know how to look him in the face. It soon became obvious that Papa would neither eat his lunch nor sit down till he found me. Unable to bear the tension anymore, I came out of hiding, much to his relief and mine.

'Why were you hiding?' He asked.

'Papa, I ate your corn,' I said, looking at my feet with my heart thumping.

Papa did not respond, and I stood there, not looking at him.

After a while, Papa stooped gently before me, in a manner that made our heights appear the same, then he said, 'Promise never to hide from me again, no matter what.'

Papa raised my chin so we could make eye contact, sealing the agreement. He did not scold me about eating the corn, his concern was that I should not deprive him of my company. We proceeded to eat his food together as though nothing happened.

That day has remained etched in my memory.

PART I

Finding My Roots

Becoming my Father's Daughter

How does one start a story of happenings that had not been experienced, things that existed before they were born? You would have to open your ears to the lips of those who saw the events unfold, listen to things said and those not said, question and prod elders to reach further into their memories. You would also need to look through piles of documents and pictures, conduct research and arrive at conclusions. To know of my first days in this world, I looked through the eyes of the one who knew me first. My mother.

Let me tell the story as my mother told it.

I was born on Tuesday 29 January 1952, the fourth child of my Father, Dixon Kanu, known as DK to many, and the fifth child of my mother, Hope Onwenu. My eyes first saw the world in my mother's hometown of Obosi, in present-day Anambra State. It was the norm in those days for wives to go to their parents' home when babies were due, to be near their caregiver mothers.

My Father, DK, was a busy school teacher and a politician. He had short teaching spells in Amichi and Onitsha in Anambra State, Okpare in Delta State, Arondizuogu his home town in Imo State, and Diobu, which is a town on the outskirts of Port Harcourt, Rivers State. He eventually taught in Port Harcourt in 1951. As a teacher, he served in different capacities throughout his career; he was Vice-Principal of Baptist High School and Principal of Enitonia High School in Port Harcourt. This busy schedule made it expedient for my mum to give birth to me in Obosi, which also had a good maternity home, run by Mrs Ikeazor.

Hope Onwenu was hoping for a boy. Boys were and still are very important in Igbo land for connubial safety. I was the third daughter after my brother Richard, but Papa could not be bothered about the boy-girl thing. He welcomed every child as a gift from God and celebrated their birth in the same way. My mum was bothered, though, for in the patriarchal Igbo society, as a wife and mother, she needed as many sons as she could bear. One was good, but a second was even better. My mother pretended to be happy, but Papa was elated, I was told, and took to me as if I were his soul mate.

I was given two names: *Onyekachi*, which poses a rhetorical question 'Who is greater than God?' and *Akuchukwu* which means 'God's wealth'. The surname *Onwenu* means 'The Owner'. I imagine that my birth was celebrated, just like those of my older siblings. They had our parents' love in several doses. However, according to my mother and relatives, it seemed that upon my arrival, I greedily cornered all of my father's love for myself.

Now, let me tell the story as my siblings remembered it. Every morning, Papa stood in front of our house at 35 Moorehouse Street, Port Harcourt to say goodbye to his family. Just before getting into his car, Papa and I would perform our early morning ritual. He would open his right palm with different coins in it - a farthing, the smallest in size and value; the penny, the largest of them all; the sixpence and the shilling. The farthing was insignificant in size, so I never went for it, rather I would always choose the penny. It was the largest coin in the collection and it had a hole in the centre, which fascinated me. Whilst making my choice, my siblings would send signals trying to convince me to pick the shilling, which had the most value. For a long time, I never heeded their advice.

One day, I did and only then did I discover that it could buy infinitely more than the fascinating penny. In 1956, the shilling was a lot of money for a four-year-old to 'blow' in one day. Every morning, with my coin in hand, I was the toast of Moorehouse Street, our friendly neighbourhood, where everyone knew everyone else, and news spread quickly from one ear to another. I had not started school then, so my days were spent on the playground, cooking imaginary food with small tin cans as my pots and weeds as my vegetables.

I had a cousin named Goddy, who was ten years older than me. He would let me slap him, any time I had my shilling just so he could help me spend it. My sister, Ijeoma, would offer to give me a piggyback ride to the street corner where groundnuts, bananas and sweets were sold. All the kids in the neighbourhood knew about this ritual and would join the merry procession. The target was, of course, my precious coin. Once it was spent, everyone dispersed and normalcy returned. This abandonment often elicited an outcry from me, particularly as I was always left with precious little of the goodies purchased with my money. Whenever I raised the alarm, all concerned would have to take the best option open to them. They would leave the vicinity immediately, the reason being that Papa hated to hear me cry, and took no prisoners.

You would think that since this experience was a regular occurrence any time my father was around, I would learn to see people for the freeloaders they were. They were only interested in my shilling and its purchasing power. But I never learned. It did not matter because I knew that as long as I had Papa, I would have my regular supply of shillings, and everything that was attracted by it.

From my experience, I learned my first two lessons in life that my father tried to teach me in his patient and loving way. The first lesson was that not all that glitters – or fascinates, in my case – is gold. The second was that moments in the spotlight are fleeting.

In the evenings, Moorehouse Street became a playground. The street and sidewalks were turned into a football pitch and tracks were drawn for racing. I was not great at these competitions; nevertheless, everyone had to cheer me on. My siblings happily applauded me as the fastest kid on the block, even if I were only capable of leading from the back. They would shout 'Onyeka, wake up! Onyeka, wake up!' while others ran ahead of me. If not, I would collapse to the ground, refusing to complete the race I never stood a chance of winning.

If I did not hear the cheering, I felt like the attention had moved from me and I did not like that. A searing cry would follow, and my father would, in the twinkle of an eye, appear at the playground to investigate. Everyone would again take to their heels. I was an oppressor of sorts and an irredeemable prima donna.

I have often wondered what would have become of me, had my father lived longer and continued 'loving me to smithereens', the way he did for the first four years of my life. However, a story comes to mind, told by others, of an event that happened when I was two and a half years old. It tells me that yes, my father would have continued with his indulgent treatment of me, but that he would have drawn the line where necessary.

As a child, I was slow in walking. I got around by moving my buttocks on the floor. One day, Papa just got fed up with my inability to make even the slightest attempt to crawl like most babies, let alone walk. He made a harsh comment in Igbo: 'Ndii ihe e n'achichighari n'ani?' which means, 'Why are you wallowing on the floor like this?'

6

I did not understand a word of what Papa said, but I felt the sharpness of his remark. I was told that I simply rose to my feet while at the playground the next day and began to walk.

It was our dear neighbour, Mama Nnee (Mrs Okaro) who first saw me walking and raised a happy alarm. She also gave me a penny for my springing that delightful surprise. Could this have led to my fascination with the penny, the huge coin with a hole in the middle, and which had traversing triangles like the Star of David? Probably. Remarkably, I never crawled. I went from shifting around on the floor to walking on my own, simply because of a 'rebuke' from Papa.

While my Father, DK Onwenu was not the type of parent to fight his children's battles when they were at fault; he seemed to have made an exception with me. He did so repeatedly and without apology. According to my brother, the only time that he intervened for another of his children was when the school janitor slapped him without reason. My brother had slumped and had to be revived. Encouraged by his classmates, he ran home and reported the matter to our father.

Papa arrived at the school, St. Cyprian's School, Port Harcourt, with his police orderly - which he was entitled to as a legislator - to the terror of the school principal and the offending janitor who, by this time, was shaking like a leaf. With full apologies and assurances that such would not repeat itself, my father let the matter rest. Papa had no objections to his children being disciplined with the whip if they deserved it, but the heavy-handed slap from a much older and bigger man was uncalled for. My brother was the toast of his mates for quite some time, for helping cut down to size a bully disliked by many.

In December 1955, I stood beside the vehicle that was taking my siblings to visit our maternal grandparents. Waving goodbye with my parents, I knew that I would now have Papa all to myself. I do not remember feeling sad at being left behind. As we bade them farewell, my small left hand in my father's big right hand, I felt safe.

I found several things fascinating about Papa. He was light-skinned with slightly blonde hair, almost like an albino but without other accompanying traits. I am told that he took after his mother, Mgbeke Ukwu. The other thing was his inverted navel. On many late afternoons, I would be found trying to understand this navel: Why was it different? I would touch, feel, push and prod it. The navel was so deep that it could take numerous items like groundnuts and small stones. I stuffed as many of these items into Papa's navel as I could. I did this to measure its depth to see whether it was five-small stones wide or ten-groundnuts deep. My relentless disturbances never perturbed papa, nor did he ever seem tired of it. He put up with my buzzing presence, indulging my questions and pestering.

There was another one, a call and response game that we played. It was a wordplay that twisted our tongues and tested our patience.

'Onyekachi, *gbogodom, gbogodom gbom*,' my dad would start. 'Papa, *gbogodom, gbogodom, gbom*,' I would reply.

This would go on until the pronunciation of '*gbogodom*' would become stretched, more complicated and more difficult for me to mouth. 'Onyekachi, *gbogodo m gbogodo m gbogodo m gbom gbom gbogodom*,' or something like that.

Then, I would start crying with frustration and Papa would make it simple again, giving me a packet of sweets to compensate me for my trouble.

I look back and wonder what the essence of this activity was apart from relishing each other's company. This conclusion is based on the fact that the words had no meaning and the game was really about nothing. But then again, it was about everything. It was about love.

There were times when we shared our love with the world. I remember when my father was campaigning for a place at the House of Representatives in 1955. I was almost four years old. I was like many other children, the type who easily took off their clothes. Whenever Papa was going around the neighbourhood, speaking with people and talking about his plans for the future, I always went along carrying a 'Vote for Us' placard, but with parts of my body barely covered. It was not solely a vote for him, but a vote for us indeed. Papa and I later agreed on a pact: I would only go with him if I were fully dressed. That pact marked the end of the politician and his naked young daughter who campaigned for him.

Papa loved me and I knew it. I do not doubt that he and I were soul-mates. If there is such a thing as reincarnation, my father and I must have been in each other's lives for ages. There was a certain joy that I felt deep inside me when I was around him and I could tell that he also felt the same way. He had a busy schedule, so I waited for him to return at odd hours when he would share his meals with me. I ate chunks of meat from his soup as he happily watched and I had eggs as well. According to an Igbo myth, these should not be given to children or else it would predispose them to an insatiable appetite. The child may be tempted to steal if their parents could not afford to provide these delicacies all the time. Now I know the real reason meat and egg were prohibited - adults probably just wanted all the good stuff for themselves. Papa ignored the myth and shared his meals with me. He also shared his beer which I drank from a teacup with a spoon. Nothing really mattered, except that we shared company like friends.

I was also made to feel a part of whatever he was doing, even if he were in the company of others. I would be there when the Mbonu Ojikes and the Mbadiwes would visit.

Today, what do I feel about Papa's love? It was genuine and unique; it cannot be replaced or replicated except with God's love. I will be speaking in calculated ambiguity if I say I blame my father for the love he showed me. Even after the birth of Nnenna, my younger sister, who sadly died in infancy, Papa's affection did not shift an inch from me.

One day, without warning, everything changed. Death came through a road accident and severed the cord between us.

On 10 December 1956, Papa was involved in a car crash on his way back to Port Harcourt. There had been crises between politicians and teachers; the teachers were threatening a strike. Being the Teacher/Politician that he was, with a deep understanding of the dynamics of the situation, he had travelled to Aba to stop the strike action. On his way back, driving his Chevrolet Impala, he veered off the road and crashed into one of the oil bean trees that adorned the sides of the highway. Beside him were provisions he was bringing back to me. He died an hour later at Aba General Hospital. He was 40 years old. I was one month shy of my fifth birthday. Nothing remained the same. Everything changed.

You do not easily forget a love like the one Papa and I shared. Though brief, it was intense enough to last me a lifetime. Even though he was with me for just a short while, memories of him, deep and potent, would cast a lasting shadow. For me, he remained alive, lurking everywhere in my thoughts, breathing anew in the stories of him that followed me whenever I met people and they realised whose daughter I was.

My Father's People: The Onwenus

Onwenu is an uncommon name. As mentioned earlier, it means 'The Owner'. My paternal grandfather, the first Onwenu, was born at a time when farming and trading were two of the primary means by which people earned a living. He was born in Arondizuogu village, into a large family with many wives and even many more children. He was the only child of his mother and his father's favourite, hence the name, 'The Owner'.

That name rattled his siblings, causing them to relate with him with some sense of discomfort. In effect, they began to make permutations about the future and their inheritance. What if their father favours Onwenu in property sharing over them? What would become of all their years of going to the farm and working just as hard? Did they work for this only child of his mother to take all? These thoughts made them hatch a plan to get rid of him, conniving to use him as collateral for a loan from a neighbouring village.

In those days, the Aros, like people from Arondizuogu, others in the diaspora and homeland Arochukwu were called, had a practice of using humans as collateral for loans. So, off they went on the appointed day. Young Onwenu, oblivious of his brothers' ploy, went with them like a lamb being led to slaughter. For him, it seemed like a typical day at the farm. After several hours of walking through the bush and narrow paths, they arrived at Ndianiche Uno, the village from which the other Ndianiche villages sprung. There, they handed him over to a wealthy trader in exchange for a loan. As was the practice, he would only be returned to his people once the loan was repaid. If for any reason his brothers defaulted, his fate was sealed. He would have to contend with a lifetime of servitude or worse still, slavery.

In a rather fortunate twist, however, Onwenu found favour in the sight of his hosts. He learned to trade in various commodities and did well in his master's business. He did so well that he was adopted as a member of the family. It was as though by his coming, the host's family became blessed. When his brothers had repaid the loan and expectedly requested to have him back, Onwenu refused to return. What if his brothers could not repay the loan? His master could have sold him into slavery. The very idea of going back to live with his brothers, who had betrayed him seemed unthinkable. So, he decided to strike out on his own.

That was how Mazi Onwenu, originally from Ndimoko village in Arondizuogu, chose to remain in the Nwankwo clan, in Ndianiche. Not much, however, was known about his personality. Even though Christianity was gaining a foothold in Igboland, Onwenu was a staunch traditionalist with a commanding will. Once, when he was about to make an offering of a chicken to his god, a hawk swooped down and carried it away. An older cousin told me that Onwenu confidently ordered the hawk to return the chicken, and it did.

Mazi Onwenu had two wives. The first, Mgbeke a fair-skinned woman, gave birth to three children – Charles, Juliana, who is fondly called Mama Aba, and Dixon Kanu, my Father and Flora who passed away as a child. The second wife had only one daughter, Mabel, who left home as a young girl and never returned. She also never made contact with the family again. Though we were aware of her existence, we never met her or her family and I never quite understood why. I did ask, and I was told that she wanted it that way.

The Onwenu brothers, Charles and Dixon-Kanu, were close. Neither of them did a thing without the knowledge of the other. They made decisions together regarding the family. My father was usually the financier. He was the educated one and raised all his brothers' children. He even paid for Charles' excesses by financing his taking of more wives whenever asked.

Mama Aba, whose name was Mrs Juliana DanChimah, had a loving relationship with my father. Despite her being older by five years, it was as though two lost friends had reunited whenever the two of them were together. They would spend time together telling stories. Mama Aba made sacrifices so that my father would get an education. The hardworking woman did all kinds of odd jobs such as cracking and selling palm kernel, and fermented cassava meal.

Papa repaid the favour by training her four children in school. Mama Aba's children - Samuel, Godfrey, Grace and Phoebe - lived with us at some point.

DK Onwenu:
The Candle That Burned So Bright

I knew my father for only four years and eleven months. The gaps that existed about my knowledge of him were filled by stories from my mother, siblings, and relatives. It also came from those who knew him and were recipients of his kindness at one time or the other.

Dixon Kanu Onwenu was born in 1916. It was an era when getting an education was not particularly fashionable for many families. He could have naturally followed in his father's footsteps by becoming a trader. My father was more inclined, if not bent on getting an education instead. He had a vision that was greater than his immediate environment.

Young DK attended St. Andrew's Primary School Obinetiti, Arondizuogu from where he proceeded to Abagana Central School, Anambra State, about 50km away. Papa was attached to a family whom he served as a house-help while attending school. There he became eligible for the First School Leaving Certificate Examination.

My father was not one to relent or be deterred. He proceeded to acquire his Lower Elementary Certificate, an admission prerequisite for Awka Teachers' College. There he could pursue his Higher Elementary Certificate Programme. Awka College was reputed for producing very good teachers and scholars. Since my dad was not privileged to attend regular secondary school as we know it; he applied for and wrote the London Matriculation Examination via correspondence. He passed at the first attempt. In 1943, after he graduated from the teachers' college, he qualified to be a headmaster.

That was how he ended up at Amichi Central School, Anambra. Many more students enrolled in the school after his arrival; the more they came, the smaller the classrooms became for them.

One of the few lands that remained vacant and available for use was a forbidden forest or *ajo ofia* as it is called in Igbo. It was believed that no human being could enter *ajo ofia* and survive to tell the experience. It was this forbidden forest that the town offered for the school's expansion. Headmaster DK, fascinated by that offer, swung into action. He led workers into the land, had the trees cut down and built the school there.

Initially, parents were suspicious and worried about what might happen to their children in the now rebranded 'evil forest'. Many days passed, days became weeks, weeks became months, and nothing happened to the school children. As a result, more parents sent their wards to the school. Enrolment grew, and the quality of scholarship put Amichi indigenes in an enviable position compared to their neighbours. To this day, the people of Amichi remember and cherish the name DK Onwenu. They have extended that love and respect to me, personally.

So important was Headmaster Onwenu's work in Amichi that when it was time for him to leave, the elders of the town offered him a bride, a beautiful woman called Udu. Suffice it to say that, there was nothing strange in this practice. It was a period when women were betrothed as gifts for marriage to express appreciation, and also as a way of cementing relationships. It was doubtful however that he was attracted to the young maiden offered to him.

15

Our people have a saying: 'You do not bring close to the nose that which you are not ready to eat'. DK appreciated the gesture, but respectfully declined the offer. It was my Uncle Charles, who married the woman in his brother's stead. She became his third wife and gave birth to his first male child. Thus, the Amichi connection remains with the Onwenus.

As headmaster of Amichi Central School, Papa continued to seek personal development through education. This he did by preparing for his Advanced Level Examinations, through an overseas correspondence college (Wolsey Hall). In 1944, he wrote his A-Levels examinations in Economics, History and British Constitution, and passed. In 1946, his application to Fourah Bay College, Sierra Leone was accepted. This was no mean feat. Fourah Bay was the only University College in West Africa and Nigeria had only twelve admission slots. DK attended the college with other prominent Nigerians such as Late Pa Ajasin (Former Governor of Ondo State), Bishop Segun, Permanent Secretary Okagbue, Dr Alex Ubezonu, Principal Samuel Ogoazi and Revd. Ransome-Kuti, who was a few years ahead of them. DK's classmates at Fourah Bay called him 'Professor'.

Those were the days when a community's pride rested on their ability to come together to send their best students abroad for further studies. Different people brought money and expertise to ensure that children from the community, even though not theirs, received education abroad. It was crowd-funding of sorts that existed before GoFundMe, and the new media arrived. Chinua Achebe captured this phenomenon better in his second novel, *No Longer at Ease,* relating how the people of Umuofia pooled resources together to send the brilliant and precocious Obi Okonkwo to study in Britain.

In 1949, DK graduated with a Bachelor of Arts Degree from

Fourah Bay College and proceeded to Durham University at Newcastle-Upon-Tyne, England, where he had a one-year stint studying Law. In 1950, he abandoned the course and came back home as a result of pressure from both the family and the Arondizuogu community. They all needed him. Before leaving Durham though, he acquired the professional qualification of Fellow of the Institute of Commerce Birmingham (F.I.C. Birmingham).

He returned in 1950 to become the first principal of Iheme Memorial Grammar School Arondizuogu, Imo state. I reckon that this first job was like a first fruit offering, a way of giving back to the community that helped fund his education abroad. Being the restless type, DK Onwenu left Iheme in 1951 for Dennis Memorial Grammar School Onitsha (DMGS), where he was the Head of the English Department. In 1952, he was transferred to St. John's College, Diobu, a suburb of Port Harcourt. His stay at St. John's was also brief. In the same year, he left for Baptist High School, Port Harcourt, where he was the Master-in-Charge of the English Department and the first Nigerian Vice-Principal. There he taught many who went on to become important personalities in the country. Some of them were Ambassador Dele Cole, Chief Guy Ikokwu, Alabo Tonye Graham-Douglas who was former Minister of Tourism and Culture, Dr Walter Ofonagoro a former Minister for Information and Mr Chidi Ofong a former Managing Director of National Directorate of Employment.

In 1955, my father joined the Enitonia High School Port Harcourt as Principal. He not only got the school approved, as it had not been since its inception in 1932; he relocated it to its permanent site at Borokiri. Then the school began an upward swing towards academic excellence.

My father was a man of many parts. As he made his contributions in education, he also pursued a political career. Even though I cannot tell exactly why he went into politics, it did not seem that money underlined in any way, his motivation to occupy public office. We were not wealthy but we were comfortable enough as he paid not only his children's school fees but those of his nephews, nieces and other people. The Nigerian political system was still, relatively speaking, a sanitised space. Politics was for patriots, not for sycophants, and not for the mindlessly avaricious.

It all started when he was elected the Principal Secretary of Igbo State Union in 1954, an organisation that was the apex cultural representative of the majority of Ndigbo. Being well educated and eloquent, his friends advised him to seek political office. One of them later commented that I should never dream of matching DK Onwenu's public speaking skills because 'the grounds vibrated when he spoke'. I was told that my father's oratorical depth during the parliamentary sessions as a member of the Federal House of Representatives was widely acknowledged by all and sundry, including Abubakar Tafawa Balewa himself who referred to him as 'Old Teacher' every time the latter rose to speak. Papa's political career rose meteorically. He climbed the ropes pretty fast, but it all fizzled out quickly too, no thanks to his devastatingly premature death.

To begin with, he ran in the election of councillors for Port Harcourt Local Council and won. He was eventually elected the Deputy Mayor under Richard Okwosha Nzimiro's administration.

Not content to remain at the Local Government level, DK showed interest in contesting for the membership of the Federal House of Representatives. He did so under the National Council of Nigeria and Cameroons (NCNC) platform and was pitched against a tough opponent, Barrister Nnonyelum of the Action Group. He was an incumbent and a bulwark of an opponent.

Despite the odds, my father won. Even though his austere campaign was no match to Nnonyelum's fat purse - a man who campaigned in a convoy of cars - Papa simply relied on his ability to lucidly articulate the programmes he had for the constituency. It must be remembered that this was a political dispensation, where society could still discern and appreciate commitment and leadership qualities in prospective officeholders, even when they may not have the money to throw around. Had the same election been held today in Nigeria, my father would most probably have stood no chance against his well-moneyed opponent. This victory ensured that DK Onwenu became the first legislator to emerge from my hometown, Arondizuogu, even though he represented the constituency of an adopted town.

Papa lived on the fast lane, as though he had a premonition that he did not have a lot of time to spend on earth. His life which moved with the swiftness of a car in a high-speed race, had agonisingly come to a sudden halt. Nonetheless, DK's journey was epitomised by his accomplishments in such a short time.

My father was like a candle. He knew that lighting other people's would not put out his own. So, while he burned bright, he encouraged others to also shine. Besides his educational and political pursuit, he was extremely benevolent and was happy to give away the shirt on his back so that the next man could be clothed. He was a man of the people, especially the underprivileged. It was pleasing and soothing for him to know that someone had derived pleasure from what he had done. Yet, just like a candle, the more it burned, the faster it melted.

Don't Mind Them, Your Father Owns This Place!

This story falls within the realm of events that cannot be explained. For me, it was a poignant mystery totally unexpected, and strangely comforting as well.

DK Onwenu's relationship with the people of Amichi was very special. Though he served as the Headmaster of Amichi Central School in the 1940s and died in 1956, they never forgot the positive influence he had on the town. My mother would always remind me of this special bond. '*Ndi Amichi na nnai adika*' meaning 'Amichi people and your father shared a special bond,' she would often say.

Sometime in 2018, I visited the town for the burial of a friend's mother. My friend, Pastor Amaka Maduneme, and her husband were very supportive when my mother passed away in 2011. They led a powerful delegation from Amichi to her burial in Arondizuogu, at a time when severe fuel scarcity meant that a lot of people could not move around much. Pastor Amaka's mother's burial took us from Lagos to Amichi as part of a powerful group of friends from The Fountain of Life Church, where we all worshipped.

When a mutual friend, Nkechi Ali-Balogun, suggested that we make the trip together, I felt compelled to warn her that hanging around me in Amichi; she would be inundated with stories about my father and what he still means to the town. I warned her that the people would fuss over me, not because of my 'celebrity' status but because of the memory of DK Onwenu. She simply smiled and waved it off. However, I am not sure that either of us was prepared for a particular incident that took place.

We had been at the wake of this elderly woman who had attended Amichi Central School, which my dad helped to establish. We sang and danced up a storm, keeping our spirits high, and comforting the family for what was still a difficult goodbye.

During the burial proper the following day, Nkechi and I arrived for the service together. As we came down from our common ride, an old woman wearing a white blouse and a wrapper that was true to Igbo tradition, approached us from nowhere, it seemed. She looked like she was in her late 70s; she was quite erect and walked without difficulty. She called out my name, 'Onyeka!'.

As I turned, she walked past Nkechi and stood in front of me. She spoke with deep confidence, these words: '*Gbakwafa nkiti no nnai nwe ebea!*' This means, 'Take no notice of them; this place belongs to your father.'

The old woman exited the scene as quickly as she had entered it, leaving behind a bewildered audience of two. Nkechi and I looked at each other with an unbelieving mien trying, in the split seconds that followed, to decipher what we just heard. We are still unable to. What I understood from her utterance was that I was home in Amichi.

Nkechi Ali-Balogun and I go back to our days as Youth Corps members in 1981. We participated in a group community project of building a culvert somewhere in Yaba, Lagos. We spent much of the time gossiping while the men did all the heavy lifting. We have remained friends since then. Nkechi is not the sort of person who suffers fools gladly; she calls a spade, a spade when she sees one. Perhaps if she had not been around to witness this event, I might have wondered if indeed it happened.

My Uncle's Wives And The Lessons They Taught Me

At this point, I must reflect on the wives of Uncle Charles. One of the best decisions I took on returning home from the

United States of America in 1980 was to put my mum and Uncle Charles's four wives on a monthly stipend. This started as soon as I began to earn real money – in 1982. The stipends did not end until the last surviving wife passed away in 2014. They were my family as I had been raised to believe, and they deserved to be provided for in their old age. I was not the only one doing so, but I felt it was my duty to contribute.

In the process of taking care of these women who referred to me as 'Mazi' because I represented my father to them, I learned many life's lessons. Let me tell you about these women in some detail.

Mama Comfort (Grace)

She was Uncle Charles' first wife and, therefore, the matriarch of the Onwenu family. She kept an even keel, working closely with my mum, her mate from across the aisle, the other branch of the family. When we arrived Arondizuogu trying to escape the war that was threatening Port Harcourt where we live, she looked after us like a beloved and trusted guardian.

Mama Comfort was full of wit and wisdom. She would take us to pick *udala* or African cherry, the sweet, succulent fruit that is also called *agbalumo* in Yoruba. We learnt from her that tradition forbade the plucking of the *udala* fruit from the tree. Only those that had fallen to the ground could be picked. We would set out at 5 am to search for *udala* fruits, our paths lit by *akpulu akpu* - local candles made of palm fruit chaff moulded around bamboo sticks. We needed to be careful out there; you were not quite sure if the spirits had vacated the fruit trees before your arrival. They too, we were told, liked to eat *udala*.

After the first season, Mama Comfort was wise enough to drop out from our *udala* picking team. My sister Ijeoma, who could get away with any mischief, had the knack of pushing anyone down to take the *udala* they may have been aiming for.

'How would I explain to the world that an *okibili* (old woman) like me, instead of staying in bed, sustained injuries because she went on an *udala*-picking adventure with her children?' Mama Comfort reasoned aloud. It was all done in jest and love.

Mama Adene

Next in line was Mama Adene. She was my favourite and everyone knew it. She had no child of her own, and for this reason, I adopted her as a mother. I did for her everything a child would do for her mum. When she passed away, I took care of her burial as was expected of me. Adene loved my father very much and that was one of the factors that drew us close. Papa, she told me, treated her with a lot of compassion and care. We would stay up late at night each time I visited, and she would tell me stories about her beloved brother-in-law, my father.

I would keep her company and ply her with her favourite drink, Calypso Rum, a sweet mixture of rum and coconut. In the small hours of the morning, she would stagger back to her quarters, after waving a finger at me for getting her nearly drunk. Yet at daybreak, she would rouse me from sleep with a bowl of *achara soup* (grass stem soup) peculiar to the people of Isuochi, her hometown. She was my pal.

Mama Goddy

Mama Goddy (Udu) was the young maiden betrothed to my father by the people of Amichi in appreciation of his sterling service as the Headmaster of Amichi Central School. Since my father was not interested in marrying her, my Uncle Charles did instead, as his third wife.

Mama Goddy and I did not have a strong rapport. She was

distant, though fiercely loyal to my mother; they were both from Anambra State. Anambra and Imo were two major sections of the Igbo people who rarely intermarried in the early days. She was also the custodian of the Onwenu land history. She knew where the boundaries of every piece of land was and who owned what.

During the Christmas holidays, it was customary for families or churches to hold events for returnees or holidaymakers to 'polish' their 'aka' or 'also known as' names with a fee. This was a way of raising money for various projects. Such an occasion came up in 1999 and I decided to 'polish' a name I had been known by in my immediate family circle – 'Nwunye Nnia' (her father's wife). I paid a tidy sum for it as well.

Before I left the arena of the ceremony, Mama Goddy had taken a shortcut home and arrived slightly before me. I walked in on her telling my mother how I had brazenly taken a name that put me in competition with her. Sister laughed and told her that my father gave me the name and that I had a right to it. Mama Goddy was visibly disappointed. In spite of this and many other acts of unfriendliness, I had a special fondness for the woman. She was a feminist and that endeared her to me.

Uncle Charles had a rule that his wives had to serve him a stick of his favourite brand of cigarette with his food. This was notwithstanding the fact that they had to provide the food themselves. He gave them land for farming and, as far as he was concerned, that was all he should do. Mama Goddy was the only wife who refused to go along. So adamant was she that she actually got away with it. There was nothing my uncle could do. She earned my deepest respect for that act of rebellion.

Mama Egbuniwe

Mama Egbuniwe (Mgbocha) was my uncle's fourth wife and perhaps, the most hardworking. With five children, she had to be. Nonetheless, I believe she was made that way. She was also the most generous. Every morning when we were at home in Arondizuogu, all the Onwenu wives would congregate at the DK Onwenu compound next door to banter. My mum would serve tea and sandwiches and our neighbours would join us, with some staying for lunch and even dinner. On her way to the farm, Mama Egbuniwe would stop by early, with a gift of kola nuts, garden egg and peanut sauce, a traditional peace offering. Then on her way back from the farm, she would bring yam or cassava tubers, vegetables, fruits; anything from her labour. She never called on us without a gift. Her greetings were short, but heartfelt. Mama Egbuniwe would head back to her hut to cook for her brood. She was a delight to watch; focused and untiring. Her generosity stood her out.

There was yet another wife who did not stay. She was called Mama Esther. Her only child, my cousin Esther Onwenu-Uba whom she left behind, was cared for by the remaining wives who treated her as their own. Such was the atmosphere in which Onwenu children were raised.

My Mother's People: The Nwokoyes

There is a picture of my mother's family that comes to mind as I write this. From left to right is my uncle Nathan (Njio), my grandfather Ogbuefi Godson Nwokoye - whom we fondly called Papa Nnukwu - sitting cross-legged in a black suit. Next to him is his first child, Sophie. In between Sophie and our grandmother, Mama Nnukwu is Ernest, the baby of the house. On my grandmother's left is my mother, Hope, and standing next to her is Dorothy.

As centrally positioned as they are in this picture, so were my grandparents, Papa Nnukwu and Mama Nnukwu, in their house. They reigned supreme, wielding discipline with love. Theirs was a close-knit family where everyone looked out for everyone else. It was a home where discipline and the Christian ethics of piety, hard work and selflessness were expressed. If you did not work or failed to attend church service, you lost your place at the meal table for that day. It was as simple as that.

Let me tell you about Mama Nnukwu.

She was born into the Anyiwo family of Aro Egbuoma in Imo state, into the polygamous family of Mazi Anyiwo. At that time, Irish missionaries based in Asaba, Delta State had made inroads into the Igbo country, east of the River Niger, preaching Christ and establishing schools. Mazi Anyiwo was known for not sending his children to school. He considered Christianity the white man's religion, and education was something he looked upon with great suspicion. The missionaries relentlessly implored him to send them people from his household who would benefit from the mission's work. He appeased them by sending his slaves. Fascinated by this knowledge that she was barred from getting, Ucheime, as my grandmother was known then, aided by her mother, resorted to sneaking away to learn from the missionaries. Her fascination soon turned into genuine interest. Thus, she became what her father feared most – a Christian.

Knowing quite well the kind of Father she had, Ucheime was sure that she would never be allowed to openly practise her new found religion under his roof. She ran away from home at fifteen and went to Asaba, where she was sheltered by those who had converted her. It was during her stay with the missionaries that Ucheime became baptised and christened Margaret. Years later, she met and married my grandfather, a tall, dark and handsome tailor-hunter from the nearby village of Obosi, Anambra State.

Papa Nnukwu was famed for his hunting skills. It was said that he killed birds of prey by aiming at their shadows. He timed the bird as it flew by trailing its shadow on the ground so that when he eventually raised his rifle and pulled the trigger, he never missed. Perhaps it was the stories about the famous hunter who shot without missing that warmed Mama Nnukwu's heart towards him; I do not know. Whatever it was, my maternal grandparents understood each other. They had eight children, one of whom was adopted, a rarity at the time. Unfortunately, they buried five of those children in their lifetime.

Papa Nnukwu and Mama Nnukwu were the definition of true love. Just watching them as a child made me laugh. Whenever my grandfather saw his wife sitting together with their two daughters, Hope and Dorothy, he would always suspect that he was the subject of their conversation and would wade in.

'*O gwagokwa unu na mu ada eweta ego n'uno a, mana olozogo ji na ede di n'oba?*' He would ask. This translates, 'Has she told you yet that I do not provide upkeep money in this house, forgetting our barn is stocked full with yam and cocoyam?'

While Papa Nnukwu complained, the sisters and their mother cooed into each other's ears, as though to confirm his suspicions. Many times, though, their conversations were not about him.

Dorothy and my mother, Hope, were the closest of the Nwokoye children. It was as if the two women were bound together by an unseen cord. Even in the family photograph described above, they stood close to each other. They had a ten- year age gap between them, yet that tended to bring them closer, rather than separate them. The sisters wore the same style and colour of clothes and were always in each other's company. They ran businesses together, vacationed together, and 'ruled' jointly in their father's house, the Nwokoye family, as bulwarks and protectors of the heritage.

Today, I think about their relationship. It was similar to what existed between the Onwenu brothers; blood so thick, nothing could come between. They had a love that could run through the toughest obstacles. Their love was so strong it could do no wrong. There were times, however, when their love became complicated, and even difficult. As I think about this, I also think about my siblings and the love that existed between us. I think about how love flows within a family, and how sometimes, other things mix with it, even as it flows.

While growing up, my mother inundated me with stories of my origin and about her hometown of Obosi, as well as its conflicts with the neighbouring Onitsha. Some of these stories were historical, while others were imaginary. One such tale started way before she was born, but became interwoven with her own experiences and imagination.

Back in the late-1800s and as recently as the 1960s, the people of Obosi were perpetually in conflict with Onitsha over land at their borders. Each town claimed ownership. The conflicts were often bloody and prevented people from going to the farm. It also disrupted relationships between the people of the two towns. Obosi people decided to use native wisdom to create an early warning system so that they would know when Onitsha warriors were advancing or burying charms around the border areas. The town consulted its oracle, which revealed that human sacrifice to the gods was imperative. The soul of the person sacrificed would remain perpetually on guard, warning Obosi people of impending danger.

An elderly woman volunteered to be the sacrifice. She had lived a full life and had many children and grandchildren. She wanted to ensure that with her death, Obosi people would no longer fall prey to the marauding Onitsha warriors. She was called *Agadi Nwanyi*, the Old Woman.

She kept guard over Obosi against intruders and anytime there was danger, she was said to send out an alarm by screaming '*Obosi Adiikeogu! Obosi Adiikeogu! Aka akpalu unu ee!*' which means 'Obosi, the weakling! Obosi, the weakling! You are in danger!'

There is another explanation for this, however. The progenitor of Obosi was a man named Adikeogu. He is immortalised by the fact that the main market there is named Afor Adike, after him.

For a long time, Obosi women of traditional religion had ceremonial days when naked; they would deliver bundles of dry wood to the front of a hidden part of the ancient forest, at the boundary of the town. This place was called *Okwu Agadi Nwanyi*, 'The cave of the Old Woman'. The wood was meant to keep her warm, while she kept watch over the town.

My mother told me how she and her sister once encountered *Agadi Nwanyi* on their way to gather firewood at the outskirts of town. Early that morning, before dawn, she woke up Dorothy, so they could quickly be on their way to the forest. Deceived by the brightness of the moon, the sisters felt no fear whatsoever as they went on their way. The path to the forest was eerily quiet. There were no other people in sight, nor could they hear greetings or banter from those who should have been on their way to their farms at that time. The sisters went on nonetheless, knowing that their lonely walk was preferable to Mama Nnukwu's smackdown, which would definitely be their reward for not completing their chores before school. It did not take long before they realised that they were not alone.

They saw, right in front of their path, a grey-haired and shrivelled old woman, leaning on a stick. Her *ogodo* or wrapper was loosely tied around her shrunken body as she kept herself warm beside a fire. At that moment, the sisters realised that they had left home earlier than usual. It was still the time when visitors from the spirit world were rounding off their worldly outings. Surely, the being in their presence was not of this world.

They were numb and rooted to the spot. *Agadi Nwanyi* said nothing. Somehow, the sister's knew that the apparition in front of them meant no harm, yet they were transfixed. Soon they heard voices of others on the footpath and turned to look at the owners. After this distraction, the two girls turned around to where *Agadi Nwanyi* was, but she had disappeared. There was no trace of the huge fire with which she had been warming herself.

What my mother and her sister experienced was an attempt by *Agadi Nwanyi* to save them from harm. They had left home too early and were on a lonely path, easy prey to the elements of the forest.

Permit me to share another story about another old woman: Mama Nnukwu and her love for me.

We visited Papa Nnukwu and Mama Nnukwu very often, although Obosi was quite a distance from Port Harcourt where my family lived. There was this dance that I was known for as a little girl. It was called *Nwa Aginesi* – My Little Agnes. Having spent most of my Christmas holidays at Obosi, Mama Nnukwu would always request this dance of me, and I would usually play the reluctant entertainer, who needed to be cajoled.

'Nne, bia gbaalu m egwu,' she would say, pleading that I come dance for her.

I would usually stand where I was, arms akimbo and looking at her, expecting to be egged on a little more. My grandmother would throw in some ripened fresh bananas plucked from a corner of our compound. I would munch on the banana but persist with the *nlecha* or feigned reluctance of not wanting to dance.

'Ayollo o bu mma eje ogu,' she would cajole, as she psyched me up by calling me the beautiful bird.

I would smile. That seemed always to be the deal-breaker. Mama Nnukwu knew when I was ready. I reckon it must have come from years of routine, of doing this same thing with her on every visit, every year. At that moment, she would start to sing:

Nwa Aginesi mu o Ah eh!
Nwa Aginesi mu o Ah eh!
Onye isi nkpucha
Na o na edebelu mu oku muo Ah eh!
Onye aka nkpucha
Na ona edebelu oku muo

A ga m agbaji agbaji! eh!
Gbaji e! Gbaji e!

The chant is loosely translated 'My Agnes, the bald one who keeps my pots, I will break whilst dancing. Break, break, break!'

It didn't mean anything, but the more she sang, the more excited I became; the more excited I became, the more I danced. It was a dance that involved a rhythmic interplay, between my moving hands and feet, and grandma's voice. It ended with my hands on the floor and a smile on my face. My smile seemed to pass quickly through the space between us, planting itself onto her face. Thus, she would beam a wide and endearing smile. I would then run into her open arms, taking in the smell of her body and her large breasts that were so comforting.

On the contrary, a grandnephew whom Mama Nnukwu raised, received a different reaction from her. It was another song, with a different delivery and outcome. Chukwudozie sang anytime and anywhere he was called upon. He would belt out the song with no persuasion. Shortly after, Mama Nnukwu would readily dismiss him.

'*Chaa n'uzo na egwu gi enwero ngala*,' Mama Nnukwu would say. 'Give way! Your song is bereft of swagger.'

In those early years, I began to learn the lesson of situational awareness in performance. Tease your audience, make them really want you, and when you finally appear in front of them, make everything count. Make it so memorable that they will take a part of you with them. Not too much, only a part; that deepens their craving for you as they continue to thirst for another performance.

The Real Ochie Dike

In old age, my mother was known as *Ochie Dike*, which means 'Warrior of Old'. This was indeed the title of a song she wrote for her mother and which we recorded together in 1988. It remains a hit in Nigeria, so many decades later. My mother received befitting royalties for the song, given that it was mostly her intellectual property. She was a tough negotiator too. No Mothers' Day celebration would be complete in Nigeria without a rendition of the song 'Ochie Dike Nne m'.

The real *Ochie Dike*, however, was Margaret Nwokoye, my grandmother, the first woman to erect a one-storey building in Obosi. She was an active leader of women both in the church and in her community. One of her best friends was Dr Alvan Ikoku, the educationist. She supplied food to his college, Aggrey Memorial College Arochukwu, where her first daughter, Sophie, was educated.

Mama Nnukwu had a sister whom we called Mama Obele, which translates to 'Small Mama'. Her proper name was Mrs Agnes Okonkwo. Perhaps this may explain why Mama Nnukwu was so enamoured by my song *'Nwa Aginesi'*. The sisters were friends and business partners; together they undertook the supply of food items to Aggrey Memorial College.

Mama Obele lived in Abakaliki where they sourced items such as rice, beans, *garri*, and dry fish popularly known as *azu mangala,* which were supplied in bulk to the school. It was a gruelling journey they made from Obosi to Abakaliki, and then to Arochukwu, huddled in the passenger seats of the lorry, enduring all of its discomforts. The roads to these remote places were not the best, but these two women bore their troubles with dignity and pride. They also made very good money. That was how my grandmother became the first woman to erect a one-storey building in Obosi.

After the burial of my grandmother, it was with Mama Obele that I stood at the back of my grandparent's house, to mourn her passing. The house was a medium-sized bungalow or *obi*, with an adjoining house that belonged to my uncle, Ernest. A one-storey building stood majestically in the front of the premises facing the street. Uncle Nathan, 'Njio', occupied that one. It was specifically built for him. The kitchen was a small elongated hut behind the *obi*. It had a main kitchen and a smaller one attached to it for Uncle Nathan's wife, Vicky. Nearby was Papa Nnukwu's yam barn; however, this was dismantled after his passing in 1975.

I wanted to spend some time in this courtyard where the kitchen was situated. It was the centre of the house, where Mama Nnukwu ruled. From there, she fried and sold *akara;* her delicious bean cakes reputed to be one of the best in Obosi during her time. My brother Richard, as a boy of six, had been entrusted with a wrap of *akara* balls to deliver to an elderly man next door. Along the way, he began wringing out the oil in them and licking off the same. By the time he got to his destination, the *akara* package had turned into a shrivelled shadow of its original self. The displeased customer sent little Richard back with the wrinkled contents. I guess he thought he could eat the *akara* without really eating it. That was how he was found out.

Across the kitchen and the huge grinding stone beside it, were some very big earthen pots, half-buried in the ground. We stored water in them, which we fetched from the Idemili River during the day. This was used for everything but drinking. The drinking water was fetched separately and stored in pots inside the house.

Once, while we were visiting for Christmas, my grandmother noticed that someone had put a clutch of bitter leaves into one of the pots of water designated for cooking. She was furious and wanted to know who had done such a thing. My sister, Ijeoma, probably about 10 or 11 years old, felt inexplicably guilty. Jumping up, she asked a question in self-defence.

'How can I do that to the water pot of a woman like me?'

'A woman like you?' My grandmother asked and then fell apart with laughter. Imagine an old woman being compared to an 11-year-old? The matter, of course, fizzled out.

Mama Nnukwu's kitchen and courtyard held a lot of memories for me. I remember the *nni oka* or cornmeal, and *ogbono* soup with *oha* leaves. There was the ubiquitous *onugbu* or bitter leaf soup, which was the signature soup of the household. There were always *onugbu* shrubs around the compound, not to mention the rich assemblage of fruit trees - banana, plantain, *ube* the African pear, guava, mango, and coconut – all of which grew generously around us.

To stay with my grandmother, you could not be a lazy person. Everyone had assigned duties which included going to the river to fetch water, going to the forest for firewood, washing dishes, washing clothes, grinding beans for *akara*, and grinding pepper and other ingredients for cooking. These were the unforgettable experiences we could not acquire in Port Harcourt. I imagined that it was in this courtyard where Mama Nnukwu held sway that she listened to people's problems and then delivered her wise counsel.

A distant cousin of my mother's, whom Mama Nnukwu loved greatly, would visit with his Yoruba wife, obtaining life's pointers along the way. Chief Emeka Anyaoku, the former Secretary-General of the Commonwealth, always reminded me of his close relationship with my grandmother. She succeeded in persuading the Anyaokus to have yet another child, their youngest; advice which they remained grateful to have heeded. Their only regret was that Mama Nnukwu did not live long enough to see the child she helped bring into the world.

I am quite sure that my grandmother, having married into a land far away from home, would have been especially welcoming to Mrs Anyaoku, who is Yoruba.

As I stood gazing at the kitchen with Mama Obele and with all the memories flooding back, it suddenly dawned on me that a major part of my life had just ended with the burial of Mama Nnukwu. This was when I broke down and cried. Mama Obele put her hand on my shoulder. She was never the openly affectionate type, so that meant a lot. She simply asked me to dry my tears and let my grandmother go. I was really crying for myself.

My grandmother was in the place where she had wanted to be for a long time. Each time she received the news of another's death, she wondered why it was not yet her turn. If you wished her more years, she thanked you but signified that she was ready to go home. She was already 86 years old when I saw her for the last time, before leaving for further studies in the United States of America in 1971. Although I was not able to see her after almost ten years, I did send her my first allowance as a Youth Corp Member. It was a mere ₦200. But it meant a lot to her, I was told, and she blessed me for it.

My maternal grandmother, Mama Nnukwu, passed away on 23 December 1980.

Years before, precisely in 1971, just a few weeks before my sister Ijeoma, my cousin Ifeoma and I left Nigeria, Mama Nnukwu called me aside and extracted a promise from me that I would look after my mother, her daughter, in her old age. I had no idea why she chose me for such a pact, but she did and I tried my best not to let her down.

My grandmother was very good at giving out appropriate and prophetic names to members of her family, and she was proved right as the names fit. A few examples would suffice. She named my mother: *O me na nwata,* which means 'A person who does great things at a tender age'. Azunna was called *Nwa Ogalanya tijie odu,* which means 'When the child of a rich man breaks an elephant tusk, it is simply replaced'. I was called *Ayollo obunma eje ogu* and Ijeoma, my immediate elder sister, was named *Ori okuko sajem,* 'A chicken-eating sergeant'. She was named after a police sergeant who was known for something rare in his days, the frequent slaughter of chicken, an expensive thing to do. Ijeoma protested and refused to take on the name. She was therefore given another, *Ebunyiaku,* 'One who carries great wealth with her'. As far as I was concerned, the first name suited her just fine and I called her that whenever I wanted to tease her.

I grew up with three maternal uncles, Nathan 'Njio', Ernest and Joseph who was adopted. I found it quite fascinating that my grandparents were so open-minded to adopt a child from another village who had been abandoned in Obosi. Joseph's real father from the neighbouring town of Ojoto was a hot-tempered, itinerant farm labourer who lived in Obosi. He murdered Joseph's mother and brother and escaped, leaving the helpless lad behind. My grandparents took him in. When his father came back for him years later, he refused to go with him.

This act of kindness, unprecedented as it were, would come back to haunt the Nwokoye family. Joseph became a destabilising element and an enemy to the family from within. He claimed that he was the first and real son of Godson Nwokoye, my grandfather, whom he said had an affair with his mother. It was a lie of course, but lies, when often repeated, can cast a shadow over a person's reputation. This lie was meant to taint my grandfather's name and cast him as an adulterer.

The matter was finally decided in court in 2009 in favour of Ernest, when Joseph failed to provide any proof or witnesses to buttress his claims. Njio was the first son, followed by Nnaemeka who died as a young child. Ernest was next in line, before Joseph. He should have been content with that but he wanted to have Ernest disinherited.

Of my three uncles, Njio was the kindest. He was protective, generous and caring. He ensured that we always had a great time while on holiday in Obosi. During Christmas and New Year celebrations, all supplies of fireworks, toys, snacks, and treats came from him. Njio hated to see or hear any of us cry. From the vantage point of his veranda which overlooked the field of St. Andrews Church, opposite the house, he kept watch over us as we played. A young fellow who sought to bully us once learned of Njio's protectiveness towards his family the hard way.

My uncle Njio dropped out of the Anglican Church as soon as he was free from his parent's tutelage and provision. He could not have done it earlier or my grandmother would have starved him. What is more, to the embarrassment of his parents who prided themselves as stalwarts of the Anglican Church, Njio preferred to take the Ozo title. This title is given to prominent members of society. It is a 'secret society' of sorts, not acceptable to the church as it was considered a heathen practice. The Ozo title holder was immediately ex-communicated.

Ozo confers on its holder certain privileges and obligations, as well as rules of behaviour. Even more bewildering was Njio's bearing the mask of a powerful masquerade, which after his death, no one has mustered the courage to touch. However, my grandparents loved their son and felt they had no choice but to forgive him, even as they prayed that God would forgive him.

Njio's death in 1972 was a huge blow to the family. With his death, my grandparents had buried five out of their seven biological children.

My Mother, My Sister

If my mother were to tell you her story, she would start with her date of birth. She was born on 6 January 1919, in Obosi and like many children born into Christian families, she was given a Christian name, Hope, which some people preferred to call the Igbo version, Nchekwube. However, her story would be incomplete, except told by my grandmother.

The day she was born started like every other day. Margaret, her mother, had risen early to go to the market. There are four market days in the Igbo calendar: Eke, Orie, Afor, and Nkwo. That day was an Eke day. In the past few days, the child in her stomach had kicked more furiously, especially at night, keeping mother Margaret awake most of the time. As she dragged herself up from her bed, she felt pangs of jolting movements in her stomach. She dismissed them since it was not the first time that she was feeling such discomfort. She had her first child Sophie, so she knew what the proper onset labour felt like. This one did not feel like it. She got up, took her bath and headed out to the market.

The more Margaret moved, the more the pangs came. This time, more rapid and acute. Then all of a sudden, her feet became rooted to the ground, refusing to move. Women who were also passing by, immediately gathered around her. With their wrappers, they protected her from public glare, and with their words of comfort and support, they gave her strength. Thus, into their waiting arms slipped a baby girl – breathing and crying. So, there, on the way to the market, my mother was born. She was given the middle name Mgbeke meaning 'One born on Eke market day'. But my mother hated the name. You called her Mgbeke at your own risk.

At the time of her birth, there was a bad wind blowing around Igboland, and indeed the world. It carried a deadly disease: influenza, a highly contagious viral infection that afflicted the respiratory passages. Margaret caught it, became ill and was unconscious for some time. Margaret's mother was on hand to nurse her daughter and the community assisted in taking care of my mum.

'Has that child been fed?' A woman going to the stream would inquire before taking a seat in front of the house.

My great-grandmother would hand baby Hope over to a nursing mother who would suckle her. When it appeared the baby was well-fed, satisfaction sparkling through her eyes, the woman would place her on her shoulder till she belched.

'*Nno o*,' she would say in greeting, as she handed Hope over to her grandmother who was busy nursing her own child back to health.

On the hour, another woman would come by, put down her basket and ask about the child, to find out how she was doing and if she had suckled. That was the society in which my mother grew up. '*Ofu onye ada azu nwa*' is a popular Igbo saying which means 'Raising a child is never a single individual's responsibility'. In my mother's case, the entire community raised her.

The bad wind eventually passed, mother and child were again of sound health, and Hope grew into a healthy young girl. She excelled in sports, especially in races, and was known to do house chores and farm work with resounding efficiency. Hope was stubborn and opinionated, while her elder sister, Sophie, was gentle and soft-spoken. Hope made up for her sister's calmness with her boldness.

She loved her siblings and they supported one another in their life's endeavours; Hope also stepped in quickly when there was a lapse in the family.

In 1944, Sophie died in mysterious circumstances. She was 28 years old and still single; a graduate of Aggrey Memorial College in Arochukwu, she was one of the few females to have had the opportunity of high school education.

My mother, Hope Onwenu, did not attain higher levels of education. She had a First School Leaving Certificate or 'Standard Six' as they called it in those days. For a woman, that was not so bad. You were expected to get the most basic level of education before continuing to your husband's house for the education that never ended. The more Hope grew, the more she transformed into a slim, tall, dark woman with a curvaceous 'behind', which in the family is known as *kpongem*; powerful butts that stood high and robust and never dropped even with age.

These were days when women were married off early. At 19, Hope married a young man from the illustrious Obionwu family in Obosi. The story goes that her prospective mother-in-law had seen her working hard at the farm and noticed that Hope finished her assignment way before anyone else. This recommended her highly as good wife material. She married Davis Obionwu, but the marriage did not last. Death came on the brink of their first wedding anniversary and took her husband away. The young pregnant widow was inconsolable. Eight days later, she gave birth to a girl. She called her Azunna, which means 'Born after her father's death'.

Hope quickly pulled herself together; she had to be strong for her daughter. I imagine that even as a child when she felt all was lost, she had the will to survive. Thus, she returned to the farm and her job as an Elementary School teacher. This was how things were when she met my father.

Hope, The Power of 'Kpongem' And DK

There is only one version of the story of how my father and my mother met. In the family, it is called 'The Power of Kpongem'.

It goes like this...

At the time DK was ready for marriage, it was the normal thing for people to recommend possible spouses to the men. If they found someone they felt was a perfect match, they would tell you and perhaps invite you over to see the woman yourself. When DK was ready for a life partner, there was a certain renowned Igbo educationist called Ahamba. He was the author of the famous Igbo children's book *Okeke Tara Ose Oji* and also the father of Mike Ahamba (SAN), an accomplished member of the Nigerian Bar. Headmaster Ahamba, my father's contemporary and good friend, invited him to visit from his Okpare station in Delta State to look at a certain young lady.

DK was all too happy to oblige once he got the message. At the first available opportunity, he got on his bicycle and rode from Okpare to the Headmaster's office in Obosi. After exchanging pleasantries, he sat with his back to the door when Hope, unaware of this entire plot, walked in. DK beheld this elegant young lady with a graceful gait and a firm backside. She had all-round confidence. He quickly nodded in agreement. Hope never heard of this story, this plan, until DK came to propose.

When Hope announced to her father that she wanted to marry

a man from Arondizuogu, Papa Nnukwu was not very pleased. Why not marry someone from Obosi? As his favourite daughter, her father's resistance was not surprising. Papa Nnukwu simply did not want her to move too far away from home. Marrying an Arondizuogu man would mean just that. Meanwhile, Papa Nnukwu forgot that he trekked with his kindred from Obosi to Aro-Egbuoma in Imo State, to ask for the hand of Margaret Anyiwo, my grandmother. The things we do for love.

On one fine morning in 1943, at St. Peters Church Ndiawa, Arondizuogu, they took their vows, promising to be there for each other, in sickness and in health, in wealth and in lack, until death did them part. In their wedding picture, my father stood wearing a double-breasted suit, his hair parted to the right, and in his left hand, a hat. My mother, her arm resting on her husband's wore a long, white wedding dress, her hands gloved in white too, and her hair wrapped in a small veil. Mother had a half-formed smile on her face. Father looked at the camera, assured and ready to begin the lifelong journey with the woman beside him.

As if in protest, Papa Nnukwu did not attend their wedding. However, it did not take long for him to realise that he had been gifted the best son-in-law ever. Papa Nnukwu found that his earlier assumptions and fears were unfounded and getting to know DK changed it all. Their relationship quickly exceeded the artificial bonds of father-in-law and son-in-law and grew into a father and son relationship. In the young man his daughter brought home, Papa Nnukwu found a rare and exciting human being.

As soon as they got married, as it was with many in their generation, they started having children. It was Richard Chukwudum that came first in 1944, just as World War II ended. Two years later, in 1946, my sister Zoe-Dibugwu was born. Shortly after, DK had to travel to Sierra Leone to continue his education at Fourah Bay College. My mother went with him and the children stayed with her parents. It was not a strange thing for grandparents to raise their grandchildren for a while.

For two years, my father attended college while my mother learned to cook and keep a home. When she returned to Nigeria in 1949, she was pregnant with their third child. She called her Ijeoma, which means 'Good journey'. It was a name most fitting to the realities of their situation. They had travelled and had returned safely and with good news. In 1952, I came along. Two years after me, Baby Nnenna Onwenu was born but she did not stay around for long. She died at six months.

As DK and Hope raised us, their children, they were also surrounded by other people's children whom they raised as well. Some were related to us by blood, whilst others were not.

Everyone in the house called my mother 'Sister', an endearing term to show respect. My mother's younger sister, Dorothy, started this trend. Among the children, it was Richard who started calling our mother 'Ita', his version of 'Sister' and every other child then followed suit. Seeing that our mother was called 'Sister', it became natural to us. She never tried to stop us and it did not mean anything to her if we did not call her 'Mummy' or 'Mama'. It certainly did not make her feel any less our mother.

That was how my mother became 'Sister'.

My parents' love for each other was never in doubt, yet they had their fights like all couples. Like the tongue and the teeth that settle their quarrel whenever it is time for a meal, my parents settled their quarrels fast.

45

Hon. DK Onwenu was a charismatic and good-looking man. My mother said he lit up any room he walked into and that women always noticed. She was wary of the ladies and tired of him constantly arriving home late at night. One day, our mother decided to accompany him to one of his political meetings. At least, she could also learn about what was happening in the polity. One cold harmattan night, as they drove around, he stopped at every opportunity to say 'hello' to every Tom, Dick and Harry. My mother wondered why it was important to greet everyone.

'That's politics,' he said.

That night, she understood how and why DK always arrived home late. She saw first-hand how long and tedious meetings could be. Much of it came across to her as long-winded and unnecessary chattering. She felt how exhausting it could be to listen to people talk with barely any end in sight. My mother was more of an action woman than one of talking. She soon got bored with it all; that was when she accepted that he was meant for that space and she was not. However, she was always his first lady with all that it took to fulfil that role.

The next time Papa invited her to another political meeting, she smiled at him and responded: 'No, thank you!' Papa also smiled. The two of them had come to an understanding that when it came to each other's social life, they inhabited two different worlds and the best they could do was to support each other in their respective dreams and ambitions.

If there was a real fight between them, my mother was usually the aggressor. She told me herself. Once, Papa had come home late; it was one night, too many. On this night, she served him dinner but dumped the tray of food on the ground, turning around and leaving almost immediately. Papa got up and walked away. In Igbo land, after wider family consultation, my mother's offence would attract a fine of a goat or chicken, depending on the offender's financial standing.

For Papa, there was no need for family consultation; he just refused to eat any meals cooked by my mum until a full apology was rendered. Consequently, Papa would cook his own meals. He made his delicious jollof rice, red to the eyes and yummy on the taste buds, which we preferred to our mother's. The trick was that Papa used up every available ingredient and more meat than my mother, the typical home manager, would use. We were not too happy whenever my parents made up, because Papa's meat- galore rice would disappear.

After a while, my mother would tender the appropriate apologies and things would return to normal. No matter how late Papa returned, she would place his tray of food on the dining table in the sitting room and sit on the chair beside him as they exchanged tales about the happenings in each other's day. I know because I was always lurking around, waiting to be called to join Papa in eating his meal.

While Papa went around from school to school being Headmaster, or from town to town as a politician, my mother, a trader, went from market to market looking for the best bargains. Sister had eyes that saw the finest gold; she also had the bargaining skills that could get her the best buys. More so, she had the tongue and temperament of a good salesperson. She traded in gold trinkets, *ankara* and george wrappers which are the mainstay of any Igbo woman's wardrobe. She could convince anyone to see value in whatever she had to sell. Most of the time, Sister had more money than her politician husband. She often came to his aid when he needed extra funds. He would promise to pay back the loans, but never did.

Love has a Slender Frame

I had little memory of my mother until after my father's death. This was the extent to which my father's love overcame my heart and encircled my life. It took over every inch of me, so much so that there was scarcely space for another. I will let my siblings tell how they remember our parents.

Azunna was much loved by Papa, as I am sure he loved all his children. He took care to make sure that she received special attention because she was his stepdaughter. Azunna appreciated this and never forgot it.

My brother Richard felt Papa was too hard on him. It was understandable as his first child and only son, that there was a weight he had to carry. He was expected to be a greater version of his father. With the benefit of hindsight, it would seem that Papa was trying to drill into him the consciousness of his responsibility to himself, as much as he was to be responsible for his younger siblings. Yet, Papa's shoes were so big for even the finest of humans to fill. Papa always expected Richard to bring home the best reports from school. When he was not impressed with the school report, he would compare Richard with his mates, even the older ones. At times like these, my mum would step in to defend her son, urging as vigorously as she could that the boy be left to be a child.

Zoe was Papa's ardent follower. She did not reckon with our mother or anyone else for that matter. He remained her hero and the last reference point for all things, academic and political. In everything, she strove to impress him. She was a proud Onwenu and Papa was always proud of her schoolwork, something she threw in Richard's face all the time. Those two never really got on; as far as Zoe was concerned, she was better material for a son. Ijeoma's memories connect to my father through a regular hospital ritual. As children, Papa was in charge of taking us to the clinic to be dewormed. On this particular occasion, which stood out in Ijeoma's memory, he took her alone. I remember a particular medication we were made to take regularly. I believe it was called Chenopodium. It had a horrible taste and you had to hold your nose to drink it. You were then given a slice of orange to take away the bad taste and that was the only thing you ate for most of the day. This was all Ijeoma remembered.

There was one incident in which my mother featured and that I remember very well. This was early 1956. Sister was ill and was admitted at Anua General Hospital in Calabar. Papa took my siblings and me to visit her. I would learn in later years that she had a miscarriage with complications. Anua General Hospital was supposedly one of the best at that time. I stayed in the car and did not see my mum during the visit. The trip was memorable because as usual, Papa's presence meant that we had any and everything we wanted.

My mother returned home from the hospital a week later with a present for me. I remember this for some reason. It was a small wooden stool. After that miscarriage, Sister continued to make attempts to have another male child. She persisted against the advice of my father and the doctor. My mother was a stubborn woman, not easily persuaded when her mind was made up. She had the last miscarriage just a week before my father died.

In some ways, my mother's insistence on having at least two

male children was understandable, given the high value placed on male children by the Igbo tradition. A woman had no stake in her husband's family or a right to his property without a male child. She had no inheritance and no claim to her father's property either. After all, she is expected to be married off, anyway. However, if there is no male child in the family, one of the daughters may remain unmarried to bear children. Hopefully, she would have a male child to carry on her father's name. In Arondizuogu, this is called *Ihanye nwanyi*, the designation of an unmarried daughter who would bear children for her father's family.

Even though my father, a highly educated Aro man, could not be bothered by all these traditions, my mother knew that if he died before her, his family would lose all if she did not have a male child. While Richard, her first son opened the door to the Onwenu family for her, to take a seat there, she needed to have at the very least one more son. This would make her position in her husband's house unshakeable. It was some form of an insurance policy.

Although Papa's life ended suddenly, my mother would be present in mine for many decades more. I would come to respect her as a special bundle of talent, my biggest and most irrepressible cheerleader. She was a renowned songwriter, an actress, as well as a master storyteller. I learned to sing in harmony even at the tender age of three, as we made the rounds of fundraising concerts for Motherless Babies Homes in Port Harcourt.

When my mother sang hymns in church, her voice could not be mistaken. Her melodious renditions would often hold the congregation spellbound. In full synergy with the organ and choir, her voice rose with that of the congregation into a crescendo, a vocal offering to God. She had a sonorous voice like her father, Godson Nwokoye.

My father called her 'HO', an abbreviation of Hope Onwenu. After my father's passing, we children jokingly called her 'Madam Ekeocha' after a woman in Abakiliki who featured in Drum Magazine in the 1960s. She had the habit of carrying a gun and ruled her roost as a Commanding Officer.

My mum, elegant, good-looking and fashionable, was a go-getter. For my siblings and I, she was the first and greatest example of a liberated woman in action. She lost her second husband at 37, yet she raised her five children and several nieces and nephews. She quickly stepped up to become both father and mother to her wards. Even though her husband's death was both sudden and mysterious, there was no time to sit around and mourn. In her never-say-die spirit, she took full charge of her immediate family and the extended one.

Through Papa's death, I saw that while love could be such a strong force, it also had a slender frame. With his passing, our family began to see people for who they really were. My father's death shattered me for a long time, especially when my mother recounted the incident that led to it.

The Path to Death

Most times, when death calls, it gives no warning. It does not give you time to prepare. It burrows through the door of your house like the typical unwanted guest. Even when you tell it you have no seat to offer it, it says not to worry, that it has come with its own. When it visited us in our house at Port Harcourt, though, we felt that some three strange men invited it.

Here is how it happened.

The evening was no different for the children. We played on the street, enjoying the last minutes of a lazy and pleasant day. Ijeoma had cooked 'play soup' - a mud broth made from sand, cassava leaves and water, all stirred in a discarded tin can. She played 'the mother' and our neighbour Osinomumu, whom we also called *Aka Ngu* as his right hand was bent outwards like a hanger, played 'the father'. Ijeoma made us, 'the children', eat lizard meat. It tasted like chicken. We did not know any better but I suspect that Ijeoma did. She never ate any of it. My mother only found out years later. She wept.

We waited for the usual call up to head home for dinner at 6 p.m. Papa was in town, so I was also looking forward to sharing his meal. That meant big lumps of *anu na azu* – meat and fish – which I would then brandish before everyone else, basking in the privilege of my special relationship with Papa. Instead of the call, however, our much older cousin, Patience, began rounding us up to witness some strange happening at the house. Our compound contained two houses. Ours was in front, facing the street. A smaller house in the back belonged to the Ozi family. However, we all shared the same entrance.

Mr Ozi and his wife had been particularly unfriendly lately. The landlord, Mr Onumonu, had sold the house to them, without informing us. Papa had started to build our house in a different part of the town and just needed three months to complete the first floor so we could move out of our present premises, but the Ozis could not wait. They wanted us out immediately.

Papa, in his usual manner, maintained a friendly disposition. He doubled up efforts at getting the new house habitable. My mum bore the brunt of the Ozis' antagonism and unwarranted aggression. She suspected that the matter was a lot more complicated than a spat between neighbours and told Papa so. She was provoked daily with name-calling. She was spat on and hissed at by the Ozi children. My mother was a firebrand who would have responded ordinarily, but Papa implored her to keep her cool. Nevertheless, she remained vigilant.

The curious spectacle that Patience was calling us all to witness was the arrival of three strange men who alighted from a black Morris Minor taxi. They entered the Ozis' house, walking backwards. One of the men had very long hair, another had breasts like a woman, and the third had a limp. Shortly after they entered the house, we heard them loudly pounding in a mortar and calling Papa's name. The older children and cousins were alarmed, but I did not understand why.

At about 5 a.m the next morning, Papa and I were woken up by loud banging on the door. It was my mother. I usually went to sleep early and would settle into Papa's bed. I was always taken to the children's room later at night when he came to bed. That night, however, I was not. It turned out to be our last.

Papa had been up most of the night, trying to reassure my mother who had kept vigil, monitoring the activities of the three strange men. He tried to convince her that she need not worry about Mr Ozi's visitors. My father did not believe in witchcraft, or that anyone could harm him through incantations or curses. That early morning, the three strange men were in our garage, which was at the front of our house, under a small veranda. Again, they were reciting incantations and calling out my father's name. That was why my mother was at the door, frantic.

'What are you doing in my garage, Mr Ozi?' Papa called out, finally addressing the issue of the strange goings-on.

'Sorry, Mr Onwenu,' Mr Ozi answered. 'My wife is an *ogbanje*. The native doctors say she buried something in this area. She will die if we do not find it.'

*Ogbanje*s are reincarnates who die young, and then return again in a coming and going that never ends, causing pain and anguish to their parents. Locating their buried token breaks the cycle.

It appeared from all indications to be an unusual and contrived tale, but Papa bought it, or so it seemed. He let them continue and went back to bed. My mother was screaming at the Ozis, calling them all sorts of names. Not satisfied with her husband's reply, she hurriedly grabbed her wrapper and securely tied it around her waist with a headscarf – an indication that war was afoot – and ran off to fetch our pastor. She returned with the pastor in tow, to counteract whatever it was Mr Ozi and the three witches were doing in our compound.

The three strange men were spreading some black substance on the ground floor of our shared compound. My mother, the pastor and Mama Nnee, our beloved next-door neighbour, started pouring palm oil over any spot they found the black stuff. There was panic everywhere. The children watched the entire drama from the stairs and windows.

The Ozis and their guests had now retreated into their house, and the compound was a mess. There had been a war between palm oil and the black stuff, and we weren't sure who had won.

Papa suddenly emerged from his room and walked up to my mother, a dishevelled shadow of the attractive woman she normally was. He held and comforted her. To her bewilderment, he declared that he was now going to show her how powerless the Ozis and their witch doctors were. Papa marched into the Ozi's living room and shook the hands of the witch doctors, announcing that he was off to Aba for a meeting with the Teachers Union.

My mother was shocked. She could not understand how Papa could be so naïve. The pastor prayed, while my mother insisted that Papa would not drive himself that day. Our loyal driver, Simeon, who also lived with us, was summoned by my mother to drive Papa to Aba. That may have assuaged my mother's fears. However, on getting to the site of our new house on Degema Street, Papa asked Simeon to stay behind and help the construction workers, while he drove himself to Aba.

Looking back, Papa's actions on the morning of the day he died made no sense. I am inclined to believe that, whatever the Ozis and the three witches did, by the time Papa shook their hands before leaving for Aba, they had him.

It was late afternoon on 10 December 1956 when the devastating news came to us: Papa was dead. His brand new Chevrolet Impala had crashed into an oil bean tree, *osisi ukpaka,* many of which adorned the Port Harcourt-Aba Road. The doctors of the Aba General Hospital were on strike. My father had suffered serious internal injuries and bled to death before help could get to him.

We would later find out that before the news got to us, it had reached his sister, Mrs Juliana DanChimah, also known as Mama Aba. Her love for Papa extended to everything that concerned him, his wife and children. My mother could do no wrong. Mama Aba was her greatest champion and protector, in the wider Onwenu family, and would often take my mum's side during quarrels with Papa. Because Papa had so much love and respect for his sister, my mum often reported his infractions to Mama Aba, who would very quickly arrive Port Harcourt, battle-ready, to find that her brother had beaten a retreat to avoid confrontation.

On the day Papa died, Mama Aba's youngest child, Stephen, the only one of her children who had not lived with us, bumped into Papa on the road. The Chevrolet Impala was unmistakable. Stephen flagged my father down and was rewarded with two shillings for his effort. When news of Papa's accident and the fact that he had been rushed to the Aba General Hospital came, it was Stephen who broke it to his mother. He recalls it decades later, as if it had just happened. He had rushed home because he knew the danger in allowing some other, and perhaps undiplomatic person, do the job. On seeing his mother from a short distance, he blurted out the news.

Stephen suggested that they needed to prepare a meal to take to Papa in the hospital, insisting that it was only a minor accident, but did not succeed in pulling the wool over his mother's eyes. When she heard the word 'accident', her wrapper immediately fell from her waist. She knew that she had lost the love of her life, her beloved brother 'Dikison'. Mama Aba never quite recovered from this loss till she passed away in 1988.

Port Harcourt came to a standstill. Offices shut down and people thronged Moorehouse Road. A delegation of Arondizuogu men had arrived at our house and disconnected our radio, before other people arrived. They told my mum that my father had been involved in an accident, but was alive and was asking to see her. That was partly true. Papa's car had veered off the road and he was pinned to his seat by the steering wheel. An expatriate, who was the only other person who owned a 1956 Chevrolet Impala, rescued him. He was driving by when he spotted Papa's car in trouble.

Even before the wise men from Arondizuogu had finished their story, our compound was filled with people, neighbours, friends, relations and political associates. The unthinkable had happened; a political and academic shining light had been snuffed out. Everyone was thrown into unexpected mourning. My mother had to be given tranquilisers to keep her calm, for there was palpable fear that she may drown in her grief when she still had children to care for. We, the children, were taken away to the house of a relation, Mr and Mrs Ajagu.

The Ajagus did all they could to maintain a semblance of normalcy. Mrs Ajagu began to cook a pot of rice and chicken, a meal that was guaranteed to distract. Yet we could still tell that a disaster of terrible consequences had taken place.

We left Moorehouse Road with the Ozis in a celebratory mood. Mr Ozi dusted up his gramophone and put on a record. I can still remember the music, with the lyrics that said something like this: '*Umunne m, ihe na-atu m egwu bu onwu,*' which loosely translates to 'My people, what I am afraid of is death.'

When the crowd began to grow, the Ozis retreated to their living room. Mr Ozi was walking backwards, like the three witches before him. The three strange men were quickly rushed out of the compound, their dubious mission accomplished.

Papa Goes Home

In 1956, mortuary and embalming services in Nigeria were not as developed as they are today. People were buried soon after they died, and my father was no exception. He died in the afternoon of 10 December 1956 and by nighttime, we were on our way to Arondizuogu. We picked up Mama Aba, who was with his body at Aba General Hospital. I sat sandwiched between the two most important women in my father's life, Mama Aba and my mother. We sat in the front of a Mercedes 911 truck which sounded and looked as rickety as the name people called it – *gwongworo*. My siblings were at the back seated on wooden planks, balanced across the two sides of the vehicle.

Normally, such a family trip to the village was planned. We would have been in Papa's Chevrolet Impala or some other decent vehicle. Yet here we were, swooped up by the urgency of the occasion, accompanying our father's hearse home. His car was lying at the side of the Aba/Port Harcourt Road. The bashed fender was still lodged against the oil bean tree. We stopped at the sight of it. The only damage was in front where it collided with the tree. The women in our entourage let out a chilling wail that stoked up even more grief.

The *gwongworo* conveying Papa's corpse suddenly lurched to a stop at the bridge over Imo River. The engine would not start, no matter how hard the driver tried. The driver kicked, the conductor pushed, yet the vehicle did not budge. Everything had come to an abrupt halt. The entourage could not proceed unless the *gwongworo* moved. The crickets chirped noisily; the fireflies flew around; the stars sat bright in the sky as we stood there, waiting and praying for a miracle. Some of the 'wise men' from Arondizuogu who were accompanying us home got out with their torches and tried to help.

'Go and speak to your brother,' they told Mama Aba. 'Tell him to allow the homeward journey to continue.'

They said that my father's spirit was resisting the journey as he was not ready to go home, but we had no option than to keep going, as he had to be buried that day.

Mama Aba got down from our lorry and approached Papa's corpse.

'Dikison, *nna m*,' she called out to him, tenderly and endearingly. '*Ayi ya anaba*,' she continued as she pleaded with him, calling him her father and begging him that it was time to let go.

At that moment, total silence swept everywhere. It seemed as though even the crickets were afraid to chirp. The driver kicked again, the lorry made as though it was going to start, but burped and jerked to a faint stop.

Then in a comical elder sisterly way, in a manner that only Mama Aba could have mustered, she threatened him.

'E *chokwahu ina, aya m ahapu ghu ibe a, nawalu*,' she said.

She told him that if he refused to let go, she would abandon him there, somewhere in the bush. That did the trick. What Mama Aba did not achieve with her pleas, she did with her threat. The lorry suddenly roared back to life and lumbered into action. We were on the move again.

This happened two more times before we got to Ndianiche

Obinetiti or Ikpa Nwahihia Arondizuogu, as the town was then known. I remember because my mother used to tease Papa about the name of his village, Ikpa, means 'Home', and Nwahihia means 'Child of the Grass.'

It was a tortuous and sad journey to my father's village. The roads were bad; some parts were waterlogged, much as our hearts were. At 5 a.m on 11 December 1956, we arrived.

Arondizuogu was covered in a cloak of darkness and harmattan was beginning to set in. Papa's death was a huge blow to the town. A tragedy made worse by the fact that within two weeks, Arondizuogu had lost two other illustrious sons – the iconic Mazi Mbonu Ojike of the 'Boycott the Boycottables' fame and who also was my father's best friend, and Mazi F O Mbadiwe, brother to Dr K O Mbadiwe. Mazi Ojike was a member of the Eastern House of Assembly and Mbadiwe, was a member of the Federal House of Representatives. Papa had been named the next Minister of Education and was to be sworn-in in January 1957.

I was almost five when Papa died, but everything that happened remains etched in my mind. Through the mist from the harmattan haze, I could make out the faces of the many people who had come to bid my father farewell. They were all crying inconsolably. Uncle Charles was devastated. He had to be held down by four *dimkpas* or remarkably strong men, but even they could not. Who could blame him? His world had come to a crashing end. Here was a brother for whom he could do no wrong and who humoured his every caprice. Papa raised all his brother's children and never complained about him marrying more wives than he could fend for. He just wanted Charles to keep at whatever made him happy.

That morning, the air was cold with our bodies shivering and our teeth clattering. Everyone looked ashy for the harmattan wind was the kind that made one's skin look as though they wore a white cloak. My siblings and I positioned ourselves around the fireplace in the kitchen area at the back of *Nnukwu Uno* or the main house. *Nnukwu Uno* or *obi* was where the man of the house lived. One or more of his wives could live there as well, but the wives mainly lived in the huts surrounding the *obi*.

'*Bia nu hu ebe a na-awu papa ahu.*'

My cousin Goddy was calling us to come and see where they were preparing Papa for burial.

Mama Aba was cuddling her brother's upper body. She was crying and talking to him at the same time. She was washing my father's corpse, aided by other people I did not recognise.

This was a disturbing sight for me. I knew something was happening; my father had died, that was clear. I did not understand, however, how it would affect my entire life or that I would never see him again.

The next thing I remember was seeing Papa lying-in-state on an iron bed covered in *akwa george* or Madras cotton, the traditional cloth of the Aros though imported from India. It was tied all around the bedpost. Papa had a smile on his face. I reasoned later that he must have been at peace at the point of his death.

No one explained death to me. No one cared about me. I might as well have been a fly on the wall as I witnessed and took in the happenings around me. Even though I could not fully appreciate the gravity of what was going on, I knew that I was now part of the horde and special to no one.

During the harmattan season, when the early morning cold was at its peak, it was not unusual to find people in the village sitting around the fire either preparing breakfast, boiling water for a bath or just warming themselves up. It was so in the morning after Papa's burial. Visitors and mourners were still pouring in from faraway villages and food had to be prepared for them. It was mostly *igbulu* or mounds of cassava meal, to be eaten with different kinds of soups such as *achi*, *ogbono*, *egwusi* and *onugbu*. The mourners looked forward to the food as they usually arrived hungry and tired, having trekked long distances from their various villages. In Arondizuogu in 1956, you were a king if you owned a bicycle, not to mention a car. Once the mourners had wailed for a bit, someone would ask them to proceed to the back of the house, where they would be fed.

'*Gbahigebe nu na owuwa ka unu rie ihe.*'

This was a signal for them to take a break from the mourning.

It was quite fascinating for me, a child who only knew the city life, watching these mourners roll up large chunks of fermented cassava meal. I never imagined that a human being could swallow that much. I watched as they made *akpu* into huge balls with their fists and swallowed them with vegetable soup.

Papa was mourned by everyone, the poor and mighty alike. He was reputed to be comfortable in the company of all. From the old women with whom he would crack palm kernel nuts, to the very young to whom he gave colourful magazine cut-outs, as well as his political associates with whom he shared the vision of improving the peoples' lives. They all gathered in the small byway of Ndianiche Ikpa Nwahihia to bid farewell to an extraordinary man, Honourable Dixon Kanu Onwenu aka *Ogbufo* which means The one who clears a path. Even that moniker was powerful. DK was ahead of his time and he truly cleared the path for others to follow.

Out on my own, I moved around to observe groups of mourners, listening to their conversation. I also visited Mama Comfort's hut where my mum, hair now shaved, was made to sit on a mat on the floor in sack clothes, surrounded by my uncles' wives and other local women. The air was heavy with grief and no one seemed able to console the other.

My siblings and I sat around the fire on small kitchen stools warming our small bodies. My sister Zoe had reserved one of the stools for herself before I arrived at the fireside. It was therefore hers, but I sat on it without asking questions. Zoe returned shortly after and was quite incensed that I had taken her seat. She pulled it out from under me and to steady myself, I landed buttocks first, right beside the fire. I was burnt but not too badly. The scars, however, have remained. The burn was treated with engine oil.

Two days after falling into the fire, I saw a stubborn wasp building a nest on the mud walls of *Nnukwu Uno*. My eyes followed it as it buzzed back and forth. Its nest bothered me, so I poked it with a long stick. I did not see it coming. I never expected that a wasp, a small insect, could harm me and that was exactly what it did. Suddenly, the mother wasp came out of its partly destroyed nest and went straight for my forehead. I screamed as it stung me and gave me a big swelling. Thus, for the rest of the burial period, I walked around with a swollen forehead and a bum on fire. If my hand was not on my head, it was on my buttocks.

My grief over Papa's death was a period of prolonged consternation. It all seemed unreal; I kept hoping that it was a bad dream from which I would wake up. I missed my Papa and no one could fill the deep and gaping hole that he left in my life. At Arondizuogu, I still believed that I would go back to Port Harcourt and Papa would be there, waiting. I believed that I would walk into the living room and hear his affectionate call, '*Nwunye nnia!*' But that was never to be again. All I have are the memories: the games we played, the coins, the gifts, and the love.

My vivid memory of the details of Papa's presence often surprised my family, but it should not have. Papa was the centre of my life.

Surviving Papa

Given the fractured relationship between the Ozis and us before Papa's death, we had to move out of 35 Moorehouse Street immediately after his burial. My father had not completed the foundation of our own house at Degema Street before his death. We had no place to go. With five children, five relatives, Papa's driver Simeon and two helpers, Sister had a real challenge on her hands.

Mrs Nzimiro came to our rescue.

Papa had served as the Deputy Mayor of Port Harcourt under her husband in 1954, before he contested and won the election into the Federal House of Representatives. Our families were particularly close. Mrs Nzimiro was our hero. She gave us accommodation in the boys' quarters of one of her houses on Hospital Road. She was a mentor of sorts to Sister, who respectfully referred to her as Mama Nzimiro. Mrs Nzimiro, a business tycoon, extended considerable credit facilities to my mum. It was a mutually beneficial arrangement, but she did not have to be so benevolent.

Sister, being a stylish trendsetter, was able to market and sell products quickly, albeit with the assistance of my older cousins, Patience and Baby, and my eldest sister Azunna. At some point, my mother added the making of bed sheets and bed covers to her offering and soon, with profits from trading, she was able to complete the ground floor of our house on Degema Street and we moved in.

We never forgot Mama Nzimiro for her unbelievable kindness. My family maintained a close relationship with her and continued to visit her in her old age until she died in 1989.

Despite my father's popularity and contributions to the development of Port Harcourt and the impact he had on other people's lives, his widow and children got little help from those in a position to offer it. My mother lamented that instead of support, she got advice to sell my father's property. Many 'big men' offered to buy it at an auctioned rate. Others proposed marriage to her; after all, she was a very good-looking 37-year-old widow. Rather than be distracted by the attention, my mum decided to focus on what she felt were more pressing priorities: her children's education and her husband's legacy. Those became her legacy.

Papa Nnukwu, my maternal grandfather, came to live with us for six months. My mother shared with her father, much the same kind of relationship I had with mine. The image of my tall, dark and handsome grandfather, walking around the house and overseeing the on-going construction work was most comforting. He was also on hand to tell us stories.

Our driver, Simeon, refused to leave us after Papa's death. The two had a special relationship. Papa would not eat at an outing unless his driver had been fed, and Simeon was fiercely loyal to his boss and everyone related to him. He stayed on and even brought his new wife to help cook for the entire family. She was a tall and stately woman with a huge mole at the right corner of her mouth. She made the most delicious jollof rice, and its taste stayed on in our mouths long after the pot was empty. Sister had feared that Ijeoma might be tempted to raise the issue of the big black mole, and warned that she would be skinned alive if she did. Sister need not have worried. Ijeoma was too busy enjoying the jollof rice that she forgot about her usual mischief.

Just a few weeks after my beloved father was gone, no one in the family loved me as much. Certainly, my mother was emotionally absent. She was too busy grieving and my siblings were all dealing with their own grief as well. I was no longer the girl that had a lot of money to spend every day. I ceased to be the centre of anyone's attention. While this was going on, Sister did the unthinkable – she sent me to school.

And I did the thinkable: I resisted.

It was not unusual for most young children to resist school, especially for the very first period of that experience. We had spent much time at home, playing around and felt that all of life was a playground. My sister Zoe had a phobia for chicken. When my parents left her and Richard in the care of my grandparents in Obosi as Papa studied in Sierra Leone, in addition to Mama Nnukwu's other duties of the day, there was a most important one. She had to chase away all the free-roaming chicken in the neighbourhood on the way to school. None, not even a chick must be seen around or there will be no school that day.

So, when my drama started, it was not strange. Every morning came with a new performance, a new way to resist. To prevent the drama, Sister took to bribing me with special gifts – umbrellas, bags, toys and books – anything she could lay her hands on. I took the gifts, but would quickly lose them and the drama would start all over again. Of course, my mother's patience ran out and the cane came out. I went to school by force. I ended each school term with just my Bible in a torn bag. After this, my mother took to calling me '*Nwunye Pastor*' which means 'Pastor's Wife' as I would have lost all my belongings except the Bible.

I started school at St. Cyprian's/St. Peter's School, Port Harcourt when I was five years old. Both schools were one entity, sharing everything but locations and names. Classes were held simultaneously and pupils spent equal time in both places. My earliest classes were at St. Peters, which was farther from my house. We walked to school. St. Peters School was located next to the cemetery; what a place for a five-year-old to be just a month after the loss of her beloved father.

There was a funeral procession almost every day. We saw caskets mounted high on shoulders or in cars, with family members sniffling into handkerchiefs while following the hearse to the graveside. Everything reminded me of Papa's death when everyone who came out for him cried till there were no tears left in their eyes. As no one had taken the time to explain death to me, I was left to figure it out on my own and I was at the mercy of my own imagination. I would lie on the grass, close my eyes and hold my breath for a while pretending to be dead, and wondering what it felt like to die.

There was a rumour-mill in our school, built around stories and myths about ghosts that have refused to rest, of ghosts that were roaming around looking for their killers. Sometimes the rumour would have it that the head of the 'Federation of Ghosts' had sent a notice that they were holding a convention and the school had to close earlier than usual. Once someone raised an alarm, there would be a sudden stampede that would lead to school closure. No one would bother to investigate these rumours; fear was pervasive among teachers and pupils alike. However, I suspect that they were started by lazy students who used them as an excuse to get out of school early.

The first three years of school were particularly difficult for me. I preferred to stay at home and play in the sand, but Sister would have none of it.

While I struggled with my memories of Papa, there were

attempts by other institutions that encountered him to immortalise him. Enitonia High School named one of its structures, DK Onwenu House. Port Harcourt Municipality named a street DK Onwenu Road. However, during the Nigerian Civil War and due to the general hatred for Ndigbo, the street was changed to Winston Churchill Road. That singular act erased my father's contributions to the development of Port Harcourt.

Nevertheless, being erased from public memory did not mean being erased from the life of his family. Papa's developmental strides remain etched in our memory and in the minds of all who knew him.

I have not forgotten. I never will.

1 Degema Street, Port Harcourt

Onye ga enye m uno?
Dodotila tilaa tido
Onye ga enye m uno?
Dodo tila tido

Everybody sang and clapped, chanting, 'Who will give me a house? Do-do-ti-la-ti-do' as each person stood to defend his or her side of the wall, inside the rectangular courtyard. The game involved having to run over to the other side in an exchange of territory with the person opposite you. There were usually four persons, two on each side. However, there was always a fifth person in the centre, trying to get a territory.

This was 1 Degema Street, Port Harcourt, the house that my father started, but which was completed by my mother. This was where I grew up. In it is buried memories of my formative years as a little girl who had lost the love of her life; a little girl who would grow up to be me. It was a most interesting place. All who lived there felt like family and many were positively affected by the Onwenus, especially Madam Landlady, Mrs Hope Onwenu, the fear of whom was the beginning of tenant wisdom.

By 1958, my mother had completed our house. It was a sprawling one-storey building, one that helped pay our school fees. The front of the building, on the first floor, was rented out for commercial purposes. Rooms and flats were rented to small families and single persons. My family occupied one wing but even then, there was a room set aside for rent. It was reserved for those who needed my mother's special attention, like the West Indian schoolteacher who lived with us for two years.

We soon received a guest: Uncle Charles, Papa's brother. Uncle Charles was an interesting person, sly and cunning as a fox. He was not a particularly nice man but my father loved him, and I guess he loved Papa as well. In contrast, Mama Aba disliked Uncle Charles intensely. And the feeling was mutual. The relationship between Uncle Charles and Papa was so tight, that no one – not even their wives or their sister – could come between them. Unfortunately for my mum, Papa Goddy, that is Uncle Charles, did not like her much and did not hide it. He found it objectionable that Sister was from Obosi, and not Arondizuogu, and that she spoke a different dialect of the Igbo language. Papa Goddy tried very hard to convince my father to marry a second wife, one of his choosing, much to Sister's chagrin. Fortunately, this was one area that the two brothers did not agree on.

During Papa's burial, it was as though Uncle Charles' life had ended: he laid on Papa's coffin and insisted that he wanted to be buried alive with his brother. He had to be restrained physically from jumping into the grave. He was even on suicide watch for a while, but he recovered. Although Papa Goddy did not like my mother, he sought to marry her after Papa's death, in the Igbo tradition of *Ikuchi nwanyi* – to lock down a woman in the family. For the second time, my mother would reject this particular tradition, and we all had to be smuggled out of Arondizuogu with the help of Mama Aba, a few days after Papa's burial.

As soon as he was sober, Uncle Charles came to visit us in Port Harcourt. While staying at our house, the house a widowed mother had struggled to build after her husband's death; he sold another piece of land belonging to my family. The land in question had been bought with money from my mother. Uncle Charles sold it for a tidy sum running into thousands of pounds. He collected the payment in cash and had it hidden under the bed, in our guest room. We only found out about the sale after he left Port Harcourt. When Sister approached him, Charles Onwenu was unapologetic. He said that he was entitled to all that belonged to his younger brother. It did not matter to him that my mother had his late younger brother's children to raise, as well as five of Uncle Charles' children, who at the insistence of Mama Nnukwu, she continued to raise.

Knowing that Uncle Charles would eventually come for our house, my mother took steps to secure it, making herself the sole owner. Sister sought legal help from her lawyer, Barrister Obiora, to prevent Uncle Charles from taking everything and kicking us out into the streets, which he was capable of doing. This was done with the help of Mama Aba, my aunt.

Charles Onwenu soon became a stranger to his brother's family. He never came to visit again and we had no reason to visit him in Arondizuogu. One afternoon in 1964, eight years after my father's death, news came that Charles Onwenu had died. No one cried. We, the children, carried on with our games, laughing and jumping about until my mother stopped us and asked that we reflect on the fact that we had just lost a close relative. But we hardly knew him, and we did not understand why we had to quieten down and mourn someone we did not know.

Sister effectively became the head of the Onwenu family. She continued to raise the children and played a strong and supportive role for Uncle Charles' wives. You do not abuse an Onwenu woman and get away with it. Hope Onwenu was known to confront any abusive man who thought that because the two Onwenu brothers were gone, they could 'mess' with their wives. She became the defender of the extended Onwenu family.

To return to how my mother kept our family going after Papa's death, she always impressed it upon us, the children of Mazi DK Onwenu, to look out for the rest of the extended family. We watched her provide for many, paying school fees, affording them financial assistance, feeding, clothing, sheltering, and lending them emotional support. My siblings and I, having seen this protective tendency all our lives, continued with that tradition as we grew up. As it often happens in life, there were times – in fact, many times – that those good deeds were repaid with ingratitude.

Occupying one of the apartments at 1 Degema Street were the Obioras. The Oguta-born Barrister Obiora had just returned from the United Kingdom with his young family. He was a brilliant lawyer who loved his beautiful wife and three daughters. Our families became very close. Ngozi, the eldest daughter, was my age. I became so close to the Obioras that I spoke the Oguta dialect. Ngozi and I even 'married' the same husband, on the same day, at age nine. His name was Chibueze, the last child of the illustrious Ikokwu family who lived nearby on the adjacent Hospital Road. We could see their house from our balcony and they could also see ours from theirs.

At 11, Chibueze was a dashing, handsome boy. His elder sisters and mine were friends. His parents were revered in the Port Harcourt society. One day, while playing around, the sisters gathered pieces of discarded cloth from a seamstress who had rented a workshop in the front of our house. They made wedding dresses for Ngozi and I. Chibueze wore an old suit. We all went around the neighbourhood, singing, and dancing. Some older people, including our parents, even gave us money. This was Chibueze's song:

> Ladies and gentlemen
> You use to see my wives
> Just look on top of my facing cap
> And see my American wives
> Singa little ma, singa 1
> Singa little ma, singa 2
> Singa little ma, singa little ma,
> Singa little ma, singa 1

How Ngozi and I ever agreed to such an arrangement, I do not know. Yet there was never any rancour. I guess because everybody knew that it was a play marriage.

Ngozi also taught me a life lesson: unless you are asked, do not stick your neck into another person's business. We were in Primary Three and Ngozi's younger sister, Alex, had just joined us. One day, during a break period, I saw Alex being pummelled on the ground by an older girl. Without thinking, I threw myself into the fray. Playing the role of a big sister, I began hitting the offending girl, giving Alex a chance to escape. I was not exactly a physically strong person, so the girl turned on me and gave me the beating of my life. Ngozi, who was watching nearby, quickly snatched up Alex and they both ran away, leaving me to my fate. Realising that I was on my own, I had to swallow my pride and beg my way out of the quagmire.

My house had become too small for a growing family that now included Sam, Dr Leslie Obiora and others. Besides, Barrister Obiora had become hugely successful and had built a house of his own. The two families remained close.

I had another best friend in primary school, Beatrice Aham. She lived two streets away and we visited each other doing homework together or plaiting our hair during school breaks. Beatrice came from a humble background. Her parents were honourable people. She had a brother with a deformed hand and I always felt bad about that. Her mother, a lovely plump and fair-complexioned woman, always brought home snacks for us from the market. Beatrice and I parted after primary school as we went to different secondary schools. Her family moved away and we lost touch completely.

I finished primary school early. I was in the first set of Primary Five pupils allowed to take the First School Leaving Certificate Examination, which is only taken by pupils in Primary Six. Not only did I start school early, at age five; I also passed the entrance examination for secondary school at age 11, at the same time with my cousin, Ifeoma, who was four years older than me.

One of the lessons I learnt in life was in Primary Four when I was ten years old. Everyone in my class could beat me up, except for one girl, Joy Agina. She was a beautiful, plump girl, and the only child of her mother. A pampered and reserved kid, Joy would always sit quietly in class and avoided trouble at all costs.

One day, when I should have been studying, I decided to redeem my image of being the most physically weak in class. The only way to do this was to prove it by beating Joy in a fight. I called her out, but Joy would have none of it. She reminded me that our mothers were close and would not be happy to hear that we were fighting in school. She begged me to please let peace reign, but I would not listen. The mere fact that she sued for peace meant that she was afraid, I thought. Thus, I became even more adamant and grew more confident that I could defeat her.

After her pleas fell on deaf ears, Joy had no choice but to step up to the plate. By this time, the whole class and many others had gathered around us in the playground, excited by the brewing tension. Everyone was full of anticipation as to how this one fight would go down and whose favour it would be decided. I had to prove myself.

We were given the countdown to a contest. 'One, two, three...' but before I heard the word 'Go!' Joy had picked me up with great speed and thrown me to the ground. The contest ended as quickly as it had begun, amidst the jeers of the entire class. If there were any doubts as to whether I was the weakest, such doubts were finally erased and Joy Agina suddenly began to move around with a new swagger in her gait.

The fiasco taught me the futility of underestimating an opponent, no matter what. You never know what hidden strength lurked behind their screen of humility.

In Honour of Globe Motors, Chief Willy Anumudu

We were age mates and classmates at St Peters School Port Harcourt. He came from the well known family of Chief Anumudu, a transport magnate back in the 1950s.

In Class Four, when we were both eight years old, Willy had a crush on me, but I did not know it. Every day after class, just as we sang our closing song which loosely means 'We are closing from school. 'Thank you' to all our teachers':

Anyi agbasa go
Akwukwo Ekene diri
ndikuzi Kuziri anyi o
Akwukwo

Willy, instead of closing and covering his eyes with his palms, would be busy shaking his finger at me in warning that he was going to get me – for what I did not know – but ostensibly to get me to notice him. I would see him through the openings of my fingers and would position myself to be out of the door in a jiffy. Willy would then chase me down the road, all the way home; his house was on Hospital Road not far from mine on Degema Street. One day, he went too far and threw a stone at me, so I reported him to my mother. She wasted no time. Taking me by the hand, she matched down to the Anumudu home to launch a report to Willy's mum who was a friend of hers. As she made the report, the 'culprit' was nearby taking it all in. When my mother warned, as parents are wont to, that if he threw stones and blinded me, he would have to marry me, Willy replied: 'but that is what I want.' From then on, we understood the reason for the harassment.

Having been outed, Willy became my defender in school. He no longer chased me down the road; he protected me so that no one else could.

Failing and Rising

Good grades are door-openers anywhere, and my case was no exception. My good results opened the doors to several secondary schools but Sister preferred Amumara Girls Secondary School in Mbaise, Imo State. It was a boarding school owned by the Anglican Church, far away from Port Harcourt. This was to ensure that I would not come running back home at every excuse. On the trip to school, if you missed the only bus plying the route once a day, you had to travel by bicycle, with luggage strapped to the back. It was a rough ride on an uneven, untarred and bumpy road strewn with potholes and pools of water.

Though it was my mother's preference to send her children to schools outside Port Harcourt where we lived, my siblings had better luck than me. Azunna and Ijeoma attended Ovom Girls Secondary School Aba, which was the town next to Port Harcourt. Richard first attended St Augustine's Grammar School Nkwerre, Imo State which was far away, but he also attended Dennis Memorial Grammar School (DMGS) Onitsha for his Higher School Certificate. The town was next door to our maternal grandparents in Obosi. Same with Zoe who attended Ogidi Girls Secondary School nearby.

Why did I have to go to school in Mbaise where I sometimes had to travel by bicycle? I have no idea. The fact that it was an Anglican school with a strict regime and far away from Port Harcourt, may have all tied up with my mother's perception of what I needed to take school more seriously.

One day, when I returned from Amumara for the third time in one term and on account of a bout of malaria, my mother called my attention to a young girl hawking bread nearby. Pointing to her, she said to me in a matter of fact tone, 'This is who you will be if you do not stay in school.'

After that, I grew used to an Anglican boarding school's deprivations and bore my cross in quiet resignation, as did most other students.

On my first day in boarding school, my heart sank as I watched the bus turn back and leave. I was barely 12 years old and alone, on my own, for the first time in my life and life at Amumara was brutal. Independence was foisted on us. The conditions we were exposed to made us grow up fast, and we became independent, not by choice, but out of necessity.

Having spent idyllic Christmas holidays with my grandparents at Obosi, I knew how to fetch water from the nearby stream and run other errands. But nothing prepared me for the strict regime that Anglican secondary schools were known to unleash on their students.

The rising bells rang at 5 a.m. We would quickly say personal prayers and then rush to the stream with a bucket and basin, as well as a head pad to carry both. We had to walk for two kilometres, part of which was a steep hill. We would put some water in the basin with some green leaves to steady it; a full bucket of water was put inside the basin, and more leaves to cover the bucket to prevent water from spilling. I brought back enough water for myself and for my school mother's personal needs. A school mother was usually an older and senior student who provided some form of guidance and emotional support. In return, she may receive support from the younger student by way of washing her clothes and fetching water from the stream. There were the odd occasions when school mothers would help themselves to the younger students 'provisions' such as milk, sugar and biscuits.

After attending to your school mother's needs, you had your bath before doing more chores such as cleaning the hostel. A bland breakfast of *akara* with corn pap was served in the school dining hall. Some students brought their sugar and milk if they could afford it. We all could at the beginning of the term, but ran out of provisions and pocket money by the second month.

The school had different fruit trees – cashew, oranges, avocado and many others. We helped ourselves to these even though it was against school rules. You could pick any fruit that fell to the ground, provided you could prove that the fruit did not fall on account of the vigorous shaking of its tree. Amumara's rural setting was a blessing in the sense that we were always able to pick wild berries of different species when in season such as *icheku*, *utu*, and *udala* the African cherry found all the way down the path to the river, which was surrounded by bushes and farmlands.

After our morning chores and breakfast, all the students would proceed to the main hall. The Principal and teachers joined us for our morning assembly. In 1964, I played the role of hymn starter with two other girls every morning. We continued to do this until schools closed in 1967 as the Nigerian Civil War loomed.

I was active in various school activities. I was a member of the debating team and the choral group. I was the only junior girl allowed in the senior debating team and I worked hard to justify my inclusion. I was also good at sports; the long jump was my forté. Drama and writing got my full attention as well.

In 1965, when our teacher-coach failed to show up at a statewide Festival of the Arts and the Amumara Choral Group had to go on stage, I quickly stood in for her and conducted the choir in the way I had observed her do time after time. We received a thunderous ovation and won our first title ever, a third-place award. We came home victorious, though thoroughly exhausted. Our hired bus lumbered into the school compound under the cloak of darkness at 9 p.m from Owerri, surviving countless kilometres of terrible roads to get us back to our school.

At 10 p.m, just as we were settling down to sleep, after the excitement of reliving our victory to other students, the School Principal, Mrs Inyama, burst into my dormitory, accompanied by our boisterous matron, Mrs Odocha and the teacher-coach. I was roused from sleep with a hug, carried shoulder-high around the surrounding dormitories as a great symbol of resourcefulness. There, high on someone's shoulders, surrounded by cheers and applause, I felt really proud of myself.

However, my heroics were quickly forgotten a week later. As usual, my name was on the punishment list for some transgression or the other, usually talking in class. It was expected every Saturday and I did not disappoint this time around. The announcement of my name was usually greeted with a sigh 'Mmmmmmm!'

Stories of rivalries between Anglican schools close to each other abound. It is often between boys schools and girl schools. Amumara Girls Secondary School was paired with Ife Boys Grammar School.

These boys often threatened to beat us up on our way to the stream, especially if we had just visited another boys' school for any academic or social outings. Such visits were arranged between Government College Owerri and us, for example. We preferred them to the 'local boys' of Ife Grammar School. The boys never beat us up but we were always wary of them. We went to the stream in groups. Ife boys were just jealous.

Easter at Amumara was memorable. Good Friday was solemn, but Easter Sunday was joyous. There was always an enactment of the discovery of the empty tomb by Mary Magdalene. This enactment was so good; the mystery and secrecy of who was playing the angel at the tomb so well-kept, one could easily believe that the Lord had indeed risen right there in Amumara Girls Secondary School.

> At 4 a.m, shouts of '*O bili wo!*' which means 'He has risen!' woke us up. This cry was interjected with '*Okpara ya. Ka o ji gbaputa anyi. Obili wo, Obili wo. Orara ndu ya nye onwe. Jesu ebili wo*'. These were shouts of elation at the resurrection. It was with rapturous joy and goosebumps that we ran to the simulated graveside. With our lanterns and candles in hand, we sang all the way, led by our matron. The angel was wrapped in white bedsheets and knelt at the head of the grave. There was no electricity in Amumara, so the scene's ambience was enhanced by the breaking dawn, half-lit, half dark. It was eerie, surreal and deeply moving.

Amumara Girls Secondary School was a tough environment for me to grow up in, and I grew up toughened. Independence is a double-edged sword. It can give you a sense of freedom but also a sense of responsibility. It may slip through one's fingers while one basked in the illusion of it. A person could feel in control of her time and spend it anyhow. I got away with not studying, hoping to pass my exams with natural intelligence and inquisitiveness.

I did well during my first year, but failed in the following school year. Failing humbled me and made me realise how unfocused I had been. I was the first in my family to fail a class in secondary school. Now, I had to share that class with those who came to Amumara a year after me. It was a big blow that brought with it a shame to shake off. I lost my verve and my self-confidence. It was catastrophic as I felt I had been humiliated before the whole world.

The month before the epic failure, I had teased another classmate who was herself repeating Class 2. Her name was Anara; she was a much older girl and had seized my *Record Song Book,* a prized possession with the lyrics of popular songs by great artistes such as The Everly Brothers, Elvis Presley, Pat Boon, Doris Day, Jim Reeves and many others. Sometimes, the compilers used the wrong words to approximate what they thought they heard on the cracked records. We sang along anyway. The use of radio was not allowed and there was no television in the school.

For entertainment, the matron allowed a gramophone every Thursday in the Assembly Hall. We played the latest highlife tunes by Rex Lawson, Celestine Ukwu and Osita Osadebe.

When I demanded to have my songbook back, Anara refused to hand it to me. In anger, I taunted her for failing her exams. I had touched a raw nerve and she dealt me a slap on the face. We were both hurled off to the Principal's office, and charged with 'two fightings'. Our punishment was suspension for a fortnight. On my way home to my mother in Port Harcourt, I stopped over in Aba to collect letters from family and friends, who appealed to her not to 'kill' me. Those letters saved my life.

That was how I gained the dubious reputation of being the first to be suspended in my family. Not long afterwards, I added another notorious feather to my cap by being the first to fail a class in secondary school. That failure, however, turned my life around. I promised myself that never again would I not live up to my capability in anything, not just schoolwork. I resolved, there and then, never to take things for granted.

Visiting Day happened once a month and my family was usually a 'no show'. The journey was exceedingly long and uncomfortable. Besides, my older siblings were all in school themselves and my mother was not the visiting type. She was too busy earning a living for the whole family. However, I had a first cousin, Mama Aba's youngest child, Stephen DanChimah, who made it his duty to visit. He usually came with canned food such as baked beans, peas, sardine, corned beef and bread. He would also augment my pocket-money to purchase items from the school canteen.

Everyone should have a cousin like Stephen. We have maintained a close relationship all our lives. Stephen's first child was named after me.

One Visiting Day, Sister sprung the mother of all surprises on me. She surfaced. It was during my repeat of Class 2. Though it was a pleasant surprise as I was certain that she would not come from Port Harcourt empty-handed, I was anxious. Whatever her reasons were, it was a most welcome development. She looked good alighting from the black Morris Minor taxi she had hired from Port Harcourt. She was elegant; the colours she wore were soft and classy. I felt proud to be her daughter.

Nonetheless, the thought that dominated my mind was that something crucial must have made her come. My anxiety was justified when I was summoned to the Principal's office. With each step, my heartbeat became louder as though it would burst out of my chest. I had a query to answer: a 'love letter' that a boy had written to me. It had drawn the Principal's attention who in turn, contacted my mother. That was the reason for the visit.

To be clear, I did nothing to invite the boy's attention. He had sent a necklace – the kind you would find in a crackerjack box – in a letter, I had not even seen, let alone replied. That fact did not deter my mother and Principal from giving me a dressing- down. My brother joined the condemnation crew as soon as I came home on holidays. The family had been informed about my 'wayward inclinations'. I was told in clear terms that it should not repeat itself. It was truly bewildering. I had no contact with my admirer; yet, I was blamed for his attention. It was perplexing how no one wanted to hear my side of the story. Many years later, way into my 40s, my brother apologised for his role in that blanket condemnation I had suffered. I appreciated his apology.

There were times during my formative years, mostly in my teens, when I wondered if my mother was truly my mother or someone who had adopted me. I have heard friends speak similarly about their mothers. I misunderstood Sister's strictness to mean dislike, without appreciating how all of it was motivated by a sense of love and duty. With no father in the picture, she had to be both man and wife at the same time. This meant that my mother bore a greater sense of responsibility for our well-being than would have been the case if our father were alive. I know that now. All she did, she did out of love for her family. She attempted to raise us in a way that prepared us for the future which lay ahead of us.

Though we were a middle-class family with my father's 'big name' to live up to, Sister knew how to stretch whatever money we had to accommodate everyone's needs. She had done that all her married life. One such way was the ability to select clothes for her family from a cheap source, the 'Bend Down Boutique', or second-hand clothing. In Port Harcourt, it was called *okrika*, which is also the name of a town in Rivers State. My mother was so good at this cost-saving venture that she made it appear as if the clothes were bought from the best fashion outlets abroad. At Amumara Girls Secondary School, I was accused of being arrogant, because my mother was 'rich'. These people could not have imagined the struggles we were going through.

Being misunderstood by my peers and associates, even older and richer people, has been a regular feature in my life, one that I have learned to accommodate in my stride.

My Amumara story cannot be complete without this one, which I call 'The Fake Prophecy'.

While I was repeating my second year, and at a time when the Christian Students Union (SU) was flourishing in the south-east, a false prophetess arose among us and terrorised students with her false claims and accusations. Her name was Miss Inyang. Early one morning, she came to my dormitory with Matron Odocha to prophesy about me. She said that I would die if I had another abortion. I was still a virgin, but somehow I knew that no one would believe me, so I kept quiet. I was a charming and attractive girl who was often deliberate about looking good. This probably made it easy for some to assume that men were after me. They did not know about my mum and her strict upbringing. Weeks later, I was vindicated. It happened that Miss Inyang was the one who was carrying a pregnancy and was merely projecting her anxieties on me. She had to leave the school.

The year 1967 came with rumours of war. One day, the school bells rang at an odd hour for a General Assembly. One of our senior girls, Abiodun Abidogun, was to return to the western part of the country with her family. They were Yorubas based in Enugu and were no longer safe among us due to the reaction to the pogrom, which had started in the North. We bade her a tearful goodbye. We had been at school together, with no rancour or discrimination. Now, we were being pulled apart by events we had no hand in, nor control over.

Not long after Abiodun left, the rest of us had to go home as well. The political climate in the country was fast deteriorating and the school could not guarantee anyone's safety.

> I was leaving Amumara but I knew that I was not going to miss it. When I started school again at National High School Arondizuogu in 1969, I jumped a class. I started at Class 3 instead of Class 2, and I was at the top of my class. That was how God nullified my failure. I simply caught up and moved on. I had learned that lack of preparation and being too carefree could lead to failure. I was not focused on the ball, and I suffered the consequences. Luckily, however, I was happy to have learned the lessons of failure without having to pay a costly price for it. That is what I know now as grace.

Self-Discovery in Port Harcourt

Life in Port Harcourt before the Nigeria-Biafra conflict was simple and secure. There was a sense of community and no discrimination whatsoever. Everyone was simply a human being, and not seen through the lens of ethnicity, language, dialect, religion or even country of origin. Port Harcourt attracted people from all over Nigeria, Africa, the Caribbean as well as Europe. It was not strange for families to bond through their children's friendships, or because they attended the same church or school. We were held together by the thread of community.

This sense of togetherness also found expression through discipline. If any of our parents caught us doing something wrong, they would discipline us on the spot, usually with a strong admonition, and then report the matter to our parents, who would likely punish us further. I call it the 'double effect treatment'.

There was a quiet, West Indian teacher from Barbados who took up residence at 1 Degema Street, in a studio apartment on our side of the building. She was single and did not know anyone in Port Harcourt, so my mother took her under her wings. She was safe from everyone, except Ifeoma my cousin and Ijeoma, my sister. One day, the pranksters came up with something new.

If you are familiar with the food condiment called *ogiri* – fermented bean seeds – you will know that it has a peculiar and pungent smell that not everyone appreciates, even though it makes a better tasting *onugbu* or *oha* soup. Ijeoma and Ifeoma took to surreptitiously rubbing a small amount of *ogiri* on the doorpost of the poor, unsuspecting teacher. It drove her nuts, trying to figure out what the smell was and where it came from. The pranksters watched from a safe distance, all the while laughing at the lady's discomfiture.

One day, she confessed that she had had enough and was going to move out. My mother heard about it and knew exactly what the problem was and who had caused it. Well, it was *'sekpulu ani chinie aka gi enu'* – kneel and raise both hands up – for the two rabble-rousers, for the next two hours. They were also grounded for days, for good measure.

By this time, Ifeoma and Ijeoma had become too big for spanking; they had become immune to it too and would not cry. Ifeoma, who was a year older, would openly encourage Ijeoma not to cry, infuriating my mother further. She, therefore, had to devise a more effective punishment.

I also recall one day in 1962, when an American lady came to see my mum. She was researching African women and their survival instincts and came over for a chat. We could tell that someone important was coming by the way my mum went about preparing for the visit. There was good food, plenty to drink and a family meeting to issue instructions on respectful behaviour and an acceptable code of conduct. The American lady had a wooden leg, so Ifeoma and Ijeoma were warned not to approach the lady with any awkward questions.

Sister thought she was well covered and went about receiving her special guest. They spent time talking and it looked like they were having an interesting conversation. The time came to introduce the family and we were called to the living room to greet the visitor. Then the unexpected happened. Ijeoma was desperate to confirm that the lady had a wooden leg. As she approached to greet her, Ijeoma dropped an object on the floor near the woman's leg and proceeded to pick it up. So far, so good, until we heard a hollow sound from the wooden leg. Ijeoma had dared to tap it, to find out if indeed it was wooden.

You can imagine my mother's embarrassment. I cannot remember what Ijeoma's punishment was for her inquisitiveness, but it did not stop her from such pranks thereafter. Ijeoma was Ijeoma and Papa decided early in the day to let her be. This was why he called her 'Ome abu nso' – the One who did as she pleased. She was always capable of the ridiculous. She pulled off all manner of stunts. As long as it was not dangerous, Papa said to let her be.

There were periods of high spirits and camaraderie at 1 Degema Street too. Holidays were major events; Sister would slaughter a hefty goat or ram and cook food for the tenants and neighbours. On offer was her signature dish, vegetable salad or 'nwongwo ihe ndu' as some of the tenants called it. A local mix, which was made with the head of the goat and its entrails, was served; everyone got a bit of this much sought-after delicacy called isi-ewu, no matter how small. It was a communal feast and something to look forward to. The kids usually fed the tethered goat for days to 'fatten it up' before the day of slaughter. This was part of the fun.

Our house at the intersection of Degema Street and Hospital Road was a beehive of activities. Friends came and slept over, mostly my brother's friends, many of whom had become members of the Onwenu household. One could well imagine what my mother's food bill was at the end of each month; however, it was a healthy atmosphere for all.

There was not much to look forward to in terms of entertainment in Port Harcourt in the early 60s. A few streets away there was Rex Cinema which specialised in Indian films. We knew all the songs even though we did not understand the language. Lido Night Club was available to adults only. The minors settled for the Girl Guides and Brownies or the Youth Club at St Peter's Church. Television which arrived in Nigeria in 1959 came on for just six hours, from 6 p.m to 12 midnight. We were only allowed two hours of it on any given day. Storytelling, debates and political discussions took up our time. While all this was going on, there was a free flow of the usual snacks of groundnut, banana, doughnuts and sandwiches from Kingsway Stores.

Sister taught us money lessons without deliberately setting out to. My brother Richard's story after passing his Higher School Certificate Examination explains this better. He had a fairly good result in 1965. Sister most unexpectedly rewarded him with the princely sum of £34 sterling which he could spend as he wanted. His salary as a school teacher at Enitonia High School was £22 a month.

Soon, word got around that he had so much money. Like bees to honey, Richard's friends began to gather at the house for all kinds of peer meetings, after which they all trooped to the dining section of Kingsway Stores for refreshments. This happened so frequently that the cafeteria manager, Mrs Onwuamaegbu, who also happened to be Sister's friend, reported the trend to her. Sister, aware of the source of her son's sudden wealth, predicted that it would soon dry up. And this was exactly what happened.

He spent the £34 in less than two weeks. Sister, who also thought that Richard was saving his earnings from teaching, was shocked to find out that he had 'blown' that as well. He paid for his extravagance. She did not buy him any new clothes when he went for further studies in Belgium. He had to wear hand-me-downs. This was a big deal and a source of great disappointment for my fashion-conscious brother. It was also a clear example of how parents in those days knew of their children's activities, even outside the home, through communal parenting. If a child escaped the parents' eyes, they were unlikely to escape the eagle eye of collective surveillance.

As I already observed, there were times when the spectre of strictness my mother maintained towards me was so intense that I would pause and wonder whether or not she was my biological mother. Yet there were also times when my mother demonstrated such a great measure of understanding and respect for me that went beyond the confines of a mother-daughter relationship.

I must now tell the story of Ralphael Obioha's birthday party. In 1966 I was almost fifteen years old. A close family friend, Raphael Obioha, was celebrating his 21st birthday, a landmark age. The L N Obioha family was prominent in Port Harcourt. Mazi L N Obioha, the legendary self-made palm oil merchant, industrialist, political financier and Arondizuogu patriot, played an important role in my family after Papa's death. He facilitated Richard's sojourn to Belgium before the civil war broke out. From there, Richard found his way to London, then Chicago. It was thanks to him that my brother was not killed during the war.

Raphael Obioha was a gangling, good-looking chap, the toast of young ladies in Port Harcourt. His party was the talk of the town. Everywhere was agog with anticipation as friends prepared for this special birthday party. I was not invited, neither was Ralph's sister, Eunice, a good friend of mine. We were considered too young. Brother Ralph had warned Eunice and I that he would walk us out of the party if we dared to show our faces.

I observed as everyone got ready, taking it all in and wishing that I was a few years older. I did not know that my mother had been watching me all the while. She quickly organised a navy- blue chiffon dress for me, and gave me her necklace with multi-coloured stones. I wore my pair of black shoes and Sister dabbed my face with a little make-up. I looked and felt good, although a little subdued with fear of expulsion from the party I was not invited to. My mum knew what she was doing and got my older siblings to acquiesce.

To the party, I went. As I sat in one corner, hoping that the celebrant would not notice me; my siblings were all having a great time and even forgot that I was there. I began to think that Eunice was far smarter, staying at home. I was way in over my head. This company was beyond me.

As part of any respectable birthday celebration, a dance dedicated to the celebrant with a female guest of his choice was one of the highlights of the soirée. It allowed the celebrant to play Prince to a Cinderella.

From the corner of my eyes, I saw him approach, looking dashing in his tight-fitting pair of trousers and matching Sopedo shoes, the type with the long, pointed tip. I thought to myself; this is it. I braced up, closed my eyes, and waited for the marching orders. To my dismay, what I heard instead was, 'Excuse me dance.'

He did not recognise me. My mum had done such a good job that he was convinced I was a new catch. We were, of course, the connoisseur of all eyes until Raphael realised that he had been hoodwinked. Nonetheless, he did not throw me out. He took it in good faith, even if I had deprived him of the opportunity of landing a new catch with his first dance. I was more of a sister than a possible girlfriend.

It was a defining moment for me. I knew I was still too young, but I realised that I would become an adult in time, not too far from then. It ended up being my coming out party, as well as a birthday party for Ralph Obioha.

That throbbing music from the party that night was soon replaced by another kind of music: the unpleasant drums of war. It came and dispersed people across the country. It put an end to the smiles on many faces, and abruptly ended millions of lives. It ensured that none of our lives remained the same ever again.

My parents wedding photograph.

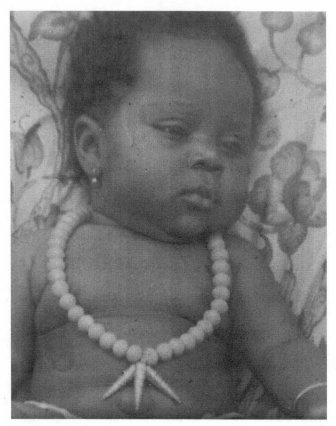

Onyeka Onwenu Baby Picture

Her husband called her HO(Hope Onwenu). My mother.

The Power of
'Kpongem' -
Hope Onwenu,
aka Sister.

Hope Onwenu
At 40

Hon. DK Onwenu - Papa - graduation from Furrah Bay College Sierra Leone

Papa and I

Our last family photo including Àzunna and our Onwenu cousins. Goddy was missing in action. He came home late.

From left to right Ijeoma, Onyeka, Richard and Zoe 1955.

From left to right Ijeoma, a friend, Ifeoma, Pearl Amobi and me, hanging out in Obosi during the early months of the Biafra War - 1968-69.

Ijeoma. Sister and I just before leaving for the US in 1972.

Amumara girls. I played a lawyer in a theatre skit. Stella Nwaubani beside me.

DK Onwenu after winning the election into the Federal House of Representatives
in 1955, in Portharcourt

DK Onwenu,
Okotie Eboh
and other
NCNC party
faithfuls in
Warri in 1956.

My maternal grandfather-
Ogbuagu Godson Nwokoye-
aka Papa Nnukwu

My maternal grandmother
Margaret Nwokoye- aka Mama
Nnukwu

DK Onwenu

DK Onwenu's grave in Obinetiti Arondizuogu

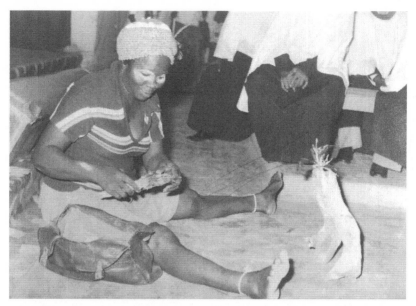

Even Before Nollywood. My Mother As An Actress - In A Drama Skit At A
Church Play. She Played The Role Of A Witch Doctor.

My Mother Receiving An Award For Marrying Outside Her State Of Origin

Grandma. Tijani and Uncle Richard at his
christening in Lagos in 1986

Obiora Mkpaaru - my mother's cousin who was
killed during the Biafra war

On stage with sister

Sister in her 90s - still
winning awards

Sister goes home in a blaze of glory

PART II

The War Years

The Drums of War

I was only fourteen years old in 1966, yet I had dreams of my future. Although I had no definite plans for what I wanted to do with my life, one thing was clear: music would be a big part of it. I was already known in my family circle as the next Mariam Makeba. Many times when I sang hymns at school, I imagined myself on a large stage, mesmerising my audience as their bodies swayed to the rhythm of my voice. I was in a hurry to finish my studies, so I could indeed be successful on the world stage, like my idol, Mariam Makeba.

We began hearing the drums of war beating so close to home. The closest that children of my age ever came to war before then was perhaps in the films we watched at Rex Cinema, the old films shown on television, or the Ogoni and Kalabari antagonists who trooped from the creeks into the city after a clan war. Nothing prepared our young minds for what ultimately went down as one of the most genocidal conflicts in modern history. It resulted in the death of over 3 million Biafrans, the devastation of our homeland and the truncating of what was, for all intents and purposes, the emergence of a fast-developing region in Africa.

The rumours of war began right after the 1966 coup led by Majors Ifeajuna, Ademoyega, Nzeogwu, Anuforo, Chukwuka and few other officers of southeast and southwest origin. Nevertheless, their reasons for the military take-over were pan-Nigerian in scope

111

and the whole nation rejoiced at the news. Very quickly, however, the jubilation turned into a blame game that heralded reprisals. It was the duo of General Aguiyi-Ironsi and Lt. Col. Emeka Odumegwu-Ojukwu, both Igbo, who foiled the coup.

MY FATHER AND IFEAJUNA

Let me share with you an anecdote about my father's early encounter with one of the coup plotters, back in his secondary school days.

DK Onwenu, was the English teacher at DMGS. The students were restless. They were complaining about feeding arrangements as most students do. There was talk of 'let us write a letter to the Principal, detailing all our grievances and the things that we want to be changed.'

What made Papa their favourite teacher (if I can put it that way), was that he could relate to the students in a way that other teachers could not. He was approachable. They wanted to write a petition and did not want anyone's name to be at the top of the list, in case they are perceived as the ringleader, and then targeted.

My father came up with a piece of advice. He suggested that they sign the petition in a circle; that way, no one would know who started it and who ended it. It was a brilliant idea and it worked. But Emmanuel Ifeajuna, a student at DMGS at that time, went to the school authorities and snitched on him. My father was accused of aiding and abetting the students, which did not present him well to the school administration. Ifeajuna betrayed their beloved English teacher and he had to leave DMGS.

DK Onwenu did nothing wrong. If the students were writing a petition, they had the right to air their grievances. He just advised them to do it in a circle and not linearly. Papa left anyway.

Nigeria received her independence from the United Kingdom in 1960, a development that filled every Nigerian with hope. As an eight-year-old pupil, I rejoiced as my schoolmates and I at St Cyprians School were given free loaves of bread and tins of sardines to celebrate. This was Nigeria offering us a treat as a goodwill gesture and we thoroughly enjoyed ourselves.

I first heard the rumours of war from our tenants at Degema Street. Every morning, they would gather in clusters and discuss the looming conflict. I read leftover newspapers and magazines, such as the Nigerian Pilot. My older siblings and friends also discussed the unfolding political drama at our house. Common in their conversations were words like 'negotiation', 'Aburi Accord' and 'massacre'. Many were aggravated about the way the country was going. Through their conversations, there was a sense of helplessness, of people who could only talk, but who's views could change precious little.

Talk could not stem the arrival of trains from the northern parts of the country that brought Igbo victims of the pogrom into Enugu, Aba and Port Harcourt. Droves of Igbo refugees arrived into the south-east. Many were dead, while others were in a state of '*o di ndu, onwu ka mma*' – alive but better off dead. Many of these returnees, just like me, had their lives and dreams right in front of them. These ended abruptly. Rather than pursue our dreams, we became preoccupied with surviving the conflict. After all, one had to be alive to pursue dreams or fulfil destiny. Just hoping to make it out of the conflict became the single most important dream anyone could have.

Before this time, and inspired by the political news flying around me, I had written an article at the age of 13 criticising the Nigerian government for 'poke-nosing' into the affairs of 'Rhodesia', now

Zimbabwe. I heard of the labour strike of June 1964, of how workers demanded bigger salaries and better service conditions. They rejected the government's terms for an agreement, and the police were then deployed to quash the protests. The elections that followed were also not without bloodshed. My article was filled with the uncertainty that I felt as a child living in a country with an uncertain future. Once done, I dropped it off at the Nigerian Pilot, a newspaper owned by Dr Nnamdi Azikiwe on Bathurst Street, just a few blocks away from my house.

All smiles, I returned home and excitedly announced to my mother what I had done. To my utter shock, I did not get the applause I expected, rather she sighed, pulled me by the ears, and dragged me all the way to the newspaper's office, to retrieve the 'offensive' write-up. I did not like the fact that I could not express myself. I made a promise never to shy away from self-expression, as soon as I could get away from my mother's suffocating guardianship.

With increased killings in the northern parts of the country, more and more Igbo people arrived in eastern Nigeria with tales of woe and unmitigated terror. While all these happened, the Aburi Accord was negotiated at Aburi, Ghana, a neighbouring country.

It decided on a looser Nigerian federation and the whittling down of the enormous powers of the Supreme Military Council of the Nigerian government. It agreed to the devolution of powers to the four Regions – the East, the Mid-West, the North and the West. However, the military Head of State, Lieutenant Colonel Yakubu Gowon, reneged on the agreement as soon as he returned to Nigeria.

On 27 May 1967, Gowon divided Nigeria into twelve states, slashing Eastern Nigeria into three: East Central State, Rivers State, and South Eastern State. This meant that Ndigbo, who were mostly of the East Central State, would have no control over much of the petrol located in the Region. Four days later, on May 31, Lieutenant Colonel Emeka Odumegwu-Ojukwu declared the independence of the Republic of Biafra.

Given the political chain of events unfolding up until then, no one needed to be told that war was imminent. The Biafran propaganda machine began early enough in the struggle, to provide a rallying call for patriotism and commitment to the Biafran cause. '*Osondu agwu ike*' became a mantra, reminding all that tiredness had little place in the battle for survival. Biafrans knew that we had to fight, whether we liked it or not. Young men signed up for military service in the Biafran Army and were readily marched off to training.

I do not know how my mother knew that salt would be expensive during the war and started preparing ahead of time by making her own. We would fetch the seawater that surrounded Port Harcourt and then boil it down for its salt content. The salt looked dirty and was as hard as rock. Bleached salt was what we were used to, but my mother's version, though unbleached, was still salt. It came in handy when that commodity became scarcer than gold and prohibitively expensive. It soon became virtually unavailable. Anyone who has tried eating unsalted food knows that it tastes bland and is unpalatable. My mum had seen ahead of time and, therefore, had stockpiled enough salt to see us through the initial period of scarcity. After this, she sent us to Obosi, where we were when the war began in July 1967.

Life in Obosi was different from Port Harcourt. Though we had been there many times, those were short holiday spells. This particular visit was indefinite. Living was rustic. We woke up early to fetch water. As we passed along the footpath to Idemili River, we were welcomed by the jerky laughter and joyful screams of other kids splashing about in the water. Going to the river also had a social significance. It was here that we met up with our friends. We would wash our clothes and spread them on tree branches to dry, then would dive into the river for a bath. It was not strange to swim with the fish of the Idemili River, which we were forbidden to kill.

Now and then, masquerades came along to reinforce the maintenance of a clean environment. Anyone found at the riverbank, took part in the cleaning and generally avoided being flogged. It was fun dodging the masquerades' cane. Once your clothes dried, you made them into a sling which you hung on your back like you were carrying a child. You filled your bucket with water and chatted all the way home.

We had no idea when the Obosi trip would end. It felt like a perpetual Christmas holiday. Our friends were all home, and we took turns visiting each other. Sometimes, a group of us would be found on the narrow streets going from one family house to the other. It seemed that the same thing that chased us to Obosi, also chased them there. We were glad to reconnect with our friends, Pearl Amobi (now Justice Pearl Enejere), Onuorah Ibezue, the Iwekas and the Nwobi twins, and the Justice Nkemena brood.

Eventually, what initially felt like a holiday soon turned into a bleak nightmare as people began to leave Obosi as well. The war theatre was coming close from Asaba, across the River Niger and into Onitsha, which was only about 7km away. Another sector was coming down from Enugu trying to connect to Awka and Onitsha. We had to move again, this time to Arondizuogu.

The Great Displacement to Arondizuogu

E ven though there was a war going on, life continued. The falling of Nigerian soldiers was greeted with cheers and outbursts of joy. But the capture of Biafran towns by Nigerian soldiers was accompanied by loud wails from everyone. We were all united in our joys and tragedies, knowing that the same fate could befall anyone. We knew that staying alive, and seeing each day was a privilege, one that was not guaranteed to continue indefinitely.

It was also clear that the more Biafran towns fell to the advancing Nigerian soldiers, the closer the war got to us. With the surrender of more territory to the superior firepower of the Nigerian troops towards the end of 1967, we were firmly planted in our village Obinetiti.

Obinetiti means 'The one that lives in the middle or centre'. True to its name, the town was a cross-section where three major areas of development were linked together. Umunze, a town in Anambra State, was linked to us. Akokwa too in the Orlu region of Imo State, which was also linked to Uga, a town in Anambra. Uga was the location of the famous airstrip that aided Biafra's survival. It hosted one of the airports through which relief supplies were brought into the landlocked nation. Finally, one of the intersections led to Okigwe about 20km away. This later became a war front.

Whilst in Obinetiti, it struck me that it was only the second time I had been home. The first was for my father's burial. That was a dark tale of inexplicable loss, punctuated by wasp stings and that burn on my bum.

The war was filled with horrific tales, but there were also strong memories of a people's will to survive. There were pleasant childhood memories, as well. Chief among them was the little fish that swam in the stream that flowed from a rock. It was called *Onyenanwankeya bee Onwenu* – the stream of contentment – belonging to Mazi Onwenu.

My paternal grandfather had discovered the stream. We would go there to fetch water for household chores and in the process, attempt to scoop up the little fish. We were usually not too successful. The water from the stream was pure. It was from this little stream of ours that the Biafran leader, Emeka Odumegwu- Ojukwu and his household drank. It needed not to be boiled, distilled or filtered. It came purified. Every day, a jeep from the Ojukwu residence, which was not too far from us, arrived to fetch the water from *Onwenu's* stream of contentment.

As a growing teenager, I heard tales of my father's love for his people. I was told that each time he returned, our home immediately became an emergency pharmacy or medical centre. The wounded brought their injuries for him to wash and dress. Those who needed help with school fees, brought their children for him to see. He gave out many scholarships and promised even more. Papa taught the people the health benefits of eating fruits and green vegetables.

My father also promised to build a health centre and establish a secondary school to make life better for his people. These were promises he was never able to fulfil. Realising how much my father cared for the people of Arondizuogu, I began to feel obligated to take on some of his dreams for them.

We were still in Arondizuogu, when in May 1968, Port Harcourt fell to Nigerian troops. That was when Sister came to meet us. She brought tales of woe. She had seen death as she struggled to flee the city. Many died on the road, and many were wounded by exploding shells, mortar bombs and stray bullets.

With the loss of Port Harcourt, Biafra became completely landlocked. The economic blockade had crippling consequences on the fledgeling Republic. Huge Nigerian ships and superior naval equipment ensured that the blockade exacted maximum damage.

By this time, we felt the full weight of the war. Hunger dealt a crushing blow to millions of starving people inside the enclave. It lingered in homes where there were empty pots and even emptier stomachs. There, hunger entrenched itself. Then, without respect for the owner of the house, it invited its siblings – starvation and disease – to come in and live rent-free. To keep hunger away from our home at Arondizuogu, we embraced farming. The fact that we had land was my family's saving grace.

The Onwenu compound was filled to the brim. It had my late Uncle Charles' four wives and some of their children. My immediate family made up of my mother and two siblings were there. Brother Richard and sister Zoe, were both studying in the United States of America. Of course, there were my maternal grandparents, Aunt Dorothy and her husband Sammy Ejindu, their seven children, and Uncle Njio's wife Vicky and their four children. Mama Nnukwu's cousin, Mrs Iredu, joined us with her two children, so did the family of Dr Alex Ubezonu, my mother's cousin from Nnewi, as well as the Emekekwues, our distant cousins from Obosi.

Feeding a huge assemblage of people during the war was daunting, but we were the lucky ones who farmed. We grew yam, maize and cassava from which *fufu* and *garri* were made. There were also vegetables and legumes. Goats and chicken were reared within the compound but those disappeared after a while.

Arondizuogu, and indeed, the whole of south-eastern Nigeria were producers of organic palm oil and the plant's by-products. Palm oil has been reclassified as the most essential oil for the human body. We always knew that. Palm oil and its by-products have always been used for cooking, fuel, soap making and *ude aku* which is oil for the skin. Since my family owned land, we had many palm trees on them. These were exploited for money, food and medicine.

Within the compound, often at the back of the houses, where the women threw away ash from the firewood used in cooking meals the previous day, the soil was fertile. Families often grew plantain and banana, local pear, oranges and vegetables in these areas.

On our farms, there were different fruit trees; however, the fruits did not remain on the trees for long. If we thought it needed just one more day to ripen, it disappeared before we arrived the next morning. The *ukwa* or breadfruit was a favourite. *Ukwa* is rich in protein and is highly nutritious. The tree is valuable in Igboland and we had many of those around us. We noticed that we lost them just like the other fruits as we waited for them to mature. The normal thing was for the ripened fruit to fall to the ground, from where its owner would pick it.

One day, a guest refugee was caught picking up a huge ball of *ukwa* that did not belong to her. When she was accosted, she innocently said '*Okwa ika onye patalu, o palu,*' which means that she thought it was 'finders keepers'. That was how it was done where she came from; she was not a thief. They let her go and '*Okwa ika onye patalu o palu*' became a joke among us, which always seemed to provoke riveting laughter.

There was something about how the war drew Igbo people from across the country together. It was not strange to hear different Igbo dialects around you. The woman seen on the farm had a peculiar Awka dialect, giving her Igbo a delightful ring.

Late Uncle Charles had established a thriving cocoa farm around the main house. It yielded good sales, which supported the family for decades before the war. In a way, being surrounded by cocoa trees also provided good camouflage and protection from air raids. 'Ukwu Coco' – under the cocoa trees – was where we sat for fresh air, assembled for gossip and shared rumours and stories of war. It was where we received guests and played our games of ludo, whot, draft and *ncholokoto*, or *ayo* as the Yoruba call it. Most of our days otherwise, were spent working on the farms.

We also had civic duties to perform. Everyone – young, old, male and female – had a role to play in the sustenance of our little haven. We, the children, had to keep the mud houses clean and cool. We dressed the floors and inside walls with fresh mud and shredded banana stems. The exterior was dressed once a month. Everyone did their chores efficiently and learned as many skills as possible.

One of the skills that I learned and mastered was growing cassava tubers and processing *garri* from it. My sister, Ijeoma, hated going to the farm; she would grumble, drag her feet and find excuses not to go. However, when Sister arrived Arondizuogu some of those excuses disappeared.

Surprising, perhaps, was the speed at which my distant cousins learned the *garri*-processing trick, or so they thought. These were the children of Dr Alex Ubezonu, a Fourah Bay College trained educationist, who had married a wonderful Sierra Leonean woman, Mama Chizoba. Twelve-year-old Chizoba had been watching and observing our *garri* processing for some time, but she never had the opportunity to try it. Who would risk the burning or spoilage of even a fistful of *garri* because a 12-year- old wanted to learn the processing technique? No one took such chances during the war.

One day, however, someone left their *garri* station, so the zealous Chizoba took over and resumed the frying. The process involved oiling the big black wok with palm oil. As it melted, one would add about three cups of the first cassava meal. This would have been grated and tied up in bags for days, in a way that the moisture is drained; the meal is a little sun-dried as well. The three-cup base, well tossed in the oil, will now receive a bucketful, which is blended in until completely fried. This produces cassava flakes known as *garri,* which is a staple food in Nigeria.

Chizoba only joined the process at the last stage and began spreading the dry grains all over the place. It was a spectacle that would have probably gone on for some time until real damage was done.

'*Amuta m ighe garri, amuta m ighe garri*! I have learned to fry garri! I have learned to fry garri,' the exuberant Chizoba exclaimed.

We arrived just in time to save what would have been the loss of more precious *garri* in a time of great scarcity. That was how valuable food was. Everyone watched out for the best ways to save it, to ensure that life continued the day after. Not even a child was allowed to come between *garri* and survival.

There were also days when following sad news; we would all be united in mourning. Uncle Njio's wife, Vicky, had an aged mother whom we called Abadagu. She was known for making the tastiest *onugbo* or bitter leaf soup. It was presented in a small earthen pot. It did not contain meat, just dry fish and palm oil slightly congealed. It was indescribably delicious. There was not much of the soup at any given time, so we treasured it. As it happened, the old woman refused to leave her hometown Obosi, even after the next town, Onitsha, came under siege with shells falling all around. She was advanced in age and met her death there, though of natural causes. Abadagu was quickly buried and word sent to us about her demise.

There is nothing more painful for Ndigbo than not being able to bid farewell to a loved one in death. During the war, we often could not bury our dead. With the news came wailing from every quarter. Neighbours trooped into our compound to commiserate. Chizoba and her sisters joined in the wailing. She threw herself on the floor, crying uncontrollably as she had seen the adults do. After about 10 minutes, an exhausted Chizoba suddenly stopped, walked over to Njio's wife and asked in Pidgin English, '*But na who die so?*'

Tears turned into muted laughter as it dawned on us that she did not know who had died. She mourned as though she did because as family, we were all united in times of joy and of grief. This scenario taught me that family exists, for good times and bad times.

The Big Three

'Ifeoma *na* Ijeoma,' Sister would scream, looking everywhere for the two girls.

That call meant just one thing: these two cousins have caused trouble again. Such calls were followed by punishment. Ifeoma was Aunt Dorothy's first child, a tall, dark beauty who was given to as much mischief as her cousin, my sister, Ijeoma. Our time spent together during the war provided ample opportunity for such.

They were close in age. Ifeoma was just a year older than Ijeoma and they were more bonded than thieves. When I tried to wedge myself in as part of the team, they simply would have none of it. They involved me only if they felt that they could use me as a cover-up. My mother and Aunt were more likely to believe their story if I told it. That was fine. I could hide their secrets and provide a cover-up, as long as their scheme did not appear too outrageous for comfort. Our mothers were quite capable of severe punishments and I hated those.

During the war, Ifeoma and Ijeoma had the habit of buying chicken that was on the brink of death. They would buy the chicken cheap and slaughter it before it died. They would then cook it with stolen spices from our mother's stash, and precious salt. My sister and cousin did this in secret until I found out. Paralysed by the fear of everyone knowing, they added me to their 'chicken cooking gang'. The only problem was that I had no money to contribute toward the purchase of sick fowls. I, therefore, settled for the feet, head and other parts that others liked the least. The urge to buy sick fowls went on for months, to the extent that prospective sellers started bringing them to us in the house. This was how my mother found out and stopped the enterprise. Could this be a fulfilment of Mama Nnukwu's premonition in giving Ijeoma the nickname *ori-okuko-sagem*? The chicken-eating-sergeant? I wonder.

It was not from eating sick fowls that we got our name, the Big Three. It was from doing something more charitable – making people smile through our songs. We formed an informal singing group to amuse ourselves and in turn, the family. We were so good at it that we became the family entertainers, often called up to thrill visitors. We sang about love, of soldiers dying, of war and loss; we sang of hope in God and showed off our synchronised dance steps.

There was not much entertainment available in a place just 20km away from the Okigwe war front. Now and then, a theatre troupe would pass by on their rounds to entertain our gallant Biafran soldiers. The public was only allowed to attend by invitation. That was how we saw Sonny Oti's troupe featuring the singing sensation, Ms Orih Enyi. The performances of the group transported us for a moment beyond the turmoil that was Biafra. I was so inspired and enamoured by their act, the very emotive and moving renditions they offered, that I decided to join them and entertain army formations as well.

Sonny Oti was a famous Theatre Arts teacher, songwriter and performer. He was not a stranger to the family. He had been to our house in Port Harcourt at the invitation of brother Richard. I asked Sonny Oti to speak to Sister for her permission to join his troupe. He got a quick reply; a stern look on Sister's face that said more than her words could convey.

'*Ala o na pui?*' She finally said when she turned to me, asking if I'd gone mad.

That settled the matter. Like morning dew melting away under the noonday sun, the idea was trashed.

There were parties that we were allowed to attend as a group. It usually included Ijeoma, Ifeoma, our friends Grace and Eunice Obioha and a few others. There were wartime bands that toured the region, like The Rex Lawson's Band Boys. They came without their leader who had remained in Port Harcourt after it had fallen to the Nigerian troops.

On other occasions, we just had a DJ who provided the music we danced to. There were unwritten rules about dancing too close to a male partner. We were encouraged to maintain a 'social distance' between us and male dancing partners. Getting too close could arouse a man, so we just had to be careful. After the party, we all ended up at Mazi L N Obioha's country home, which was closer to the venues. It was a big house as L N Obioha had four wives and many children; there was always room for us. My mother had her peace of mind, knowing that we were safe.

As the war progressed, plans were put in place to get us, the Big Three, out of Biafra. That was how we met Dr Alvan Ikoku, whom we thought was a blood relative. When the story of his relationship with my grandmother was told, I marvelled. Mama Nnukwu was accused of embezzling community funds when she was the treasurer of the Town Union. Despite the lack of investigation and evidence, she was adjudged guilty and 'punished' for it by a group of powerful families who were afraid of her rising profile. Her punishment, unjust for sure, was ostracism from the community. No one could buy from or sell to her; no one was allowed to relate with her, except members of her own family. Dr Alvan Ikoku gave her a job; to supply food to Aggrey Memorial College Arochukwu, where her first daughter, Sophie, attended school and where he was Principal. That was a rare feat for a woman in the 1940s. My grandmother took the job in her stride and was very successful at it.

Mama Nnukwu's home in Obosi was a stopover place for her Aro Egbuoma people passing through to Onitsha, a gateway town and a great commercial city. She also came in contact with Aros in diaspora and worked with other leaders to promote the welfare of Umuaro. That was how she met Dr Alvan Ikoku.

We later found out that there was more that bound the two together. Mama Nnukwu and the Great Uncle, as we called Dr Alvan Ikoku, both had 'prodigal sons', Nathan Njio Nwokoye and Dr Sam Ikoku, who were themselves best friends. I am sure the concerned parents would have shared their worries for their 'wayward' sons. My grandmother was a great counsellor who would have likely dished out some useful advice to her friend on how to raise, or rather, how to survive the challenges of raising a loved but rascally son.

When Dr Ikoku's plans to ferry us to Gabon, from where we could connect to other parts of the world pulled through, only Ijeoma and Ifeoma were selected. I went with them on a 'Thank you' visit to Dr Ikoku in Owerri. He was so surprised that I knelt to thank him for his efforts, even though my name was not on the approved list. He was profoundly touched and he said so. For me, this was a major reinforcement that the lessons my mother had taught me about the usefulness of a grateful heart were not mere theories. Appreciating the importance of gratitude to others is a lesson I have held onto ever since.

The closer the war drew towards us, the more the number of those needing help at the hospitals. There were no hospitals in the real sense of the word, just makeshift spaces that shooed away death from dying people. There were wounded soldiers to treat, starving children to feed and nurse back to life, as well as wounded and sick civilians straddling the close extremes of life and death.

Towards the middle of the war, I joined the Red Cross and was trained in First Aid. I worked as a nurse's aide at a makeshift military hospital at Iheme Grammar School Ndianiche, Arondizuogu. Though it was a two-hour trek from home, the joy of adding my quota to Biafra's survival efforts woke me up every morning and led me towards the hospital. There, I cleaned wounds, made beds and washed bandages for re-use. Decades later, even though I had blanked out the images of dead and dying soldiers, sometimes the sound of their cries, with pain and anguish would come back to me. I recall patients being sewn up without anaesthesia; I can still hear their screams ringing in my ears.

In addition, I worked at a sick bay for kwashiorkor patients. It was dedicated to the treatment of malnutrition, the advanced stage of which is kwashiorkor. Patients had bloated stomachs, exposed ribs, swollen faces, hands and feet, and pale skin. A malnourished body was vulnerable to diseases because the immune system was seriously impaired.

Biafra was not landlocked, but the Nigerian government was able to mount an effective blockade that prevented the delivery of much-needed food and medical supplies to the embattled enclave through the waterways. Biafrans were being killed by starvation, the young and old among them, and even the soldiers were showing signs of acute malnutrition. As such, the soldiers were never prosecuted for helping themselves to crops in people's farms.

Through improved feeding using non-fat dry milk, dried egg yolk, cornmeal and other relief materials from Caritas International, the Red Cross and the World Council of Churches, we were able to save many people. However, many were too far gone by the time they were brought to us. Children died in my arms and I sometimes watched old men and women die from treatable diseases because we had no drugs.

I remember the smell of the one big ward everyone shared. Often, we received food aid in the forms that our people could not consume. Africans are known to be lactose intolerant, and the consumption of milk could accelerate stooling. If a person had diarrhoea, we devised ways to turn cornmeal, which our people were not familiar with, into *moi-moi*, a local dish of steamed bean meal. We did everything we could to keep them comfortable but we could not save many. The death of a child was most heartbreaking, and it occurred with tragic regularity. Death was everywhere.

Tougher is the End of a Thing

In April 1969, Nigeria captured the key Biafran towns of Umuahia and Owerri. Things became tougher; food became scarcer. It also became more difficult to keep livestock safe from humans. People relied on frogs, toads, termites, grasshoppers, locusts, rats, lizards, bush meats, small birds and anything that moved, for protein. Rats and lizards were the first to disappear from the environment. Biafrans almost ate them into extinction, but they did that to survive.

Those were the days when many relied solely on food from charitable organisations across the world. The relief materials came in trickles. It was not strange to see people with tiny limbs, distended stomachs and outsized heads. Daily, Biafrans stood in long queues for endless hours just to receive materials that could mean a postponement of their dying day. However, death could come unannounced to those queues as they were prime targets and incessantly bombed.

Towards the last quarter of the war, my eldest sister Azunna got a job through her paternal aunt with one of the relief agencies and was paid with foodstuff. My mother and Aunt Dorothy had access to some wheat flour with which they baked bread. It was the first time we would eat bread in more than a year. The bread was baked in a sand-laden aluminium pot over coals. That day, the bread felt like the first rains on parched earth. Its tang brought me delight, like the smell of rain following an extended period of drought. We were approaching the end of the war, even though we did not know it.

Biafra seemed to be at the end of its tether. Its resistance seemed to ebb away by the day. Nigerian forces gave us an unpleasant Christmas present. They had wreaked havoc by striking at the very heart of Biafra. In the meantime, more and more people died from hunger than bullets. It was not strange to see dying bodies strewn across the roads. Neither was it strange for a strong stench of death to hover around for a long time. You could not shake it off.

It was clear we were close to the end, but no one knew how it would come. Christmas came dull and barren, bereft of the love and the joys that come with the festive period. There seemed to be a dark grey to the white haze of the harmattan. It was a foreboding for what January would bring.

The New Year brought news, bad news that buzzed around, like flies around a corpse. Operation Tail-Wind, the final Nigerian offensive that shattered Biafra's already failing strength, was launched early January 1970. The attacks came from all sides: the 3rd Marine Commando Division with the 1st Infantry Division's support to the north and the 2nd Infantry Division to the south. Biafra finally caved in, its fragile resistance no longer sustainable.

On 9 January 1970, Owerri fell. Two days later, Uli, the airport town, followed. The war had already reached Okigwe, a town just 20km south of Arondizuogu. The famous Uga Airstrip to the north was incapacitated. Ojukwu fled into exile and Biafra surrendered. The 30-month long war had come to an end. That was when another war began.

Before I talk about that other war, let me first disclose where I was when I heard that the war had ended. I remember that moment very well.

The news came over the transistor radio owned by a few and operated whenever they had access to batteries. My younger cousins and I had gone to a newly discovered cassava farm, where if you paid a small amount of money, you were allowed to carry as much of the tubers as you could manage.

That day, I nearly broke my neck and arms carrying cassava. Imagine what it was like for us to have access to such an abundant supply of cheap cassava when we had no idea that such a supply existed. I balanced a huge basin stuffed with cassava tubers on my head, held it with one arm and carried another bucket of the prized crop with the other hand. My sister, Ijeoma, was, as usual, a no show. I do not remember what ailment she had feigned on that day; whatever it was, this assignment was voluntary and I took it on. As I walked home, I was confident that my mother would be impressed by my resourcefulness and how much cassava I could carry over a long distance.

As we walked up the hill that led to our *Nnukwu Uno*, I saw what appeared to be an animated discussion going on under the cocoa trees, the place where we held court. It did not take long for the words '*Agha ebie! Ndiawusa emelie!*' 'The war is over! The Hausa people have won' to be heard all around.

While there was excitement in the air, there was also apprehension. We had always believed that victory for Nigeria would come with more genocide, rape and the usual 'victor-takes- it-all' attitude of Africa's conquering armies. Biafran propaganda had increased our apprehension while experiences in places like Asaba where there had been a massacre of hundreds of unarmed civilians in October 1967 confirmed our fears. Sister was worried about her daughters.

Fairly soon, in a matter of hours after the broadcast, our general fears receded and we dared to believe that indeed, the whole war ordeal was over and our lives had been spared. We also wondered if life could return to normalcy. I was disappointed though, that no one had time to appreciate the cassava my cousins and I had brought back, and the *garri* and *akpu* – cassava meals that would be made from it. All that neck-breaking effort had been for nothing; Ijeoma was smarter after all.

I thought of the normal life waiting for us in Port Harcourt. We would just go back home, dust ourselves up from the ruins and ravages of war, and rebuild our lives. General Gowon, the Nigerian Head of State, said that there were no victors and no vanquished in declaring that the war was over. He used a particular phrase known as the three Rs – Reconciliation, Reconstruction and Rehabilitation.

I thought of the new clothes I was going to acquire, instead of the few that my cousins and I exchanged among ourselves, or the ones handed down to us by Sister; new underwear instead of the home-sewn ones we managed. Even so, we were better off than most. Occasionally, packages from abroad would find their way to us from relatives and what a blessing those were.

Now, we would have three square meals a day. Sister had cut it down to two decent meals. We had to augment our caloric intake by sourcing fresh fruits, oil palm, coconut, local pear and guava. All these were shared with our neighbours and the whole extended family of refugees. If we had precious salt, meat, fish or mushrooms, we also shared. Sister had taken to feeding Uncle Charles' young children to prevent malnutrition and any opportunistic diseases from coming in. There were a lot of sacrifices made so that as many of us as possible could survive the war.

All that had come to an end. It was a new and exciting reality, indeed. Then the news turned sour; when word filtered in, that Ndigbo were not welcome back to Port Harcourt, and could not reclaim their property as it was war booty. That 'Abandoned Property' doctrine which it was called, was peculiar to only Rivers State, and was designed to displace and economically weaken an already defeated people. Gowon's 3Rs had been no more than a cruel joke.

Lost but Never Found

During a war, so many things are lost that are never found: lives, property, peace, values and innocence. The events of the Nigerian Civil War shaped my life. I was fifteen years old when the first fires of war sparked. Two weeks before my eighteenth birthday, the fires died down. Yet, the ashes continue to smoulder in my memories.

The first thing that I lost during the war was my innocence. I was just a child doing childish things, playing around and experiencing the world as it unfolded before me. No one prepared us for the war; no one prepares anyone for things like that. Those were my formative years and they were spent in conflict and bloodshed. I never planned to see gory images of people cut open, or hold dying babies in my arms until their last breath. I did not bargain on having to hear the screams of wounded soldiers. I saw death, hunger, and deprivation. My life was turned upside-down and in the most chaotic way possible.

'The world has no conscience,' my mother's cousin, Dr Alex Ubezonu, would repeatedly say, while we sat under the cocoa trees.

For a while, I wondered what he meant as he argued with other people on the war's tactics and brutality. I wondered about Aunt Dorothy, who always brought home the sad tales. She was chronically depressed and pessimistic. Mama Nnukwu called her 'home saboteur'.

I later understood what Uncle Alex meant by the world, not having a conscience. It became clear that only a few countries of the world would stand with Biafra or support our cause, as right as it was. It became clearer to me that even though 'the world' was not a human being that could have a 'conscience', it could do grave evil by its silence.

Many decades after the war, Ndigbo are still subjected to marginalisation and discrimination, despite the 'No Victor, No Vanquished' slogan. Yet, being the industrious people that we are, we trudge on, and the world continues to have no conscience. One of the remarkable things Ndigbo achieved after the war was to maintain a sense of communalism, strong enough to ensure that we banded together and built infrastructures for ourselves, such as the Imo State airport.

There is something that cannot be taken away from Ndigbo, and that is their penchant for crowd-funding. They consider it a veritable means of development, for ordinary citizens to step up and solve a problem that the government has refused to entertain.

In 1979, during Sam Mbakwe's stewardship as Governor of Imo State, when it comprised Imo, Abia and Ebonyi States, Ndigbo decided that instead of complaining about the lack of a Federal Airport in their region, it was best to raise funds and build one for themselves.

The Imo Airport became the only one in the country built by the people and handed over to the Federal Government of Nigeria, which designated it a Cargo Airport. But an airport it remains, all the same, conveying several thousands of passengers daily, in and out of the eastern heartland.

For three years, a group of Imo patriots in Lagos led by the renowned insurance guru Dr Joe Irukwu met weekly to plan and carry out a nationwide fundraising effort needed to complete the project. It was a huge sacrifice of time, money, ideas and much more, to get the job done. Our efforts were robust and the coordinators from all walks of life were highly driven.

Artistes of Imo origin had to perform at fundraising events free of charge and my musical equipment was surrendered for such use.

I cannot think about the Nigerian-Biafran War without remembering friends and family who died in it. Many of them were cut short before the prime of their lives. They were on the upward swing, filled with hope and then they were no more. My family lost my maternal uncle, Njio.

There was also Obiorah Mpkaaru, my mother's first cousin. He was to my siblings and I, a brother and friend. He was beguiling, with an air of rascality to his fun-filled nature. Obiorah was the only son of his mother, Mama Nnewi, Mrs Mkpaaru (née Anyiwo). As a bright young mind, he was at the University of Nigeria Nsukka, when war broke out. Being the radical type that he was, he quickly joined the Biafran Army and went to war. Lt Mkpaaru was stationed near the Okigwe Front. On his off days, he would pick up the Big Three – Ifeoma, Ijeoma and I, and take us as close as we could get to the trenches, to walk where the soldiers walked. On the day that we received news of his death, I heard my grandmother cry a deep cry that I would never forget. And then, she sang a dirge for him.

I still see Obiorah in my mind's eye, vibrant and enjoying himself. I still hear his laughter as it fills up the entire room, the brightness of his face as it lights up the saddest days. I see him climbing the top of the bus that brought Richard back from secondary school, all dusty, to disengage my brother's luggage tied to the roof of the bus. Obiorah spent many holidays with us in Port Harcourt. The last time I saw him, his goodbye seemed to linger longer than usual. He had dropped us off after a visit to his base near Okigwe.

I will not forget Charlie Oguchi, one of our tenants who was a teacher at Stella Maris College, Port Harcourt. During the holidays, I would help him copy his teaching notes by hand, as he prepared for the next term. It was a paid summer job for me. Oguchi was a brilliant, young engineer who was just starting life. He was a Lido Nite Club patron, a 'good-time' boy and a ladies' man. Charles was altogether kind-hearted. Like the legendary poet Christopher Okigbo, he was killed at the Biafran war's early stages. So were many other enterprising young men, from a particular generation. There was the felling of the handsome pair of John Onubogu, his cousin IK and so many others, too numerous to mention.

Ikechukwu Anyakoha was an 18-year-old from Obinetiti. His death hit many of us hard. He was killed at the war front just months after joining the army. His young mother was devastated and never recovered from the loss. Years after the war, Ikechukwu's friends, myself included, continued to look after her. We all adopted her as our mother.

I am sure that every Igbo household lost someone dear to them, some loved ones whose departure left a gaping hole in the fabric of their existence.

Another thing that we lost was our respect for all things formerly held sacred. Before the war, Obosi traditionalists revered several animals like *eke*, the python. Pythons were generally sacred in many parts of Igboland and could neither be killed nor eaten. Killing a python was equated to killing a human being, and would draw the anger of the whole community. Worse still, the anger of the gods. It was a taboo to kill or harm it in any way. Pythons were themselves harmless. They had peacefully coexisted with select igbo communities for ages. If found in the home of a Christian, it was gently coaxed away. People simply spoke to it: *'Eke, naba na ebe a bu be ndi uka'* which means that the python should please go away from a Christian home.

However, when protein was scarce and starvation commonplace during the war, nothing was sacred anymore, not even the python. Looking back, the reverence for these animals was a way of respecting and conserving nature. It was similar to the round-about conservation approach attached to the 'evil forests' that existed in many communities, but things fell apart with the war.

The war changed us permanently in so many ways. There was a loss of morality and the reordering of priorities. For many, everything became about money; people did just about anything for money. The natural Igbo inclination for collective progress was soon replaced by ruthless individualism. It was not so much about family or the community anymore, but about getting ahead in life as quickly as possible, even at the cost of established values. It did not matter anymore how people made their money, or how they stumbled upon stupendous wealth. Money began to cover a multitude of sins. This was not so before the war.

If someone happened upon wealth, it was not strange for the family to set up a meeting to ask how the money was made. No one questions abrupt wealth anymore; rather, we celebrate it with chieftaincy titles and allocate the church's front pews to people of questionable character. We allow money to address us at family and town meetings, while the wisdom of the elders is relegated to the background.

Nevertheless, if the war brought out the worst in humans, it also brought out the best in Biafra. In that period of great suffering and adversity, we discovered how much ingenuity resided in us. We found out what we could do, and how we could squeeze something out of nothing to survive. The Obinetiti community remains dear to me for their compassion, neighbourliness and hospitality. I watched them welcome waves of refugees with open arms and love. The community would receive them with foodstuffs such as yams, palm oil, rice and whatever vegetable they could gather. These were struggling families, yet they shared whatever they had. Most importantly, they shared their love.

Biafra survived for three years manufacturing its weapons, including the famous bomb nicknamed *ogbunigwe,* which means 'that which kills in great numbers'. Biafra had its locally manufactured armoured vehicles. The budding nation inflicted several catastrophic defeats on the Nigerian Army, especially in Abagana on the Enugu-Onitsha highway. Biafra built local refineries that produced its petrol and other by-products.

The war had a way of bringing out people's true nature. Angels before the war likely became better angels, while beasts became uglier versions of themselves. Others were like shapeshifters, formless like water and adapting to any appearance that served their purpose. Whatever the war made people do, or perhaps become, it was already hidden somewhere in them.

People like my cousin, Goddy Onwenu, took the war as a great leveller which in many ways it was. He, who started living with my mother since childhood, ate her food, drank her water, and obtained an education through her, was suddenly full of hubris and disrespect. He took to calling her by her first name 'Hope' instead of 'Sister' or 'Mama'. Being the oldest man in the

Onwenu household, Goddy became the head of the family and he began to lord it over everyone else, including his biological mother, Udu. He was rude and demanding of respect, forgetting that it is earned. Sister put up with it all.

When I asked her why, she simply said, '*Nsogbu adiro,* no problem. Water will find its level again after the war.'

She was right.

After the war, due to the devastation of resources, Goddy lost his socio-economic well-being, was humbled and once again became dependent on my mum, even till she passed away in 2011.

Biafra is a story of 'ifs' and 'maybes'. Some possibilities never saw the light of day. If Biafra had survived as a nation, it would have become one of the most prosperous and innovative countries on the African continent. If Nigeria had learned from and used some of Biafra's inventions, it would have increased its chances of being a true giant of Africa, something it has always called itself but has never been.

Biafra has remained for some people a dream deferred. For others, it was an accident of history. It continues to live in the heart, a testimony to the fact that people still bear the scars from its charred remains. It is more so because Nigeria, for many years, has disallowed the teaching of history in schools and has discouraged the discussion or writing of stories related to the war.

I do not doubt that my account of Biafra might unsettle or make some uncomfortable. Nonetheless, it is my story. I lived it and I have a right to tell it to my children and grandchildren. I hope that they never get to see war and that they assert themselves and exercise their right to live as equal citizens of our country, Nigeria.

Return After War

The Nigerian Civil War was a brutal one and Biafrans on whose land it was fought, witnessed the massive destruction of their homeland. Having been uprooted from our home in Port Harcourt, we were caught up in the unjustly abandoned property saga in Rivers State. It was stipulated that every property owned by Ndigbo in the city was designated as such and could be sold or disposed of by the State Government. This policy was formalised by a decree nine years later by the Rivers State Government, even as they had sold off most of the properties by then.

When Sister tried to reclaim our house in Port Harcourt, she was attacked on the street and beaten into a coma. She survived and ended up selling the house to the first buyer for much less than its value. She invested the money in building a family house at Obinetiti.

After the war, we returned to Obosi. Thankfully, my grandparents' house remained intact but for a few bullet holes. Papa Nnukwu complained bitterly that the Biafran currency was useless, just soon after he had become 'a multi-thousandaire', money which he made from growing cassava, rice and corn. He was deprived, he said, of his bragging rights.

We were fortunate to have survived the conflict. Many were not so lucky. Some Igbo landlords in Port Harcourt died in penury or heartbreak for the seizure of their property. This they suffered at the hands of the people, some of whom were our Igbo brethren in select areas of Rivers State.

Perhaps driven by the shame of being associated with a defeated people, these Igbo people made conscious efforts to deny their Igboness. The need for Ikwerre people – who are actually people of Aro descent – to distance themselves from us was manifest in many ways. They renamed their towns with a corruption of the first letter of the word. For example, Obigbo, which means 'The Heart of Igboland' was renamed 'Rumigbo' which meant nothing. 'Umukurushi' which means 'the children of Kurushi' became Rumukurushi, and so on.

The first thing Sister did when we got to Obosi was to call a family meeting. When everyone had gathered, she cleared her throat and spoke.

'Please, help me beg Ijeoma and Onyeka,' she started. I felt as though all the eyes were on me. 'They are not helping around the house,' she continued. 'As if my life is not difficult enough, these two (she pointed at Ijeoma and I) are determined to make it more impossible.'

Sister then listed the many things she needed help with around the house, and which had been left undone. Right there, watching my mother, I knew that she was not talking about me. I did my bit, and part of Ijeoma's as well. Her appeal should have been directed at my sister, but she roped me in. What it meant was that I had to double my efforts and cover Ijeoma's lapses even better. I was responsible for washing Sister's clothes, by hand of course, before ironing and putting them away. I also plaited her hair, which I was good at. Ijeoma would never ask me nicely to do her hair but rather demanded it, and never said 'Thank you' either. She purposely never learned to plait hair, and so could not reciprocate the favour.

One day, she was particularly unpleasant in demanding that I attend to her after doing our mother's. I could not refuse, but I could protest by giving her a bad hair-do. Everyone who saw it got the message, including my mother, who fell, laughing. After that, I never had to plait Ijeoma's hair again.

Ijeoma and I had resumed school in 1970. This time, we attended Zixton Memorial Grammar School Ozubulu, not too far from Obosi. My mother wanted us close by; we were war survivors in a ravaged environment. The family's financial situation was, as usual, stretched to accommodate my grandparents and other relatives. This was the state of affairs when a package from Zoe arrived. It contained prospectuses from various schools in the United States. And it was for the Big Three.

By the grace of that all-important opportunity, the burden of years of school fees and other worries that go hand in hand with raising girl children were in one fell swoop removed from my mother and Aunt Dorothy. We embarked on the application process guided by Zoe, and I was quickly snatched up by the Baldwin School, Bryn Mawr, Pennsylvania, an elite Prep School. After one year of High School, I gained admission to Bryn Mawr College, and Wellesley College in Massachusetts, two top women's colleges in the US.

Leaving Nigeria was an opportunity to start afresh, to rise out of the ashes of war and build something new. I did not take the opportunity for granted. There is no doubt in my mind that my life would have been different, had I not had the privilege of attending the schools I did. Going to America was that action that changed my course, and I owe it all to my sister, Zoe.

Before I saw Zoe in America, however, I saw Lagos. I saw someone in Lagos called *Abami Eda* – the Strange One.

Lagos, Abami Eda

Zixton Grammar School was owned and operated by Dr Ikeotuonye. Ijeoma was in Class Five, the class in which students sat for the West African School Certificate (WASC) examination. I was in Class Four. Ifeoma attended another school, Basden Memorial. Among the Big Three, I was the first to obtain a US visa. Back then, in 1971, the process was hassle-free. Once anyone had the Form I-20, which meant that they had secured admission to a US school, the granting of an American visa became a mere formality, especially if you had a scholarship or proven support from family.

In Lagos, we stayed with Aunt Dorothy, who had moved back there with her family and lived in Surulere with her sister-in-law, the business tycoon Mrs Mercy Eneli (née Ejindu). 'It was only our second time in Lagos, the first time being when we were much too young. Ifeoma and her siblings were born there, though my mum partially raised them in Port Harcourt, all seven of them.

Before our arrival, Grace Obioha, a friend and fellow student at Zixton Grammar School, who was also a sister to Ralph Obioha of the famous 21st birthday party, had the privilege of being one of the first war survivors among us to have a glimpse of the much talked about Lagos, after the war. She gave us no rest with her numerous stories.

'Good God in tappers! This is Lagos!' she would exclaim, now and then, breaking into a James Brown dance immediately.

144

There was everything in abundance in Lagos it seemed. For those who had been so deprived of the necessities of life during the war, that meant a lot. Upon finally beholding Lagos, however, I was not as impressed as I had expected to be. It was no better than Port Harcourt, the city I grew up in; it was just a lot busier and fast-paced. We still knew the people in the neighbourhood and could stop on the streets to chat, even if they were in a car. That was how I met *Abami Eda*, also known as Fela Ransome- Kuti. He later changed his name to Fela Anikulapo-Kuti.

I had just turned into Falolu Street in Surulere when a car pulled up behind me. Seated in it was Fela. He was pleasant and introduced himself, while inviting me to his nightclub that evening. I knew that I was not going to honour the invitation, but it was rather flattering to be invited all the same.

The second time I encountered Fela was in 1984, a few years after I had returned from the United States. He had just been released from jail. Fela had been arrested for attempting to travel with his band for a gig in London with the sum of £1,600 for their hotel accommodation. Carrying any amount of foreign currency was against one of the many decrees promulgated by the Buhari/ Idiagbon military junta. Meanwhile, just days later a certain traditional ruler was allowed into the country with 53 suitcases, allegedly stuffed with the currency. The implications were many and I made these known in an opinion piece which was published in The Vanguard newspapers.

In hindsight, I realise that the government could have had me arrested for being so critical. It was not a tolerant regime at all. However, I do recall that Brigadier General Idiagbon, the second-in-command, had commented that the government would accept criticism from people like Onyeka Onwenu because 'that woman loves Nigeria'. I was touched and I longed to meet him but never did. His premature death in 1999 was a shock to me.

In any case, after Fela was released from prison, he sent a mutual friend, the journalist Onuorah Udenwa who is now a US-based pastor, to bring me to his club. I thought that he probably wanted to thank me for speaking up for him, but that was not it. He never even mentioned the article I had written in solidarity with him. Fela wanted to marry me, and I was flattered. I reminded him of the first time we met at Falolu Street and his invitation to visit his club. I thanked him for the honour of wanting me to become his consort, but I turned him down all the same.

While I waited to see him, I had noticed that his Queens – the euphemism for his numerous dancer-wives – had been looking at me with scorn. They passed by often, whispering comments about me. They were downright hostile and quite obvious about it. I pointed this out to Fela and told him that I was a possessive lover and would not be able to cope as an appendage to his harem. Fela laughed. He seemed to enjoy the idea that the women were 'fighting' to keep his affection. He did not persist with the marriage proposal, however.

It was a good night out and Onuorah Udenwa was a perfect escort. I did not stay for too long and he took me home safely.

That was my last encounter with *Abami Eda*.

Fela stood for all that was bold, creative and self-assured about Nigeria, as the preeminent black nation in the world. In a sense, he was like Lagos, restless and unpretentious. His life was an open book and his stand on any issue was always clear. He stirred up in Nigerians a certain bittersweet taste. He reminded us of how to be black and proud, even if we are from Africa where our leaders did anything but lead. The confidence he exuded as a black person, asserting himself through his music on the world stage was palpable. His radical nature of speaking out against State oppression made him the toast of Nigerians, and rightly so.

Fela criticised the heck out of our leaders and they deserved it. They still do. I could not understand, however, his philosophy or his views about women. Keeping a harem of women – 27 wives – did not coincide with my idea of love.

PART III

Going To America

The Baldwin School

There is a picture of my sister, Zoe, which I suspect she took during her early days in America. She was wearing a traditional attire called *akwa george* – a blouse and two layers of wrapper from the waist down with a head tie, all of which she covered with a jacket. That was my sister, comfortable in her own skin, even in a strange land.

I find this picture remarkable because it expresses my initial conflict on arriving in America. I do not remember what I was wearing when I left Nigeria, but I remember how I felt. I was excited beyond description, and at the same time, apprehensive of the changes I knew were coming. Yet, I was assured that Zoe would be there waiting for us – three young black women, taking their first steps on the road to a new life of discovery.

Zoe had made this journey earlier. Let me share with you, how fate conspired to connect her to someone through whom her story changed. Being raised by Sister without Papa was tough. Everyone had to work as soon as they were able to. When Zoe completed her secondary school education at Ogidi Girls Secondary School in 1965 and passed the West African School Certificate Examination with distinction, she needed to get a job to start earning money before contemplating her next move. Off she went to apply for a clerical position at the United Bank of Africa.

At UBA, she ran into an American lady called Estelle. Estelle immediately took to Zoe, pleased that she had strong analytical skills and a command of lucid, refined English at such a tender age. She could not understand the rush to throw her into the job market so early, with only a secondary school certificate's basic qualification. This was early 1966. She advised Zoe to withhold her job application form and insisted on accompanying her back home to see our mother. Rather than berate Sister for sending out Zoe so early to seek employment, Estelle prevailed on my mother to allow Zoe to come live with her in Jos, Plateau State. While at Jos, the 'plot' for Zoe to study in the United States was hatched.

In September 1966, Zoe and Estelle left for Wisconsin, in the United States. In no time, Zoe completed her prep school and gained admission into North Eastern University Boston, Massachusetts to study for a Bachelor's degree in Business Administration. She obtained her degree (cum laude) in 1971 and was admitted into the prestigious Harvard University for her Masters in Economics. Her wish to speedily complete this programme was not readily realised. Zoe was such a magnanimous creature; in the middle of her programme, she decided to bring us, the Big Three, to America for further studies.

The Pan Am aeroplane that flew us to Boston via Casablanca was my first flying experience, a most exhilarating one. Arriving in the US, everything was new and shiny. If I thought that Lagos was a step up from Port Harcourt where I was raised, nothing prepared me for the grandeur of the big cities of Boston and Philadelphia.

Before dropping me off at the Baldwin School, Bryn Mawr, Pennsylvania, my sister took us all shopping for clothes and we were spoilt for choice. She also opened my first bank account
–a savings account – for keeping my pocket money which came

from her as well. Having a bank account gave me a great sense of freedom and responsibility at the same time.

We arrived at Baldwin School one morning in September in early autumn. There was a slight chill in the air, gently cooling to the nostrils as I breathed. My skin responded with goosebumps. Zoe and I were confronted by an old Gothic building, the main facade of a sprawling compound that made up this prestigious prep school. It was established in 1888. I quickly settled down as the school term had already begun. I was a boarder in the twelfth grade, my last year in high school. It was the equivalent of Nigeria's Class Five in Secondary School.

A classmate named Amy was assigned to take me around in an informal orientation. She was to familiarise me with the environment and the school rituals such as bells, mealtimes, and classes registration. However, she did not turn up to take me to breakfast and I was too afraid to go searching for the dining hall. I went hungry. I did not have the boldness to ask anyone for help, so I missed lunch too. By dinner time, I was so hungry that I simply stepped out of my room, and followed the wafting smell of grilled chicken right into the dining hall. I had my fill of a whole chicken, vegetables, potatoes and gravy.

I could not believe that I was served a whole chicken. Wow! This was unheard of where I came from unless the chicken was from the sick stock of war-time Arondizuogu. This felt like when Papa was alive and I could eat anything I wanted. At any rate, eating rice and chicken was such a big deal whilst growing up that sometimes, children left their hands unwashed after the meal so that their playmates would know they had eaten chicken that day. They would have also smeared their mouth with oil from the meal for the same purpose. Here I was in America, being served a whole chicken. I felt like flying back home immediately, just to share the chicken story with my people, then come back to school to further my studies.

Stepping into the dining hall dressed in an *ankara* trouser and top, I was immediately aware that all eyes were on me. I was the girl from Africa, a continent that held a morbid fascination for many who knew very little about her, and which many more thought of as the 'dark continent'. The uninformed could not see beyond the obvious stereotypes of uncivilised people living in trees, dancing naked to tribal music and only eating after they must have hunted.

My fellow students were shocked to find out that I spoke good English and had a decent knowledge of global affairs. My accent was different, no doubt, but it did not conform to their expectations. It sounded more British than anything else and my classmates were quite impressed. I soon joined the school's choral group and the soccer team. It was presumed that coming from a former British colony, I would know how to play the game but I had never played soccer in my life. In Nigeria, it was not what girls did. I went along anyway, hitting the ball with my toes instead of the side of my foot. No one knew any better, except my sore toes. If my classmates had been shocked by my spoken English, they were even more surprised by my overall academic performance. The fact was that the Nigerian education system in the 50s, 60s and 70s was of international standard. Nigerian students all over the world were remarkable in their ability to compete with the best anywhere. Some of my best subjects were English Literature, Biology, Geology, History and Social Studies. I was still struggling with Mathematics as I had done in Nigeria.

My literature teacher Mrs Copeland took to reading my essays and analysis of Shakespeare regularly in class after a classmate complained that she had received a C grade while I had an A. I found favour with my teachers and school authorities who were impressed with my level of maturity. A recommendation from music teacher Mr D. Scarlet in support of my application to Bryn Mawr College, literally blew my mind when I came across it in preparation for this book. My teacher thought highly of me.

My coming to the United States and attending the Baldwin School on free tuition and boarding, was the initiative of the senior class – the class of '72. They had raised funds through various projects. It was humbling to learn of their generosity and compassion. I was chosen because of my essay about Biafra, which was part of my application.

Unsurprisingly, I felt lonely at Baldwin. I was away from home and my country for the first time, in a strange land that I had only encountered in the movies. Americans were not as communal as Nigerians. When I asked a friend for a dime to make a phone call, the lowest denomination of American money, it was given to me as a loan. My friend wanted it back. On the other hand, I would have just 'dashed' it to her, as we say in Nigeria.

Thankfully my loneliness did not linger as I soon made friends at Baldwin. I was an object of curiosity and interest. There were always many invitations from classmates who wanted to show off their African friend, me, to their families for holidays. Sometimes, I was weary of being a trophy and did not like it so much. I simply learned to enjoy my own company. This was 1971, just at the end of the hippy movement – flower power and all that. I learned a lot about American society through Television, which I watched quite a bit of it in our common room, in the company of my schoolmates.

I took part in regular school trips to Philadelphia to enjoy the latest theatre productions. With my own music turntable bought at a garage sale, along with old albums of Tom Jones, Engelbart Humperdinck, Andy Williams, Joni Mitchel and Roberta Flack, I was adequately entertained. Being by myself gave me the opportunity of getting to know and understand me. I learned to thrive on my own, writing songs and a lot of brooding poetry. All in all, it was a time to be free from the oppressive presence of my sister, Ijeoma. I liked that a lot.

Being an American prep school, Baldwin School graduates were expected to gain admission into the country's best colleges. I was accepted into Wellesley College and Bryn Mawr College. I chose Wellesley because Zoe attended graduate school at Harvard nearby. The thought of spending more years in the small and quiet town of Bryn Mawr area did not appeal to me at all. As much as I appreciated the scholarship offer from Bryn Mawr College, I wanted to be near Zoe and partake in the Nigerian parties I had heard so much about from her and Ijeoma. My Baldwin School experience came to an end in June 1972. By that time, I had established a reputation as a singer in the school choir. I had friends, some of whom were headed to Harvard, Massachusetts Institute of Technology (MIT), Duke University, Smith and other Ivy League schools.

For my graduation, Zoe bought me a beautiful white lace dress. It looked gorgeous. She was very proud of me and was satisfied with my school performance and conduct. The Baldwin School wrote to her especially, to commend those very qualities in me. I did not disappoint, and that was extremely important to her and me. Her trust was paramount; I felt as though I owed her, and I did.

Years later, my cousin Ifeoma Ejindu, was able to invite five of her siblings to the US for studies. She married and raised a family with Nkem Nwankwo, the novelist and author of iconic books such as *Danda* and *My Mercedes is Bigger Than Yours.*

Ijeoma went the academic way. She is an award-winning

professor of Microbiology at Montgomery College, Maryland. I do not doubt that without my sister Zoe's sacrificial intervention in facilitating our studies at some of the best schools in the United States of America, our lives would have been different, very different indeed.

After my graduation, I found my way to Chicago, where my cousin Godfrey DanChimah, Mama Aba's second son, lived with his lovely and wonderful wife, Ada. Godfrey had been the closest nephew to his uncle, my father. Also living in Chicago was my brother, Richard, who had only recently relocated from London, and my favourite cousin, Steven DanChimah and his family. It was a summer spent among family and friends. The holiday ended soon enough, and it was time to proceed to the next phase of my life: Wellesley College.

Life at Wellesley

I always knew that I was going to be a singer, but also a journalist or indeed any other profession I wanted. When it was time to select a major course of study at college, I did not choose music. At Wellesley, I studied International Relations and Communications. Wellesley, being a Liberal Arts College, allowed me to make selections that exposed me to the humanities, science and the arts, to ensure that I covered all areas that were either core or tangentially important to my chosen field of study.

Why choose International Relations and Communications? I was interested in people, their make-up and their relationships. I always stood for a shared humanity, the many values and attributes that we all have in common as humans and as nations. Suffice it to say that I did not think of going into politics. If I had, it would have been understandable. I had a role model in my father, but that consideration did not inform my choice at all.

I thought about the United Nations, about Africa, and the persisting scourge on humanity, represented by apartheid South Africa. Oppression reigned supreme there even when most African countries had been liberated. I was curious about that phenomenon, that tragic African story evolving so sadly at the bottom of the map.

I also wanted to understand the peculiarities that made each nation unique and how these manifested when nations worked together. No matter how well endowed, I believed that no country could sustain holistic growth without making available to its citizenry information about its functions and vision, enabling them to participate in the all-important development process.

I wanted to follow a career in the area of public service and administration. With a Liberal Arts education, Wellesley College helped prepare me for this interest. The curriculum's flexibility gave me the boldness to explore areas that I would otherwise not have bothered with. At MIT, I met Ed Diamond, a lecturer who took a liking to my writing and presentations. I took courses in Communications and he became one of my advisors. My choice of study became International Relations and Communications, with Professors Linda Miller (Wellesley) and Ed Diamond (MIT) as advisors. Every week, I shuttled back and forth, between the two campuses. Buses left each school on the hour. Wellesley had an exchange programme with MIT.

My junior year (third year) was spent at Mt Holyoke South Hardly MA, another women's school which was in a 12-college exchange programme with Wellesley. They were in turn connected to the University of Massachusetts (UMASS) in nearby Amherst. I took courses there in Mass Communications.

During my freshman year at Wellesley College in 1976, there were two other Nigerian students there: Chinelo Evelyn Irukwu, now Dr Evelyn Mbanefo, and Chinwe Dike, who sadly passed away in 2014. She was the daughter of Dr Kenneth Dike, Africa's renowned historian who was then a Professor of African History at Harvard. There was also a Nigerian Professor of Philosophy, Mr Ifeanyi Menkiti at Wellesley college.

Evelyn and I were quite close. We spent our weekends studying and cooking *okro* soup. If a Nigerian stayed a fortnight without a meal of *garri* with soup, things would rarely seem to be normal. In

1976, Boston could only boast of perhaps two African stores. It was difficult to find palm oil, an ingredient imperative for our Nigerian soup to be authentic. We did the next best thing by adding tomato paste, which gave the soup a semblance of the red colour from palm oil. We did not care; we just had to swallow something. When we could not find *garri*, we used ground oatmeal, farina or ground rice to form the molds of carbohydrate to suck up and hold the soup while our mouths and tongues did the rest. For Chinelo and I, a well-spent weekend meant getting all our class assignments done, spending some time discussing and debating issues, and then going to bed with bellies full of *garri* and *okro*, or *egwusi* or vegetable soup with spinach.

There were other students from Ethiopia, Somalia and Cameroon. We were all united in our loneliness and the surprising realisation that we did not fit in with Black America. We found no enjoyment in attending their parties, where it felt as though the men were only looking for women who had straight hair and light skin. It was hard to tell whether this was down to personal preferences or the residues of oppression finding expression in new insecurities.

The truth was that many of us who had come from the African continent to our shock, did not feel very welcomed by our African-American brethren. However, this has changed over the years. We organised our get-togethers and mixers under the aegis of Slater House, a beautiful house on the banks of Tupelo Lake, reserved for the use of all international students. Our gatherings allowed us to share our food with friends, and hold seminars or discussions about developmental issues in our various countries.

During my sophomore year in 1977, a great drought was raging in Africa's Sahel region, occasioned by the spread of the Sahara Desert into the Savannah area. There was famine and malnutrition in Niger, Burkina Faso, Chad, parts of Northern Nigeria and Senegal, in fact in all the countries with proximity to the desert. I set up a fundraising effort at Wellesley with the acronym SADVA – 'Students to Aid Drought Victims in West Africa'.

I worked with other African students to organise bake-offs, garage sales and other fundraising activities. We held talks to raise awareness about the problem. The funds were funnelled through OXFAM to meet some of the humanitarian needs of those affected by the drought. It may not have been a lot of money but at least we were engaged in finding relief.

I made an outstanding discovery in the process of this project: the preponderance of ignorance amongst many of the students about the world. A student's response to my attempts to talk to her about the immense sufferings of a large population of people in the Sahel region was: 'Them are the breaks'. It was a bit insensitive, nonchalant and discouraging. It did not seem empathetic that one looked at the sufferings of others and simply uttered the words: 'That's life.'

Yet, I also found so much kindness among the American people. That same year, the Meyer family chose me as a 'school daughter'. I cannot quite remember how we met but Mr and Mrs Norman Meyer stood in as my parents and did a good job of it. They were white and I was most definitely black, but they introduced me as their daughter without flinching and without an accompanying explanation. It was fun watching eyebrows go up and down. I spent my holidays with the family and was thoroughly integrated into this brood of very interesting people. There was Bruce the pilot who owned and flew his plane, Wendy, the musician Chris, Laura and another sister.

This singular experience taught me not to throw the wide blanket of stereotypes over people. No matter what, there was always the individual who did not represent their people's true image.

All in all, the Wellesley experience was life-changing. I remain grateful for the opportunity of studying in such an institution, with a full scholarship. As a foreign student, I earned money on campus by working in the music library. I also earned money the way most others did, as a babysitter. This enabled me to take care of my personal needs, academic supplies, travel and general living expenses.

I do not think that I quite realised the value of the education I received at Wellesley until after graduation. It quickly dawned on me that anytime I mentioned my Alma Mater, I got special attention. One such occasion was in 1994 at Nelson Mandela's inauguration breakfast in South Africa. I met the United States' Secretary of Commerce, Ron Brown. In the course of our conversation, I mentioned that I had attended Wellesley College. Mr Ron Brown excitedly told me that Wellesley women were 'brilliant'.

'I have two of them in my office,' he said. He then took my hand, and led me to Hilary Clinton, First Lady of the United States, and said to her, 'Here is one of your sisters.'

Mrs Clinton was talking to the wife of the Palestinian leader, Mrs Arafat, but quickly turned to share a few words with me. Mrs Arafat did not like the interruption one bit, and for the rest of the breakfast, stared at me with undisguised annoyance.

It also occurred to me after leaving Wellesley that I had benefited from an underlying emphasis on success at whatever one chose to do. Being a woman was not a disadvantage; rather, it was the opposite. Wellesley and institutions of its calibre have produced remarkable world-changers; it is a fertile ground for the planting dreams, for nurturing them and watching them bloom. I can say that my days there were central to the making of Onyeka Onwenu, the woman.

At Wellesley, I found confidence in the new person I was becoming and strength in my convictions.

I do not have any proper pictures of my graduation ceremony at Wellesley. I just have a few badly lit ones, like the one of me hugging my mum as she arrived with her sister Dorothy. It was so pleasant to see her and I became emotional; my face dissolving into an 'ugly cry'. I felt my father's presence as well. I had completed my first degree but there was more to come.

That same day, I left Wellesley with my friend Desseta Marsie-Hazen. Her mother lived in New York and I had some friends nearby, in Long Island. So, I hitched a ride.

New York! New York!

After graduating from Wellesley, I knew what I wanted to do: go to graduate school. How to go about it though, was the big question. I chose to go in search of an interim job. Desseta, my half-Ethiopian half-Jamaican friend, lived with her mother in New York. I was two years ahead of her in school, and she had become the little sister I never had. Through her, I got to know her family, and through me, she got to know mine as well.

After some days in Queens, I moved to Long Island to stay with a very good friend of mine, Pearl Enejere, and her husband, Emeka. I grew up with Justice Pearl Enejere (née Amobi). We spent our childhood holidays together in Obosi. Our families shared a close friendship; it began with our grandparents, Godson Nwokoye and Bernard Onubogu. The Nwokoye-Onubogu friendship was legendary; it started from their childhood and was only ended by their deaths. They called each other 'Ee eeh' and were often in one another's company.

A story was told of how they managed to impress a white man by their comical translation of an Igbo masquerade song for his benefit. The antiphonal song went like this:

Ana m o (I've got to leave now)
Ogo, Ugo, Ugo, Ugo (Eagle)
Ogbuefi, Ogbuefi (titled man)
Obele nmu o, obele nmu o (small masquerade)

The two friends translated it for the white man thus:

Call: I don go
Response: Eagle, eagle, eagle, eagle Call: Kill cow, kill cow
Response: Small juju, small juju

I am sure that the white man who was just passing by did not understand what they were on about. Still, he was so impressed with their effort that he gave the adventurous lads a gift of one shilling. That was a lot of money in those days. *Ogbuefi* transliterated means 'Killer of Cows'. That is what someone who has taken a traditional title is called because his investiture would not have taken place without his slaughtering a cow, which only the affluent could manage.

Pearl and her husband, the brilliant political analyst, Dr Emeka Enejere, hosted me for three months. It is amazing how some people come into your life and fill a void at a peculiar time. I will never forget the role that the Enejeres played in my life when I needed them. While I lived with them, I was treated with courtesy and kindness.

Emeka Enejere will demand that you fill your plate at mealtime with the best of what was available. He would say to me on my way to serve myself, *'Oburokwa iluo there imegheribe'* which meant, 'Do not go there to fool around'. He made me feel at home and treated me as a member of the family.

From their home, I commuted to New York City every day for my first job as an insurance clerk at a franchise of Equitable Insurance Company. I soon found a studio apartment on West 34th Street in Manhattan and moved in. While my ideal job would have been something in the media field, I had to make do with whatever was available to pay the bills and give me work experience.

Time was of the essence, however. My visa was about to expire in a matter of months. I had decided on graduate school but had not managed to raise enough funds for it. My insurance job was a temporary one; therefore, a stop-gap thing. It was in no way my final destination. While still on the job, something happened that I did not think was possible in the United States, given the general support for women's issues and human rights in the country. They were already mainstream concerns.

The insurance company I worked for was run by a very successful Nigerian broker. I simply walked in one day, a recent Wellesley College graduate with no real work experience, except for summer jobs in sales and modelling. I was offered a low- paying job as a clerk, which I accepted. It paid the rent of my studio apartment. I was grateful for that and I gave it my best shot. Not long after I started work, I noticed that my boss was quite a crude and rude fellow who enjoyed belittling his female workers. He said and did things that humiliated them, destroying their self-confidence and making them doubt their own abilities.

My job was not difficult and I certainly did it well. It was basically to register and follow up with new accounts that the field agents brought in. But the boss would always find fault with it. He would berate me in front of my co-workers with insults and veiled threats. Yet, I kept my cool. The verbal harassments soon escalated into attempts at physical contact. This was my first experience of sexual harassment at work.

My boss would invite me into his office and order me to perform sexual acts. I found his advances distasteful and I vehemently refused. He would then follow me out to the general office and condemn my work as substandard. The women in the office knew the drill. I later found out that he had done the same to some of them. I longed to quit but I had nowhere to go, or so my boss thought. He, therefore, intensified his efforts. Encouraged by my fellow clerks, I petitioned the Head Office, but nothing happened. I did not even receive an acknowledgement of my complaint. This was 1976 when, although aware of the issue, big organisations were still in denial regarding sexual harassment at work, or simply did not take it seriously enough.

As my boss' advances intensified, I had no option than to look for alternative employment. I sent my CV to many places, after checking the newspapers for vacancies. I just knew that I had to quit the insurance job, whether or not I got another one. My boss knew that my visa was about to expire, and thought that I would have no choice but to yield to his demands. That was when God made a way for me.

One day, things came to a head. I could no longer put up with his crude and insulting tirades, and I walked off the job. Leaving Equitable Insurance as abruptly as I did, without a backup plan meant I had to find another job quickly.

I had an American 'sister', Wendy Meyer, who worked at the United Nations. I decided to visit her and ask for advice. She was the daughter of the same Meyers who took me in as a member of their family in my freshman year at Wellesley. Wendy not only advised me, but she actually led me to the Office of Public Affairs, where I applied for a Tour Guide position. They happened to be hiring at the time. That was how I got my first proper job at the UN. The timing was not a coincidence; I considered it to be God's favour.

The Big United Nations Family

A t the United Nations, I needed a different kind of visa, that of an International Civil Servant. I quickly flew into Nigeria, spent a few days, had the requisite visa stamped on my passport and returned to the UN to begin my new job.

Living in New York City, now on East 44th Street, and working at the United Nations, I felt I was right smack in the centre of the world. The Tour Guide was the go-between who showed the public the United Nations by conducting walkthroughs around the different sections of the imposing edifice; we went in and out of the various chambers and meeting rooms along the ornate corridors lined with works of art by globally-renowned artists. There were fascinating murals, paintings and stained glass windows from around the world, and an elaborate and exquisitely detailed ivory carving from China. One, which held a pride of place for me, was the sculpture of *Anyanwu* the sun goddess by Nigeria's Ben Enwonwu.

Our role was important to the UN given how we could shape people's views and perceptions about the Organisation. Tour Guides were expected to speak at least two out of the six official UN languages – Arabic, Chinese, English, French, Russian and Spanish. However, for some of us, an exception was made. Our mother tongues were accepted as second languages. Indeed, Igbo was spoken by millions of people in Africa and the diaspora; it was a way to make our team more diverse.

Our days were busy and our schedules were mostly stacked. Tour Guides were briefed daily by top UN officials regarding topical issues and events around the world. We were encouraged to attend the Security Council meetings, the General Assembly, the now rested Trusteeship Council, for territories still under colonial administration, to keep up with happenings in the UN system. Some of us did so not just because of our job interest, but for our passion for the emancipation of the African continent. Apartheid South Africa was at the time an imperial force in the region, bullying its neighbours and occupying Namibia, which was then called South-West Africa. Portugal enjoyed South Africa's support in the repression of the freedom movements in Mozambique and Angola, while the Frontline States increased their level of cooperation in ridding the continent of repressive rule. Although Nigeria was not physically a Frontline State, it staked everything it had on the issue of ending South Africa's apartheid system. I was proud of my country.

It was during our early days at the United Nations that I met Diana Ayee. The tall, dark Ghanaian graduate of Colombia University was my friend in the new class of Tour Guides. She had a voice that forced ears to listen. She was well informed and articulate; Diana had her views on the day's important issues and was not shy to express them. I saw a bit of myself in her. We were both considered a huge catch for the Guide Unit; two self-assured African women who brought style and competence to the job.

Every morning after our daily briefings, we retired to the Guides Lounge for more discussions until we were called for a tour. We always had coffee, tea, cigarettes and refreshments available for sale, and lively discussions were guaranteed. Diana Ayee and I held the African corner with pride and vigour. We could always be counted on to promote the idea of elections in South African-held territories and the dismantling of the apartheid system.

We ensured that the image of Africa was presented in a manner that was as accurate as possible. While hunger and conflicts persisted, there were pockets of positive growth and development that could also be found at the same time. Africans are beautiful, dignified and productive members of the human race. History started with us.

Diana and I aimed to assert and educate all the time. We carried the same message on our tours and often got commendations from groups and individuals. But we also got opposition from proponents of the apartheid system. Sometimes, hecklers and even mentally challenged people joined our tours. It was not a huge problem since we had been trained to handle people of all temperaments and political dispositions. Besides, the UN Police effectively manned all our tour routes.

In the lounge, some of the Tour Guides would not mix. They stayed within their national cocoons. For instance, five women from the Soviet Union were always in their own company. We left them severely alone. The stereotype was that they were spies, anyway. This was the late 70s and the Cold War was still raging. Everyone else mingled and formed clusters of close friendships within the Tour Guide group.

UN Tour Guides were drawn from all over the world; from Sweden, Norway, The Soviet Union, China, Japan, Brazil, Argentina, Czechoslovakia, Burma (now Myanmar), Ghana, Nigeria, India, Pakistan, Ethiopia, Turkey, Algeria and Italy. We wore a special uniform for easy identification. For the class of 1978, a new uniform by a world-class designer was introduced, and I was called upon to model it for the New York Times. There is a picture of me in a fitted blue skirt and jacket, with a darker blue piping and a beige shirt. Although I had some modelling jobs as a student at Wellesley, even appearing in Women's Wear Daily, a well-known fashion newspaper, I never really enjoyed it. I always felt that I had more to be admired for than my body or poise on the runway. However, this time I was very happy to have been chosen and I wore my uniform proudly, with a big smile firmly planted on my face.

Leaving my Insurance clerk job for the opportunity of becoming an International Civil Servant, as UN employees were known, was a huge step up. It also came with increased pay and a few perks to boot. Furthermore, it allowed me to register for a Masters degree programme in Media Studies at the New School for Social Research in NY.

I met many great people at the UN, some of whom I took around on my tours. There were remarkable events in which the guides participated. The most memorable for my class was the UN/ UNICEF Concert in 1979, which featured the Swedish Group ABBA, Olivia Newton-John, Rod Stewart and the Bee Gees. It was at this concert that the two hit singles – ABBA's 'Chiquitita' and Rod Stewart's 'Do You Think I'm Sexy' – were premiered. The Tour Guides were the ushers at this huge fundraiser and we interacted with everyone, including the stars. Diana Ayee and I can be seen in a photo with other Guides and the artiste Rod Stewart

> I remember how we met. It was at a UN Event with Ambassador Andrew Young (an incredible person). Anna Frangipani introduced us and I was awestruck. Before me was this beautiful, regal woman who had the grace of a queen and a voice of silk and honey. And I struggled because, being the neophyte that I was, I

could not pronounce her name. Not for the life of me. Worse yet, for the following months, I pestered Anna to remind me of how to pronounce the name. I was not in your league but that did not diminish my interest. Anyway, it is funny how things from the past suddenly became fluid in the present. **Jeffery Amengual,** 28 November 2018

Jeffery Amengual was a very good friend of mine during my days at the United Nations. Anna Frangipani, another Guide from Italy, was a mutual friend. We were part of an interesting group of friends from all over the world. There were many others; Anna Theophilopulu, Margareta Nielsen, Jim and Judy Foster (once you were a spouse to a UN Tour Guide you were one yourself). During the summer, we gathered at the Central Park Philharmonic Concerts for some music. Everyone brought something, including great wine and food shared in congenial company. We rotated lunches at each other's flats, especially those who lived near the United Nations. My favourite dish to make was chicken in coconut milk sauce with mushroom; it was an original recipe of mine. We topped it off with a dessert of cream cheese strudel, good coffee and tea.

To live in NYC was to meet up in restaurants for meals including the Saturday and Sunday brunches, where we ate all we wanted, and sometimes drank sparkling wine to our fill. I liked to window shop and hunt for the best bargains. I was a good dresser, but without the fat purse that should accompany it. School fees came first in my order of priorities. I was good at finding bargains though, including knock-off designer wears and clothes on clearance sales. I had an eye for fashion, just like my mother.

My tour guiding years were soon over at the UN, and I graduated from the New School for Social Research with a Masters degree in Media Studies. On the surface, it would seem that living such a life was ideal and there was no better place to be at. But underneath that façade of fulfilment, there was restlessness. I had the sneaky feeling that the UN was not my destination. I sought to fill the gap with a job as an electoral officer for the much-awaited Namibia elections. Namibia was the former German, British and South African colony that should have been handed over to the UN when it was formed in 1945.

From 1977 to 1979, the UN Department of Public Information was headed by Kofi Annan, who later became Secretary-General. It was common practice that we all had lunch at the staff cafeteria with him and other UN staff. He was accessible and often listened to our many complaints about the organisation. He advised, counselled and assisted if he could. Mr Kofi Annan had advised Diana Ayee and I to put our names forward for the Namibia job. I suspect it was because we bothered him so much during briefings and discussions about how slowly the negotiations were going with a recalcitrant South Africa. Perhaps he felt that our relentless curiosity on the issue could be better channelled to a more active engagement. Diana and I made the list, but the wait was too long. South Africa would renege, time and time again, and I grew impatient.

UN Tour Guides served for two years only, except for the very few who stayed on as supervisors for an additional two years. This was to prevent them from being jaded or bored on the job. After my tenure, and to figure out my next move, I took on another job at the UN as an employment clerk where I interviewed people for work at the organization. I did the very first screening of applicants.

How Margareta Got Her Comeuppance

Margareta Nielsen (now De Coys) was a UN Tour Guide, a class below my group. She was from Sweden. She was very friendly and always good company at parties and hangouts. But she fancied herself as one who could jostle other Guides with the most outrageous, embarrassing and unexpected questions. One day, however, the table was turned on her.

It had been a particularly busy week at the United Nations one Friday in autumn when the General Assembly was in session. The air was chilly and I was rushing back from the supermarket with items for dinner with a friend. I bumped into Margareta and Diana Ayee, whom I presumed was out food shopping as well. 'Big mouth' Ms Nielsen took a look at the items in my shopping cart and asked whom I was cooking dinner for.

'A friend,' I answered.

'Are you going to make love to him?' she asked blatantly. 'Yes. Would you like to watch?' I replied, without batting an eyelid.

The look on Margareta's face was priceless. It went from preparing to enjoy my discomfiture to the dropping of her jaw in embarrassment at my quick repartee. That was the end of her jabs of embarrassing questions.

Going Home

One day in September 1980, I went for a diplomatic reception and a discussion came up. I felt that my country was chauvinistic and anti-women and I bemoaned the fact that we were not represented in government. In some parts of the country, women could not inherit property, especially in the southeast where I was born. In that regard, women were treated as second-class citizens. Yet I could never consider myself inferior to someone else on account of my gender. There was a gentleman in the room for whom it was not the first time hearing me criticise Nigeria.

'Young lady, you may be right, but what are you doing about it?' He started, his eyes fixed on me while I listened. 'You work here at the UN, and you live on the East side of New York, isn't it?'

I nodded in affirmation.

'Unless you go back to Nigeria and try to change some of those things which you complain about, you have no right to criticise your country.'

On hearing these words, I let out a nervous chuckle. It had not yet entered my imagination that I could reside in Nigeria anymore. I thought of myself as an independent-minded woman, a vocal feminist who had an unapologetic and a near individualistic disposition to life. I did not date Nigerian men and I had no plans of getting married or building a family. There were other important aspects to life, such as saving the environment and saving the world. But the more I thought about it, the more it made sense. I had no right to criticise what I had not made any attempt to improve.

Onyeka, you can no longer afford to be an armchair critic, I thought to myself. I quickly countered the argument by stating my conviction that Nigeria was not ready for uncompromising women who were stubborn and resolute in their feminist convictions.

'Who would employ me and allow me to speak my mind?' I asked.

The gentleman was quiet. He did not need to say anything more. He had made his point and I began thinking more seriously about my place in my country of birth.

That man who challenged me to go home was Alhaji Aminu Wali from Kano. He later became Nigeria's Ambassador to China from 2012 and 2015. He is a mentor to me.

'In case you consider returning, here,' he added, as he handed me two cards, one to keep and the other to give the Director-General of the Nigerian Television Authority (NTA).

I could not sleep that night. The gentleman was right. In a matter of weeks, I resigned from my job at the UN to the chagrin of friends and associates and in less than three months, I returned to Nigeria.

Onyeka at 19   Onyeka at Wellesley College in 1974

My sister Zoe - my hero

High school graduation- the Baldwin School 1972

When my mum arrived for my graduation at Wellesley 1976

Diana, me and other Tour Guides with Rod Stewart at a
Charity Concert for UNICEF in 1979.

As a UN Tour Guide

Diana Ayee and I at the UN

Onyeka 1984

On stage at MIT with the Wellesley Tupelos

Lunch with friends in the middle is Margareta Nielsen, the one with the embarrassing questions.

My mum and I - taken at the filming of the BBC NTA Documentary Nigeria A Squandering of Riches, in 1984

With Richard Taylor BBC producer recording the Links to Nigeria A Squandering of Riches In 1984

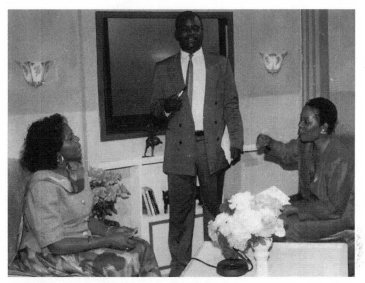

With Dr Awolowo-Dosumu on the set of NTA's Who Is On.

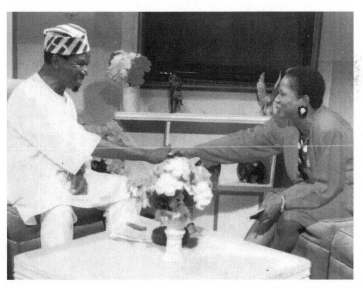

With the writer Cyprian Ekwensi on the set of NTA's Who Is On.

With Danladi Bako at NTA.

Zoe comfortable in her own skin

Zoe with her mentor Estelle

PART IV

Homecoming

Nigeria, here I come!

C oming home was like closing my eyes to all I had seen, covering my ears to all I had heard, holding my nose down and diving into the waters, unsure of whether or not the tides would be in my favour. It was a decision that had to be made, painful or not.

I had been back home in 1979, briefly, for the second time in eight years since my sojourn in the United States. That year, Alhaji Shehu Shagari of the National Party of Nigeria (NPN) had won the presidential elections. After a long military interregnum in which there had been a civil war, Nigerians had approached the polls with enthusiasm, despite the violence that accompanied the exercise in different parts of the country.

Once the country returned to democratic rule, however, the initial enthusiasm turned into apathy. It seemed as though it was back to 'business-as-usual'. Many felt that President Shagari's election had not been free and fair. Others thought that the NPN-led government focused only on projects with political implications. The establishment of federal universities in every state and the building of a new federal capital in Abuja, for example, were characterised in some quarters as 'white elephant' projects; they indebted the country and worsened the economic situation of the average citizen. These were the complaints I heard from people.

In a way, my trip home in 1979 had prepared me for the real

return in 1980. Therefore, I was not entirely shocked since I was aware that our standard of living was below what I was used to in America. Our best facilities, hotels and airports were poor imitations of what was obtainable in the western world. Our large retail supermarkets such as Kingsway and the UTC Stores may have seemed like big deals to those unexposed, but in comparison to the huge supermarket chains that dotted American cities, they were no more than roadside country shops. It was quite embarrassing that Nigeria, as an oil-producing country, was still at that dismal level of growth in 1980. In contrast, Singapore, a country with fewer natural resources, was moving faster on the road of development.

Despite our oil, we did not get our planning right from the onset. The government's penchant for borrowing, coupled with a crash in crude oil prices, increased the pace at which the economy nose-dived. Yet, many Nigerians kept their hopes alive and went to work with smiles on their faces. We had hope, but our eventual grief demonstrated that hope and oil were insufficient for national transformation. We had human capital as well, but it takes much more than that to turn a country around. Human capital, after all, cannot be efficiently deployed in countries bereft of visionary leadership.

The first thing I had to do on my return to Nigeria was to render the mandatory year of service in a scheme called the National Youth Service Corps (NYSC). It was established in 1973 by General Yakubu Gowon's administration to promote unity and national integration. Every graduate of a tertiary institution, college or university is mandated to work for one year in a State other than their own, not for a salary but for a stipend.

Without wasting time, I went straight to the Nigerian Television Authority (NTA) Headquarters in Lagos to see the Director-General,

Malam Adamu Augie. He interviewed me and sought the opinion of other directors, Dr Victoria Ezeokoli and Mr Shingle Wigwe. They all agreed to employ me and I began work as a reporter immediately.

The motivator of my return to Nigeria, Alhaji Aminu Wali, was the chairman of the United Bank for Africa. I visited his office to brief him on my successful engagement and thank him for his advice and guidance.

'Onyeka Onwenu, you have gone and done it,' I thought to myself, as I walked into his office and realised that he was a very important man.

I had been talking to him as if he were my mate; his simplicity and humility had been beguiling. I had no idea who he was at the time, but he must have given a good report of me, I concluded. Once, after a Command Performance for General Ibrahim Babangida, I introduced Alhaji Aminu as my mentor. The President called him aside as he was leaving and asked, 'So, you are the one who brought her home?'

I answered for him, saying, 'Yes, he was responsible for the deed.'

I moved in with my brother, Richard, who lived in a two-bedroom flat in Surulere. He worked as an accountant with Africa Re-Insurance Company owned by the African Union. I was grateful that I could live with him. The alternative was to live with my mother. Richard and Ijeoma, who had both lived with her briefly after their return from the United States a year earlier, had inundated me with stories of her strict rules even though they had become full-fledged adults. She imposed a 9 p.m curfew on them. Anyone who came back home a minute later found the gates of the house securely locked. They would have to scale the walls to get in. My brother's flat, I reckoned, was a much better option for me. We did not have much, my brother and I, not even a television set, just a few chairs.

Richard had a bed and I had a small mattress on the floor; that was how we lived for a while. I was working at NTA, so by 9 p.m, we would go across the street to a nearby restaurant, to buy and share a bottle of beer to justify our presence there while we watched my news reports.

We always had a Sunday brunch. Richard would invite his friends, the late Charles Egegbara and Charles Uwakaname. I would invite Chinwe Dike and Adaku Nzeribe to come over as well. The menu was usually crab meat salad, a bit of spaghetti and sauce, fried rice, chicken in coconut sauce, and fried plantain. There was wine and good conversation to be had as well.

After every brunch, the girls would jump into Adaku's white Mercedes Benz car and drive down to Bar Beach in Victoria Island. I usually sat in front with my feet up on the dashboard; a risky habit. We would wind down the windows and scream into the air; we needed to vent. We were trained abroad and then thrown back into a country where nothing seemed to work. The girls were collectively angry at a system that appeared to be standing on its head. I often soliloquised, 'What am I doing here? I know I should be here, but what am I doing here?'

I watched the wind carry my words away to places I did not know. Comparatively, things were good then, but we did not know it. I guess we do now.

My first Christmas after my return to Nigeria was interesting. My monthly stipend as a Youth Corper was N200. I had just begun my Service and had sent my first allowance to my grandmother. She had requested that we all came home for the holiday, but I could not because of my new job.

On Christmas Day, my brother and I were home, broke and alone. I had managed to prepare a small lunch, and while eating, a well-dressed woman, Alhaja Amusan, walked in. She was the landlady of our building which had four flats – two in front and two at the back. She did not know who we were. My brother had sub-let the flat from a colleague who was posted abroad, and he did not inform the landlady. She, therefore, wanted us to pack out of her house immediately. After much pleading, she relented and gave us days to raise another rent of ₦4,000, the equivalent of about $4,500.

My brother gave up, even before he tried to raise the money. I had to trust God to make a way. I had met someone who was very pleased with my work. He had expressed confidence in my abilities as a reporter, noting that I covered my stories on television without fear or favour. That impressed him even more. He was an elderly fan and when I told him that I needed help, he readily obliged, and without expectations of any kind. He is now late and I remain grateful to him. He asked for anonymity and I shall respect that. May God bless his soul.

I remember walking back home and giving the bundle of money to my incredulous brother, who heaved a sigh of relief. From then on, he began to see me as something of a problem solver, a person on whom he could rely in times of need. He would simply place his challenges on my shoulders and walk away, expecting that I would make them disappear.

It was clear from my first report on NTA that I had a distinct style. My reportage was hands-on. I worked with the editors to ensure that my stories came out just the way I wrote them. With John Chiahemen, Chris Anyanwu and Tony Ede on the Magazine programme *Newsweek*, I travelled across the country and West Africa, reporting on the activities of ECOWAS, the Economic Community of West African States.

I soon learned that not everyone was happy with my work ethics. There were times when stories I had dutifully put together were wiped, ostensibly by mistake. I considered the jealousy among colleagues some sort of professional hazard. On one occasion, I had to start my production all over again. We came out with a better version, however. A particular colleague resorted to ignoring me, refusing even to acknowledge my greetings. It was bizarre, but it made me more focused on my work.

My mother taught me to ignore seething jealousy and unprovoked ill-will, and consider them a sign that I am doing well. She made me understand that I did not need to compete with anyone but myself. Sister taught me to glorify God for other people's achievements, knowing that He has created enough room for all to thrive. Nonetheless, it was sometimes difficult to comprehend how even those who are richly endowed and brilliant in their own right could be bitter about other people's strides.

My NTA experience was the kind of introduction that I needed for work in Nigeria. It was not a question of hitting the ground running, it was a matter of 'running' in the air with speed, even before you hit the ground. Undoubtedly, there were challenges, but it was a good place to hone my skills and put all that I had learned in school into practice. It also felt patriotic, as I was contributing my quota towards the development of my country. I took to my work with a fresh outlook and vigour; just having fun with whatever I was engaged in. This was the period I got to know my country through adult eyes.

Soon, news of my work spread. Government officials and personalities knew that they had to be prepared before my interviews.

I was not alone in bringing this new wave of professionalism to the NTA. Everyone came with their A-game. We were a team of young journalists determined to improve television production in the country. There was camaraderie in the newsroom with people like Lola Alakija and Ronke Ayuba who always brought a supply of special dry meat from her mother-in-law in Kebbi State. Ruth Benemesia-Opia, John Momoh and his future wife Shola, Funmi Odugbekun and Siene Allwell Brown were the others.

It was a great learning experience for me. Some of us often congregated at Eddie Iroh's portacabin. He is a writer and television producer. There was always a great flow of conversation about events in the country while we consumed fish rolls and coffee from the Staff Canteen. Soon, the commendations began to come in, as well as criticism from those who did not like the hard questions. I was particularly excited to receive a letter from Dr Beko Ransome-Kuti, who was full of praises for my reports.

In December 1981, I had completed my one-year Youth Service assignment with the NTA. I had broken new grounds and made a small name for myself. However, I was not a permanent member of staff. I was offered a position that was below my qualifications and proven capabilities. The salary was not even enough to pay my rent. So, I turned it down.

NTA brought me back several times by designing programmes exclusively for me to anchor. Though they were good programmes, the studio facilities were below acceptable standards. They were badly designed, inadequately equipped and hardly maintained. The air-conditioners were faulty and out of commission most of the time. I am not sure that much has changed since then. I still cringe when I watch NTA; the production and technical output quality has hardly improved. Content is unimpressive.

I did not want to be subsumed by a mediocre system, especially one that failed to acknowledge its deficiencies and therefore saw no reason for improvement. I fought mediocrity everywhere I found it, and NTA gave me one more opportunity to do so. Many people were able to accommodate the minimum which I had rejected, such as the discomfort of sweating in the studios under the hot klieg lights without functional air- conditioners during production. It made me appear 'difficult', but I was only being a professional.

By the end of 1981, three things happened almost simultaneously. First, I got a job with the newly established Anambra Television (ATV) in Enugu. Second, I started work on a BBC/NTA co-production titled *Nigeria: A Squandering of Riches* and third, my music career took off.

I was invited by Chief Jim Nwobodo, the flamboyant Governor of the old Anambra State, to work with Anambra Television. He wanted the best hands at the station and I was impressed with their equipment and organisation. Furthermore, I liked the idea of being in Enugu for work during the week, and in Lagos during the weekend for my shows.

At ATV, I soon found out that I was not entirely free to conduct the kind of reporting I had become known for. I could not work without interference from my supervisors who took orders from Government House. Whoever was in power controlled everything and it was difficult to operate with my desired level of editorial fairness within such an environment. I was trained to report the news and not become a government mouthpiece.

Living in Enugu for one year though, I had ample opportunity to visit Arondizuogu and Aba, where my Aunt Mrs Juliana DanChima lived. The ATV job lasted for that period only before I got tired of shuttling between two cities and two demanding jobs.

Something which I had started at the tail end of my days at NTA and which remains an epochal piece of work for me, was about to come to fruition. I thanked the Governor of Anambra State for the opportunity to work at ATV and I left.

Nigeria: A Squandering of Riches

The day I was approached by a production team from the BBC and the NTA to write a theme song for a documentary film on Nigeria started just like any other day.

I was at home one evening when Richard Taylor of the BBC and Mr Adegboyega from NTA, came with their crew members to see me. Over coffee, we began a discussion about the problems in Nigeria. We talked about a N4bn rice import expenditure which could not be accounted for. It was a really big deal. Nigerians were also complaining about the amount of money being spent on the new Federal Capital Territory in Abuja, while many people lived in hunger and deprivation.

A few days later, the production team came back. The Third Eye Series was a BBC programme that looked at a country through a citizen's eyes. The producer wanted me to be that eye through which Nigeria would be seen. It was familiar terrain, this talking about my country, this desire to not only imagine but to see a better Nigeria.

I said, 'Yes.'

Whenever I got together with friends – Tyna Onwudiwe, Amma Ogan, Jide Adeniyi Jones, and a few others – our discussions were invariably centred around Nigeria's many problems, particularly corruption. It was excruciatingly painful to watch a country with so much promise degenerate into a failed State. The law enforcement agencies behaved as they pleased and there was growing lawlessness among the population. The Government seemed unperturbed. With crumbling facilities, underdeveloped infrastructure, a spiralling cost of living and galloping inflation, there was general discontent in the land.

I could have left the country again, but somehow, I decided to wait it out and do what I could to better the situation. Perhaps, the BBC crew saw the fire in my eyes, heard the passion in my voice and were convinced that they had found the perfect 'third eye'. All that I saw was a chaotic country, bleeding to death from corruption.

The political vampires had their fangs stuck in the country's wealth, feeding fat for themselves and generations unborn. The Nigerian Government, sensing the extent of this discontent, put out a public campaign called 'Andrew Don't Check Out' to encourage Nigerians who were leaving the country in large numbers, to remain and work things out for themselves.

In the end, apart from writing the theme song for the BBC/ NTA Documentary, *Nigeria: A Squandering of Riches*, I also wrote and presented the documentary myself.

The entire experience of working on this production was eye-opening. Even though working at NTA challenged me, this project stretched me and made me see how far I could go, and for how long. I spoke to industrialists, writers and artisans, street traders, bankers and farmers to capture the mood during a time of increasing displeasure with the economy and with government corruption. I learned something new each day as we visited oil-producing communities and saw first-hand people's experience in the Niger Delta.

The 1979 constitutional amendment had given the Federal Government full ownership of all Nigerian territory; it could now seize and distribute land to oil companies as it wanted. All that was given to the owners of the land in the Niger Delta were largely promises that were always in the 'pipeline'. These promises were hardly redeemed. We saw ecological devastation and heard stories of fishermen returning home with empty nets because the sea banks and rivers had become polluted by oil spills. We heard the sadness in the voices of the farmers whose farmlands were burnt to cinders or polluted by acid rain. We listened to the agitators who wanted more for the Niger Delta; they were growing stronger and louder, articulating their dissatisfaction with the state of affairs in the oil-producing region.

It was not the politically correct thing to do, but I felt that if Nigeria did not confront the myriad issues in the Niger Delta, it might be too late to stop the restiveness in the area. As we travelled all around the country, meeting and interviewing people across ethnic, language and religious differences, one thing shone through: the resilience of Nigerians even amidst negativity.

I remember one of the toughest interviews that I conducted. It was with the renowned author of *Things Fall Apart*, Chinua Achebe. I later heard that he had wondered how I could combine being a journalist with being a singer. I guess he found the combination somewhat incongruous.

'Ok, let me speak with the singing journalist,' he had said when the interview began.

I saw the scepticism in his eyes and heard it in his voice. However, a few minutes later, things changed. I had his full attention. It became clear to him that even though I was a singer, I could also engage in the nuances and intricacies of politics and social criticism. I was gratified to hear him say that it was the best interview he had had upon till then. That was in 1983.

In 2005, I was invited by the Chinua Achebe Foundation to

conduct interviews with two iconic personalities – Margaret Ekpo, the veteran politician and Gani Fawehinmi, a legal luminary and human rights activist. It was the last interview Margaret Ekpo granted before passing away in 2007.

Chinua Achebe remains a blessing to Ndigbo, to Nigeria, to Africa and the world, even in death.

In August 1983, when President Shehu Shagari was re-elected, there was displeasure from different parts of the country. Many people considered the election to be flawed. On 31 December 1983, a military coup took place. Nigerians were not surprised. It was a palace coup which ushered in the regime of Major General Muhammadu Buhari and Brigadier Tunde Idiagbon.

I was in Liberia for a show with Nigerian artiste Tyna Onwudiwe when we heard of the coup. I rushed to London to complete the editing of the film so that it could remain topical. *Nigeria: A Squandering of Riches* was aired to much acclaim in Europe. It received several commendations and awards. The British press was particularly impressed. It was appreciated that Nigerians had identified their problems and looked forward to having them solved and repositioning the country on the path of greatness.

However, the reception was different at home. Whilst most Nigerians welcomed the film; we received criticism from those who felt that we had portrayed a northern Nigerian-led government in bad light, and highlighted the personage of a businessman from the same part of the country who had benefited from political patronage.

On my way back to Lagos from London, a well-known businessman from Kwara State threatened me on the airplane, declaring that it was 'over his dead body that the film would be shown in Nigeria.' The documentary was aired in Nigeria, not once but twice, at the insistence of Brigadier Idiagbon, the second-highest-ranking member of the Supreme Military Council of the Nigerian government.

Though we considered that the people who featured in the film did so as Nigerians, with the benefit of hindsight, we should have paid more attention to the ethnic spread of our interviewees. There were more people lined up for interviews such as a First Republic Minister, Alhaji Maitama Sule. However, the coup took place before the set date. There had been no intention whatsoever to produce a sectional film.

At the writing of this book, It had been 35 years since *Nigeria: A Squandering of Riches* was released. It is a shame that the issues we highlighted there are still with us today. They have, in most cases, exacerbated. Nigeria continues to squander her riches and sacrifice the future of her children. The political class is unable to see beyond its selfish and primordial interests. Things have worsened progressively since 1984.

The waves of our young people still exiting the country in search of greener pastures abroad, reminds me of the famous 'Andrew No Check Out' advert. Andrew is really checking out now and with him droves of professionals, talented artistes, creative people, tech inventors and many others who would go on to enrich and further develop their host countries. As Nigeria loses some of its best talents to this unforced migration, the country stands the risk of degenerating even further.

A good many of our young people, trained and untrained, are dying while checking out to Europe. The Sahara Desert has consumed thousands, even as many more have perished in the Mediterranean Sea while searching for a better life in Europe.

Seeing this documentary again, 35 years after its production, I shudder at its candidness. It struck at the heart of the corruption that had bedevilled the country. With heartfelt and constructive criticism, incisive analysis of the economic and social changes taking place in the country, all who spoke in the film, did so with grave concern, passion and yet hope for a better Nigeria.

A respected older colleague, the actress Ms Ajayi Lycett, once described me as 'a fiercely focused woman.' Watching *Nigeria: A Squandering of Riches* again, I am inclined to agree with her. I had a passionate focus in telling a gripping story with frightening dedication. There was a touch of sadness to the film as well, one which was intensified by the fact that the documentary is perhaps more relevant today than it ever was.

Nigeria has squandered the riches she had, and the ones she did not have.

PART V

Music and Me

My First Note

nyone who knew me while growing up would not be surprised at my chosen career. There was never any doubt in my mind that I would sing and combine it with any other endeavour for which I had the talent and aptitude. My mother taught me early in life that talent comes with great responsibility; it is for the upliftment of others, as well as self. I learned my craft at the age of five. I was the little girl who sang for charity in Port Harcourt, the one whose mother encouraged to shine. Hope Onwenu, who was herself a singer/songwriter, often reminded me not to forget my music. She inherited her love for it from her father, himself a wonderful singer.

My father had an appreciation for music and the ability to efficiently multitask. Papa was reputed to engage in separate conversations with a number of people simultaneously. On his return from his studies in the UK, he brought back a giant organ that he donated to St Peter's Church Ndi Awa, Arondizuogu, the same church he got married to my mum. However, Sister was the real musician. She taught me songs and stagecraft. She took me along with her to perform at fundraising events. I was too small to be seen by the audience. Consequently, I always stood on a table next to her for visibility while we performed.

Sister had swagger, a certain stage presence. Her acting skills were unparalleled; her comedic timing impeccable; the same could be said of her storytelling abilities. She was a remarkably beautiful woman, a stunning and elegant dresser, unmissable in any crowd. Even in her old age, Sister was riveting on stage. When she was 88 years old, we were both invited by the Ministry of Information to perform at their Mothers Summit held in Abuja in 2007. As soon as she opened her mouth to sing and her clear and strong voice was heard, she got a standing ovation. I became a non-issue. Some of the audience beckoned on me to move to the side so that they could better see the real star. I was very proud of her.

Throughout the early and middle years of my musical career, it was to my mother that I would first play my songs. I valued her criticisms and suggestions, even on my costumes. I got her permission to record some of her songs such as 'Sodom na Gomorrah', 'Olu Ifunanya' (Loves work) and 'Ochie Dike' – a song my mother rapped and which remains a hit decades later. Sister and I were colleagues.

Music has always been a part of my life, but how did I make my entry into professional practice? It started in America, with a phone call. I was holidaying in Chicago with my cousin Godfrey DanChimah who was married to Sonny Okosuns' sister-in-law, Ada. One day, Sonny called their house and I picked up the phone. We got talking and I told him that I was interested in professional music. He asked me for a demo tape which I sent to him; it was my cover of 'Mack the Knife' by Bobby Darin. He liked it, but warned that jazz might not sell well in Nigeria.

Towards the end of my stay at the United Nations, another Nigerian artiste came calling. Dora Ifudu's song 'Ada' was making waves around the country. I wanted to find out from her what it was like being a female musician in Nigeria. Dora gave me a history of her struggles in the industry; she talked about the press's criticisms and unwarranted attacks and the difficulty of controlling one's productions and demanding higher value for work. I was not discouraged. With my media skills, I had something else to fall back on, if music failed. I just wanted to follow my passion.

Once in Nigeria, I contacted Sonny Okosuns, and we began planning my debut album. I was fresh in the business and had no clue about contracts or how the Nigerian music industry worked. Sonny took all the decisions for me. He selected the songs, old songs of his. However, I brought my own interpretation and twist to them. Even before a contract with his recording company, EMI Nigeria, was presented to me, we had begun recording the album with his band at the EMI studios in Lagos. There was excitement in the air about a new singer, which was me.

In those days, making an album was done with the whole band playing the song and everything recorded simultaneously. If there was a mistake, we started all over again, this continued until we got it right. Repeated takes tended to irritate and frustrate. Sometimes a recording session that lasted all night failed to capture the good tune we all longed for. At other times, serious quarrels broke out over who played the wrong notes, possibly ending the session. This was the analogue system.

Once Sonny Okosuns, the producer, felt satisfied with the basic work we had done in Lagos, off we went to London for post-production at Abbey Road Studios of EMI International, made famous by the Beatles.

In London, we drove straight to the hotel where we would be staying. I waited to be checked into my room by Charles Okosuns, my designated manager and Sonny Okosuns' brother, but he led me into Sonny's room, where my bags had been placed. I immediately asked for my own room, or there would be no recording.

Being a novice, I was not privy to the financial arrangements that Sonny Okosuns had made on my behalf with EMI. I did not have a lawyer or anyone to advise me. On the trip to London, I brought along some money for myself, which I relied on when Sonny Okosuns decided to punish me for turning him down. I paid for all my expenses on the trip. I even bought costumes for the video shoot with my own money. I decided not to complain but to get the job done.

When we completed the recording, with an overlay of the lead and backing vocals, and live guitar work, we mixed and mastered the sound. We also shot the videos of all six songs on the album. With a group of dancers and a small studio audience, no rehearsals, just passion for making music, we delivered a good performance. Everyone was happy, Sonny Okosuns included. He had maintained a hostile attitude towards me and only communicated through his brother, my 'manager'. I could not wait for the recording to come to an end.

Word quickly travelled back to Nigeria about 'the difficulties of working with Onyeka Onwenu'. A lie was told, of how I was caught in the arms of the studio engineer at Abbey Road. It was so ridiculous that I did not even bother to address it. I was comforted when Sonny's first wife, Nkechi, on seeing me for the first time, simply hugged and thanked me for what was unspoken. We both knew why I was in Sonny's bad books, even without saying a word. I decided to put that incident behind me and continued to work with Sonny Okosuns on many other occasions. He was a colleague for whom I had great respect for his contributions to the Nigerian music industry.

In 1981, I released my very first album *Endless Life*. Although it was a remake of Sonny Okosuns previously released works like 'Help' and 'Kenelum Jehova', I brought my own interpretation to the songs. I added a cover of 'Walk Right Back' by the Everly Brothers and Nigerians were introduced to the 'singing reporter' as Chinua Achebe had called me. The album release came right at the tail-end of my Youth Service. Having made a small name as a TV journalist, it was not surprising that my musical career took off aided by my popularity on television.

I started getting invitations to live performances which I excelled in. That was how I began to earn a living from music.

At the initial stage of my career, I was dissatisfied with the technical quality of our recordings. I would note, listening to the radio, that the quality dropped each time Nigerian produced music came up. It bothered me. It meant that we could not compete internationally. Thus, it became imperative for me to improve the quality of my musical output.

When I joined the industry, it was vibrant and the economy was strong. There were some capable and talented women in the field such as Dora Ifudu, a singer/songwriter, filmmaker and photographer; Martha Ulaeto, who mixed the operatic with a powerful African influence; Funmi Adams, a classical singer who blended her songs with contemporary folk music; Nelly Uchendu and her Igbo folklore, as well as Comfort Omorege, a traditional artiste from mid-western Nigeria. There was also Oby Onyeoha who brought her own flavour to African pop.

Let me give special honour to Christy Essien-Igbokwe. She started in the industry as a young girl, and rose to the top through dint of hard work and talent, both as a musician and as an actress.

She was supported by her husband, Chief Edwin Igbokwe, and Chief Olu Aboderin, the publisher of Punch Newspapers, a great patron of the arts in Nigeria. Chief Christy Essien-Igbokwe passed away in 2011.

For daring to be who they were, these women took on a lot of abuse and name-calling from the Nigerian press. I was called a prostitute and linked with as many as four men at a time. My mother, who would normally advise me to ignore bad press and focus on the job at hand, was so offended by some of the deliberate lies that she threatened to sue if I did not. I did sue and won my cases even though most of the defendants, never paid up. Years later, I realised that a lot of people might have believed the scandalous stories written about artistes like me. It may take some time, but if one remains absolutely focused, the truth will always show, I have also found out. In the meantime, one should enjoy the process by simply being oneself.

Most of the female artistes were well-educated and imbued with a sense of purpose about their music. I guess we were too uppity for the chauvinistic Nigerian press.

In choosing a musical career, I did not quite have the support of some members of my extended family. Thankfully, my mum and siblings were solidly behind me. Chief Emeka Anyaoku, the former Commonwealth Secretary-General, who is a distant cousin of my mother's, was incensed that she allowed me, the daughter of DK Onwenu, to sing and dance on stage. My mother just smiled and did not attempt to defend herself. However, when my career took off and I met him at an international event, where so many dignitaries and Heads of States were eager to meet me, he publicly confessed his underestimation of my work and apologised. It was most satisfying to hear him take back his words and come around on his earlier judgment.

Beyond the first album, I had other engagements with Sonny Okosuns. He was a humorous person. He had you in stitches all the time as he came up with different sayings; some made sense, others were outlandish. Sonny claimed that Genesis, the title of the first book of the Bible, is an Igbo word *Jee n'isi isi* and which in translation is 'go to the beginning'. Indeed, Genesis is a book of beginnings.

He was also fiery about issues concerning the liberation of Southern Africa. He sang about it, wore it on his sleeves and lived it. His passion for the freedom of South Africa was so ingrained in his life and art that we wondered and asked: 'What would Sonny sing about after the liberation of the country?' He surprised everyone and went gospel, making that genre more popular than ever before in Nigeria. Other musicians followed suit and Sonny became a pastor in his own church.

Sonny Okosuns did not possess a fantastic voice. Sometimes I felt that the delivery of his lines were off their timing and his lyrics, a bit clumsy. These judgments are of course, exclusively mine. He commanded incredible appeal and reached his fans where they lived - in their hearts. He was sincere and prophetic in the things he chose to sing about. With songs like 'Which Way Nigeria?' he captured the essence of our confusion as a nation. In 'Mother and Child', produced in 1981 by one of Nigeria's best, the late Jake Solo, Sonny Okosuns gave us a melodious tribute to motherhood. I was in the studio in London for my recording as well and watched Jake Solo do his thing. His guitar work on that album was enthralling.

There are two other stories about Sonny Okosuns that I would like to share. In 1992, I received an invitation to perform alongside other international artistes to celebrate Namibia's Independence. Namibia, formerly South West Africa, was a territory held onto by South Africa, initially administered on behalf of the League of

Nations but which it refused to hand over to the United Nations at the end of World War II in 1945.

I was to represent Nigeria, but I had no means of getting there. There was no financial compensation, so I had to fund the journey myself. Still, it was an honour to be invited. I thought that it was unfair though that Sonny Okosuns had not been invited. He had devoted a large part of his career singing against apartheid and the white South African Government behind it. I made a case for him and to the Nigerian Government to defray the cost of our trip to and from Namibia. Our prayers were answered. An airplane conveyed us and the Nigerian Ambassador to the United Nations, Ibrahim Gambari, to Namibia.

We took off from the VIP section of the local airport reserved for special passengers. The whole place bubbled with the presence of reporters, musicians and hangers-on. As soon as we moved to board the airplane, a group of journalists from various media houses approached Sonny and I for an interview. Sonny Okosuns quickly put out his hand to block me from coming forward. He was then surrounded by his band members who formed a chorus line to his left and his right as he conducted the interview by himself. He claimed to have been invited to Windhoek, and that the Nigerian Government provided him with an aircraft. I quickly walked past with my group and we boarded the plane.

Artistes have big egos and, whenever we assembled, there was always a tug of war to establish supremacy and seniority in the business. I learned never to be involved in any turf wars. I did not have to prove myself other than through my work.

In 1998, a Zimbabwean promoter Steve Chigorimbo contracted Sonny Okosuns, Christy Essien-Igbokwe and I for a musical tour of Southern Africa. We left Lagos on a chartered flight with our band members and journalists. Our first stop was Lusaka, Zambia, an independent neighbour of Zimbabwe. Zambia was in the middle of an economic recession and the naira was powerful. Though independent, the Zambians were a bit withdrawn. They were shocked that we were able to afford meals in a five-star hotel. As we entered the restaurant, the white clients there left one after the other. Soon we had the whole place to ourselves and we had a ball. We sang and danced and thoroughly enjoyed ourselves and our meal.

The staff was happy to see fellow Africans intimidate the whites with their presence, but our celebration soon turned sour. This was when we realised that the show promoter had not made solid arrangements for the tour. His investors had left him and we were stranded, all forty of us. We could no longer eat in the hotel and within days, we had to make our way by road to Zimbabwe for a performance at Harare Sheraton Hotel. The promoter hoped to recoup some money there to sustain the tour.

We got to the Zambia-Zimbabwe border too late to make the crossing. We had to check into a nearby game reserve with only two rooms available. With the threat of wild animals, Christy Essien-Igbokwe and I, and all the female members of our bands, slept in one room. All the men slept in the other. Some brave ones decided to keep watch outside the women's room. In the morning, we took turns cleaning up in the tiny restroom. Despite the uncomfortable conditions, we were in very high spirits, and the discomfort and sense of danger helped everyone bond like never before.

In Zimbabwe, we checked into the Sheraton, and the first thing we all did was to take a shower. But there were still challenges to contend with on this troubled tour. Zimbabwe was newly independent but not quite; the whites were still in control, even the police was firmly controlled by them. For some reason, the police would not let the large crowd outside the hotel enter the concert hall. After waiting patiently for three hours, the crowd began to disperse. Only after they were half gone did the authorities allow the concert to commence. We sang in a hall partly filled. In the crowd was the crème de la crème of the newly independent country and the Nigerian business community, looking to break into the new market. The audience was most appreciative of our performances and we were satisfied, but Steve Chigorimbo did not recoup his money.

From that day until we were rescued from Zimbabwe one week later, most of us were anxious about what would happen to us. The promoter could not pay and had been completely unavailable. We had all run out of money, and there was great frustration and discontent. Sonny Okosuns used his spontaneous humour to keep us all entertained. One evening, it came to our attention that one of his dancers had the wisdom and foresight of packing some *ogbono*, dry fish, crayfish and *garri* from Nigeria.

We stormed the hotel kitchen, got some sympathetic workers to provide us with ketchup and cooking oil to substitute red oil, and made us some fine *ogbono* soup. We all ate from the big pot.

On the fourth day of our stay in Harare, word of our situation reached Nigeria and the newspapers were awash with stories. The Nigerian Government soon sent an airplane to fly us back home much to our relief and appreciation. Such were the joys and pains that came with stardom. Yet this was the life we had chosen.

The Birth of Ayollo, The Beautiful Bird

The release of my first album in 1981 is not an experience I can easily forget. Looking back, I picked up a few lessons that would become useful in my entire career. First, I must read all contract pages from top to bottom before signing. Second, saying 'No' may be difficult sometimes, but 'No' should never be a word I would be afraid to use. I had to say it as often as occasion demanded. I must never remain in an uncomfortable or compromising place. If I found myself in such a position, my only option would be to quickly take my exit. As a woman, I had to be aware that some people may see me as fair game. If I respected myself, however, I could demand it from others.

My second album was called *For the Love of You*. Unlike my first, I wrote all the songs. I had gained enough confidence in the strength of my voice and my words (lyrics). The album, which was also under the EMI Nigeria record label, was produced by Berkley Jones, a seasoned guitarist who had been part of the internationally known band, BLO (Berkley, Laolu, Odumosu). When Odumosu left, he was replaced by Lemmy Jackson.

I began to scrutinise the contract I signed with EMI. It gave them the copyrights to my works and left open the important matter of how many albums I was to produce in a year. I knew something was wrong with the agreement that I had signed. EMI never furnished me with details of the cost of recording and never shared with me the records of sales either. If I needed money, I had to beg the MD for an advance, which was taken back from an invoice I never saw. I left immediately after the contract ended.

It was by no means a smooth dissolution. EMI would not go down without a fight; they took me to court. They shamelessly tendered a doctored contract. The original did not state the number of albums I would produce in a year. It had been left blank, but they filled it out to indicate two albums a year. I remember clearly while in court with my lawyer, Funke Adekoya (SAN), the MD of EMI Nigeria came to shake hands with me. I told him, looking him straight in the face, that EMI had lied. He looked thoroughly embarrassed. Although the record company won the case, they never made any claims and the matter died.

The end of my relationship with EMI Nigeria became my opportunity to launch out on my own. The music business was no longer booming in the country. For reasons attributable to the economic downturn in the country, many record labels folded up. CBS Music and Sony Music changed hands, Polygram (a Dutch company) was bought over by Premier Music, a Nigerian entity and EMI became Ivory Music. There was much uncertainty in the air, and I did not want to sign up with another recording label. I created my own called AYOLLO Productions under which my third album was released. Ayollo was the name my maternal grandmother gave me as a child when she would cajole me to dance for her. It means a beautiful bird. I now wholly owned the copyright to my music. It also meant that I had more control over aspects of the production.

In 1984, my third album, *In the Morning Light*, was started in Lagos and completed in London at the DNA Studios, belonging to the Eurythmics, Dave Stewart and Annie Lennox. Their hit song 'Sweet

Dreams Are Made of These' was one of my favourite songs of the 80s. The Fairlight System was one of the first digital programmers that allowed for the laying down of individual tracks, as well as the overdubs of live instruments. It was new and I was the first to experiment with it in the Nigerian market. I was very happy with the results. 'In the Morning Light' was the theme song of the BBC/NTA documentary, *Nigeria, A Squandering of Riches, and my album title*. In the middle of mixing one of the songs, 'Ekwe', Dave Stewart walked in, heard it and loved it. He offered to write an endorsement on the back of the album sleeve. 'Hi Onyeka Fans, listen to 'Ekwe' at least twice a day,' he wrote.

It was an unsolicited but a most appreciated gesture which let me know that I was on the right path.

The album contained hits such as 'Alleluya', 'Bia Nulu', 'I'm the One', 'Ekwe' and 'Trina 4'. The last two songs were released in the UK the following year as the A and B sides of a single by Sterns Records. 'Trina 4' was the Tartan (Scottish) infused reggae song that stood all on its own. The unique sound, produced by Kenny St George of OZO, a UK band of the 1970s, appealed to the British press.

I described my music as African pop, a contemporary blend of the old and the new. It had influences of highlife, jazz, pop and even juju. I took the album title *In The Morning Light* from my view of Lagos on arriving from a foreign trip at night. The dazzling, mesmerizing night light welcomed me, but the morning gave me a different view. This was my first effort on Ayollo Productions Label and it was completely self-funded. I relished the freedom to make both the creative and technical decisions that came with the title of Executive Producer.

Soundtracks to Our Lives

Dem say, dem say o, Na him I dey hear o,
Wetin you want make I do? Oo biko nwanne m
A no deny o
I love you proper Let dem say

Dis world we dey o Na so so wahala
Life na wah o, we know
Ololufemi o, we dey kampe
Make we do we own
And leave the rest

...*Madawonlohun*, let them say o
Jeje life Na him we want
I no go lie
I love you well, well
Make we try and make life better

Onyeka Onwenu (1987)

'Madawonlohun' (Let them say) was the first duet by two Nigerian artistes, King Sunny Ade (KSA), a veteran of the industry and myself. He was a senior colleague and an international artiste who had used the Nigerian language to tell the cultural story of our country. I was excited and honoured to work with him. 'Madawonlohum' was a love song about a couple who ignored all that was being said about them and their relationship. It was an instant hit.

Coming at the time it did, it showed that Nigerian artistes, no matter their backgrounds, could make beautiful music together. The society was just beginning to accept female artistes like me and given that it was a love song; it led many to believe that King Sunny Ade and I were involved in a love affair. But 'Madawonlohun' was just a collaboration across differences.

In 1989, KSA came calling again. This time, he requested that I write two duets. This was a John Hopkins University and United States Agency for International Development (USAID) project to increase awareness of family planning issues. We were to use music as an advocacy tool to promote family planning and responsible sexual behaviour for the unmarried.

On the back of this project, we recorded two songs, 'Choices' and 'Wait for Me'. Just as the songs gained more appeal, there was a second onslaught of wild rumours of Sunny Ade and I in a relationship that had allegedly led to a secret love child, a daughter. The rumours were so pervasive that even the Head of State General Ibrahim Babangida asked me about their veracity, though jokingly.

'Ah, not you too, sir!' I responded as everyone broke into laughter.

I took it all in my stride at first. As an artiste, I learnt to live by the reality of all publicity being good publicity. It seemed to me that putting out an official denial would further fuel the rumours.

However, I became angry when the gossip got to my four-year-old son.

The driver to one of his school friends had told my son that King Sunny Ade was his father. This was very upsetting to Abraham.

When he came home that day from school with this disturbing story, I went straight to the mother of his friend, the employer of the said driver, hoping that she would reprimand him. 'Yes! I heard it too and I told my driver that even if it were true, he should not repeat it to anyone,' she replied, to my utter shock.

'Even if it were true? You were discussing me with your driver?'

I immediately severed my relationship with the woman and all that came with her, to prevent any further damage to my son's sense of wellbeing.

I put out a statement, through my publicist, debunking the rumours. I equally addressed the issue during interviews on radio and television. It seemed to quell the rumours for some time. However, I began to receive threatening phone calls from some of KSA's female fans. On the day of the public launch of the songs at Sheraton Hotel, Ikeja, many had gathered to witness the 'official wedding' of King Sunny Ade and Onyeka Onwenu as rumoured. I daresay they were disappointed. The launch brought me much relief.

My involvement with the family planning project went beyond writing the songs and coordinating the initial production in Nigeria with the producer, Lemmy Jackson. I also toured Nigeria's six geographical zones speaking to young people in schools about the deferment of sexual activity until an appropriate age. I visited media establishments, traditional rulers, Governors and First Ladies, speaking on the importance of smaller and well-spaced families. All this, I did pro bono.

Nigeria's population continues to rise along with our level of poverty. These songs are as relevant today as they were in 1989.

Singing by Commission

My debut album was my first professional outing in music, and it would open doors for me in acting, fashion design, social activism and politics. It would also slam doors shut in my face as I dealt with negative stereotypes, long-running media battles and calumnious lies against my person. Still, music took me to enviable heights, to places where I would meet dignitaries, presidents, key world players and people on the street. Naturally, the fame garnered elevated my standing in society and allowed me to be in a network of unique and influential people. I knew that it was a gift, yet like all gifts, it came with a burden and had to be used responsibly.

In effect, I was conscious of how to use the platform that music had given me to navigate my art and my vision of social justice. I was committed to this from the very beginning. I was determined to use the gift of my voice to cheer and to uplift people, and to make my space a little better than I found it.

Throughout my career, I have found myself undertaking the writing and production of songs and music videos on topical issues aimed at uniting the country along with shared values of peace, love, and togetherness to solve national problems.

My first 'political commission', to use the phrase loosely, came from Dr (Mrs) Maryam Babangida, the First Lady at the time. She sent Justice Vicki Okobi (née LN Obioha) to me, requesting that I write a song for the Women's Day Celebration 1992, with the theme of 'Peace'. My song was titled the 'Peace Song'. Ms Regina Anajemba, a classical singer who worked with the Federal Radio Corporation of Nigeria (FRCN), had earlier submitted a song for the same purpose. It was not accepted. However, one line from it was so liked by the First Lady that she insisted that I include it in my song. It was: 'Let there be peace in our hearts, peace in our homes, peace in the nation and the world.'

It was inspiring lyrics, and I had no problem using it as requested. I needed to obtain Regina's permission to use her lyrics, and I got it. I paid her an honorarium of N3,000. I was not paid for the project. I funded it myself and funded the song's live performance at the Women's Rally in commemoration of the Women's Day Celebration that year. I later received a letter of commendation from Justice Okobi on behalf of the First Lady, thanking me for my effort.

Apart from a brief exchange of greetings at a reception in honour of the Prince and Princess of Wales held on the ship Britannia in Lagos that year, I never had a one-on-one encounter with Mrs Babangida.

At the inauguration of the African First Ladies Peace Mission in 1998, Mrs Maryam Abacha commissioned a compilation of songs for the occasion by Sonny Okosuns, Christy Essien- Igbokwe, Zaaki Azzay, Segun Adewale and me. We delivered the *Arise Afrika – Music For Peace* album. It had individual songs by the participating artistes and then the title song, 'Arise Afrika', which was jointly written and performed by all.

In the process of this production, Sonny Okosuns strangely complained to Mrs Abacha that our colleague, Christy Essien-Igbokwe, had managed to intimidate the rest of us on the project by constantly dropping her name. I cringed on his behalf because even though I knew he was right, I also knew that Christy's relationship with the First Lady had been on for a long time and they were quite close. I could have told him that his complaints would have no effect, and I would have been right. The First Lady simply laughed, thanked us and pleaded that we remain committed to the Peace project. When Christy Essien passed away in 2011, Mrs Abacha was fully represented at her funeral. Her friendship with Christy endured to the end.

As a performing artiste, I worked where I was engaged. Most of my performances were non-political at private functions, public events, fundraisers, as well as religious and social outings. Every now and then, one of those events would turn out to be a political engagement. It was always my decision to take part or not.

I want to tell the story of the One-Million-Man March and how I got involved in it. It had to do with Christy Essien-Igbokwe.

The meeting was held at my office on Isaac John Street, GRA, Ikeja. Mrs Igbokwe as PMAN President, spoke about the need to support our national soccer squad in the France '98 World Cup competition. A fundraising event was taking place in Abuja and I had been invited to perform with my band, alongside other artistes. It made sense that I did not charge my normal fee, as this was a national call and a fundraising event. So, I agreed to N900,000, which is about $5,000. It covered my band's transportation to Abuja for three days – feeding, insurance, costumes, rehearsals, allowances and fees for the band members.

We obliged out of the conviction that whatever talent we had was meant not just for one's enjoyment but also for the common good. By agreeing to what appeared to be a noble national call, I had no idea that I had been hoodwinked and that the negative consequences of heeding that call would last for many years. I had no idea that I would be termed a traitor of the 'June 12' cause, even by people who knew the truth and the sincerity of my intentions. 'June 12' refers to the nullified presidential election of 1993, which pitted supporters of Chief MKO Abiola, the presumed winner against the military regime.

Just a week before the concert, I opened the daily newspapers to find my name at the top of the list of artistes who would perform at an event called the 'One Million Man March' in Abuja. Ostensibly, the event was to support the military Head of State who was said to be intent on transmuting into an elected president. The assorted political parties who were angling for him would then work for his victory at the polls.

To say that I was enraged by this discovery would be an understatement. One of the problems artistes in Nigeria faced was the use of their names to promote events, even when they had neither been informed nor their approval obtained. I knew nothing about this event. I was only made aware of a fundraising event for the Nigerian national football team, the Super Eagles.

When it was brought to my attention that the show being advertised may well be the same as the one I had agreed to participate in, I fired off a letter to Mrs Igbokwe. I asked for clarification and threatened not to show up for the performance. This must-have put Mrs Igbokwe in a dilemma. She quickly reported the matter to the events committee at the Presidency. I soon received a call from the President's Chief Security Officer, Major Hamza Al-Mustapha. He calmly and respectfully reassured me that indeed, the event would be raising funds for the Super Eagles and that no one expected me to even mention the name 'Abacha', let alone declare my support for him. He also informed me that the President himself directed the Event's Committee to reach out to me for the performances of 'One Love' and 'Peace Song' at the occasion.

'The President sees you as someone who has demonstrated great love for this country,' Al-Mustafa added.

Based on these reassurances, I decided to go ahead and perform at the event.

I took the stage while the Super Eagles were on it and I left as soon as they did, having performed four songs, 'One Love', 'Peace Song', 'Alleluya' and 'Dancing in the Sun'. I did not acknowledge Abacha in whatever capacity; I made no comments other than to wish the Super Eagles the best of luck at France '98.

Almost immediately, a torrent of phone calls began to pour in, complete with all manner of accusations and threats. The press keyed in, lambasting me as well. I was sure that my life was in danger. Some obscure student groups threatened to storm my office and set it on fire. Others said that they would give me the beating of my life, should they get a hold of me. I quickly found out that some of these groups were being egged on by journalists, who made it their duty to 'expose' me for reasons best known to them. They spread the rumour that I had collected millions of naira from Abacha's government to support him and sing in his favour.

Some friends called me and advised that I leave town until things cooled down. Daily, articles were published in various newspapers, denigrating artistes who participated in the programme. Those who claimed that they would commit suicide if Abacha did not win the election, such as Felix Liberty, and artistes like me who simply rendered their performance according to the brief received, were all yoked together and marked for relentless bashing.

Knowing how I found myself in the programme, I was sure that I had done nothing wrong. I decided that I was not going to flee. All that was coming – the harassment, the physical assault and property loss – I had to face head-on.

I also understood why emotions were running high on the issue of Abacha transmuting into a civilian president. As a country, we had had it rough with him as a military ruler. I could appreciate the anger directed at those of us who inadvertently lent support to his regime by being at the event. It is also worth mentioning that most of the bashing I received came from the section of the country that felt particularly aggrieved that Abacha was sitting on the electoral victory of one of their own, Chief Abiola.

I decided to call a press conference to explain my side of the story and offer a heartfelt apology to anyone who felt offended by my appearance at the event. The press conference was successful. I took the journalists and students down memory lane. I reminded them of my involvement in the June 12 Movement. I was on MKO's side. I published articles in Tempo Magazine condemning the annulment of the election when most people were too scared to speak out. My articles had been so hard-hitting and critical that my mother, again, tried to stop me. She got down on her knees to plead that I stop. But I continued to write.

At the end of the briefing, the students apologised for their threats and asked me to pray for them. I did. The journalists thanked me for my openness and promised to relay my side of the story to the public. They never did. My persecution continued unabated.

This experience showed me how the truth is sometimes like an annoying fly, swatted for not advancing the agenda of the storyteller. It also seemed to validate what I thought of many Lagos-based journalists, that they perceived me as arrogant and too outspoken. My self-confidence was often mistaken for pride, and my strong views and sense of independence made me too assertive in some journalists and editors' eyes.

After a couple of decades, the furore died down and my traducers gave up. Throughout this period, those who sold-out on June 12 and betrayed Chief Abiola were hardly castigated. It was Onyeka Onwenu that needed to be taught a lesson. By now, everyone has settled on the fact that the antagonism was a waste of time. It did not stop me; rather, it made me more determined to achieve my goals. The best revenge, I always say, is success.

The year 1999 brought an end to decades of military interregnums in Nigeria. After the elections, the inauguration committee for President Obasanjo invited me to write a song to celebrate the beginning of a new democratic era. Nigeria had just come out of a period of uncertainty and President Olusegun Obasanjo, who was imprisoned by the Abacha regime had just won the presidential election. It was a prison-to-palace story and the song I wrote was 'One Nation'.

One Nation

There was a time we thought we could not go on
When our problems seemed set to tear us apart
There was darkness all around and hope was gone
But we called out your name, You saved the day…

Now here we are, a new beginning
At the threshold of freedom, the world at our feet
This is one more chance to make it all better
As we call on you to show us the way
We'll be singing

You are the One, Almighty God
Our only inspiration

A sure foundation on which we stand
You shine the light our only restoration
A sure foundation on which we stand.

Our difference is our strength,
In our diversity lies our unity
There may be many tongues, but one voice
One Nation under God.

Onyeka Onwenu (1999)

This song captured a new dawn in a country pregnant with hope. It was performed at the inauguration gala, in the presence of presidents, heads of state, royalty, heads of corporations and special guests and it was well-received. I remember waking up at 3am with the song already playing in my head. I still have the piece of paper on which I hastily wrote it as it tumbled out of me – skipping some lines to keep up with the flow of inspiration.

I got another commission from my friend and sister, Mrs Dora Akunyili. She was the Minister for Information and had received me on behalf of the Acting President, Dr Goodluck Jonathan. I presented copies of my new album *The Legend,* which contained songs about Nigeria and Abuja. Professor Akunyili had informed the Acting President that I was planning to write a song to encourage him in the task ahead. She did this without telling me, but she had the privilege and right as *Nne m Ochie,* 'one who comes from my mother's place' to do so.

I honoured her words and entered the studio at a time the Acting President was considering the question: to run or not to run, in the imminent presidential election. Dr Goodluck Jonathan loved it. He confessed, years later, that it had a reassuring effect on him. He went on to win the 2011 presidential elections by a large margin.

'Run, Goodluck Run' was recorded in a matter of minutes. It came on its own, in the studio, after the producer, Wole Oni, and I had prayed. I simply opened my mouth and started singing while Wole played the keyboard. In my prayers, I had asked the Holy Spirit to send a song that would convince the Acting President to run for the substantive election, but only if he would win. President Goodluck Jonathan was a man on the right side of destiny.

In 2013, I received a call from Rt. Hon. Anyim Pius Anyim; he was the Secretary to the Government of the Federation of Nigerian (SGF). The Nigerian Government was planning a yearlong series of activities to commemorate the amalgamation of the country in 1914. That year, the British had brought together the Northern and Southern Protectorates, and Nigeria was born. The SGF needed something emotive and rallying to drive the Centenary Celebrations and my name came up.

'Can you do it in a matter of days?' He asked. 'Yes,' I replied.

'Then, you can come to Abuja for a critique, acceptance or whatever.'

I knew that the 'whatever' meant that the song may not be accepted after my efforts. Those were the odds I was used to working with. I did not entertain any fears. I knew from whence my inspiration came, and that with the Holy Spirit, I had a perfect and inexhaustible source to draw from.

The first line of the song came and within thirty minutes, the foundation and skeletal frame had been formed. My producer, Wole Oni, understood the style of allowing the Holy Spirit do His thing through us. He was prompt in recording whatever came through me, knowing that I would have to learn the song myself and complete it a little later.

On hearing the song the following day, an elated SGF invited a few others for their critical appraisal. Some vital suggestions that invariably improved the song's appeal was the inclusion of other artistes of diversified backgrounds to give the song titled 'This Land' a 'We-Are-The-World' effect. A hit was born. It remains a very special song and one of my best. It was heartfelt, sincere and compelling. 'This Land' was recorded with the participation of eight other artistes – Tosin Martins, Omawunmi Megbele, J'odie, Zakki Azzay, Eben, Silver Saddih, Ayo, and Seun Shobo. Each artiste brought their peculiar voice and interpretation to bear on the song's rendition.

At a command performance in Aso Rock, several former Heads of State, including General Buhari, sang the chorus:

> Here we are standing tall
> Through adversity we are one
> One hundred years of unity
> Nigeria we will stand.
>
> **Onyeka Onwenu** (2013)

It was a call for Nigerians to move beyond ethnic differences and structural challenges to make the country work. Encomiums about the song continued to pour in beyond the command performance. President Goodluck Jonathan was so enamoured by 'This Land' that he made it a second National Anthem at every government event during his tenure in office.

I also wrote the theme song for Nigeria's 50th Independence anniversary, 'Celebrate, Jubilate, Consolidate'.

The 'Winnie Mandela' Song

In 1988, I found myself in a peculiar situation. Four years earlier, I had fallen in love and had a child with a man who soon afterwards had to leave the country to save his life. For my protection, I was never fully made aware of the details of the situation, but I knew that we were all in danger for something my partner did not do.

As a mother and the financial head of my immediate and extended family, I had to be strong and carry on as if all was well. As a singer and performer, it fell on me to bring hope to others through my work, while all I felt inside was deep pain. As a thirty-six-year-old woman, I would sing and dance on stage, entertaining and making crowds happy and then go back home lonely and depressed. But I would carry on, fighting to have my partner's name cleared.

Some highly placed Nigerians with connections to the government like Chief MKO Abiola and Alhaji Maitama Sule were very helpful. They intervened, though unsuccessfully. They also offered prayers, encouragement and advice. Others took advantage of the situation; it was their opportunity to humiliate or shun me. A news magazine editor who now publishes a foremost Nigerian newspaper, invited me over to his office, ostensibly for an interview about the music industry. He ended up not publishing a word I said, but wrote extensively and exclusively about my relationship with my exiled partner. A journalist who was also a 'friend' read the offending piece like many others, and the next time she saw me, moved away quickly asking me not to sit near her as she did not want to be identified with me. My partner, who became my husband, was away from Nigeria for five years. We lost everything.

Late one night, I was alone as usual, watching a documentary about the political travails of Nelson and Winnie Mandela and the African National Congress (ANC) in apartheid South Africa. I was deeply moved. It was not as if I was unaware of the ills of the apartheid regime, but the documentary laid bare the savage underbelly of the white minority government and the odious brutality it visited on Winnie Mandela for standing for her rights, standing by her man and her people.

She was defiant every inch of the way, taking a daring and vocal position against subjugation. Even in the face of the most unbelievable physical, emotional and mental torture, in the face of humiliation, intimidation, and threats to her life and that of her two young children, Winnie Mandela was not deterred. She was often yanked away from home in the middle of the night, without being allowed to make arrangements for the care of her little children. She would have no idea as to whether they were dead or alive. This was enough to break any mother but she carried on. With uncommon courage, she faced this regime of terror, insisting on her freedom or nothing. She kept hope alive for her husband, the ANC and the generality of her people. Mrs Mandela spent months in solitary confinement, in tiny spaces in remote areas. She was not allowed to bathe or use a sanitary pad during her period. She made friends and had conversations with the ants and cockroaches in her tiny cell; they were her only companions. As I watched the documentary, I wept bitterly. As difficult as my life was, it could not be compared with Winnie Mandela's by any stretch of the imagination. I could identify with her loneliness and some of her pains, though. That night, I had to put my agnst into a song. I needed to give something back to Winnie for the sacrifice of her life to the apartheid struggle. I saw it as a global one, by an African woman, brave and courageous beyond words. The song 'Winnie Mandela' was embedded in the album *Dancing in The Sun* and Nigerians loved it.

When Nelson Mandela was released from prison in 1990, I sang this song in celebration of his release. And then again, at a command performance in honour of the Mandela's when they came visiting a few months later. A surprised Winnie broke down in tears. It was the first time, some journalists said, that she had cried in public. After the memorable rendition, she greeted me with a light kiss on the lips while her husband gave me a fatherly hug.

I had the honour of attending, in 1994, the inauguration of Nelson Mandela, as the first black President of South Africa. By that time, Winnie Mandela's relationship with her husband had soured as she was accused of several grave misdeeds. No one stopped to take stock of what she had gone through and how much she may have been affected by those experiences.

On my way to the inauguration ceremony, I conversed with the white South African driver assigned to me. It was clear from that chat that Winnie Mandela was feared and despised more than Madiba himself. Her fiery spirit and charismatic leadership posed a threat to their self-serving plans for the country. They had no kind words for her. I was not surprised.

At the pre-inauguration breakfast with Heads of States and other invitees, I craned my neck looking for Winnie Madikizela-Mandela. She was not there. At the inauguration too, I scanned the front seats looking for her, hoping that I would find her lurking behind headgears and hats. She was not there either. We were leaving the stadium filled with new hope for black rule in South Africa, but I found myself thinking of my friend's unfair demonisation. At a time when there should have been a surplus of accolades for her sacrifice, there seemed to be, instead, a resentment of her person. As we left the inauguration grounds, my head a little bowed, my mind lost in thought; I heard my name.

'Onyeka!' Someone called from a distance.

As I turned around towards the voice, Rear Admiral Alison Madueke, another member of the Nigerian delegation pointed at the towering figure of a woman and a younger lady, screaming and running down to where we stood. It was Winnie Mandela and her daughter, Zindzi. The stadium suddenly stood still for a few moments, wondering who this 'Onyeka' person was, for whom Winnie Madikizela-Mandela was displaying such excitement. The duo reached me and the three of us were enveloped in a group hug, screaming and talking at the same time.

'You came! You came!' Winnie shouted, unable to contain her joy. She knew that she was the reason I came to South Africa, not Madiba.

In 2018, Winnie Mandela passed away. She was 82 years old. I watched a report on her life on CNN. There was a news clip of a recent interview where a reporter asked her if the liberation struggle had been worth the sacrifice. I saw what was for me a most poignant moment.

'Yes! We won!' Winnie Mandela said, with the unquenchable embers of defiance left in her, but beneath the words, beneath the furrowed eyebrows, I also saw deep pain.

My dear, dear friend. Indeed, we won.

May your soul find succour at the feet of the Lord. We will never forget you and your bravery. You took on an evil force on our behalf. Thank you, Winnie Madikizela-Mandela. Rest in Peace.

South Africa – When The World Came To Breakfast

I t was my music that got me there. When I received an invitation to be part of Nigeria's delegation to Nelson Mandela's inauguration, I was overjoyed. Never in my wildest imagination, especially given my familiarity with the inhumanity of the apartheid establishment, did I believe that Nelson Mandela would survive his long stretch behind bars, let alone become the President of South Africa. I also never imagined that I would get the opportunity to witness such an epochal event.

From the vantage position of someone who witnessed the official inauguration ceremony in South Africa, I offer here snippets of the events as I saw and felt them.

President Mandela's inauguration was said to be the largest gathering of dignitaries since the funeral of the US President John F Kennedy in 1963. But that was as far as the comparison went. One was a sad event, the other a joyous occasion.

At the pre-inaugural breakfast held at the South African President's official residence, the mood was one of shared accomplishment. The most commonly used expression was 'What a wonderful day this is!' indeed, it was. The triumph of Nelson Mandela, former 'fugitive', 'terrorist' and 'jailbird', who became the President, was the triumph of good over evil. He was the Moses of black South Africa, but the miracle was that this Moses got to the promised land with his people.

As I sipped my guava juice in the spacious reception hall where the stand-up breakfast was served, it occurred to me that there was no elaborate protocol. Dignitaries milled around and perhaps shared the stories of their contributions to the emergence of the new South Africa. Lord Carrington, Douglas Hurd and Prince Philip made up the delegation from the United Kingdom. The American contingent of Vice President Al-Gore, Secretary of Commerce Ron Brown, and First Lady Hilary Clinton were there. The roll call of dignitaries is simply too long for this book.

Nonetheless, I met quite a good number of them, including the Namibian President Sam Nujoma at whose inauguration concert I performed in 1989. I had a delightful conversation with Bishop Desmond Tutu of South Africa whose joyous exuberance was most infectious. I was touched by the quiet dignity of Sonia Gandhi, wife of the slain Indian Prime Minister, Rajiv Gandhi.

PLO's Yasser Arafat was there, perhaps mindful of the quest for the freedom of his people, the Palestinians. There was the huge figure of Fidel Castro, representing Cuba, the last communist bastion in the world. He was hailed for his commitment to freedom in Africa. I saw Tanzania's Julius Nyerere, a humble man of immense accomplishments. He had a quiet yet powerful draw about him. Jerry Rawlings of Ghana and his beautiful wife, Nana Konadu Agyeman were most gracious with their effusive greeting. There were two very important moments during this breakfast. The first occurred when I shook hands with the man of the moment, President Nelson Mandela. He remembered my musical performance during his visit with Winnie to Nigeria after his release from prison.

I do not know exactly what prompted my encounter with the exiled Haitian President Jean-Bertrand Aristide, but it was spiritual. I had noticed him standing at the rear of the hall. I could not help but think that if Nelson Mandela survived the rigours of prison and torture to claim his destiny, so could this man. I was moved by the yearning mixed with despondency that I saw in his demeanour. I went over to greet him and the woman who was standing next to him. Looking back, I gave him what turned out to be a prophecy; that he would be back in power in Haiti in a matter of months. The prophecy came through. From the point of that conversation, the deposed President and his companion followed me everywhere, all the while smiling.

The Nigerian delegation was one of the first to arrive at the breakfast venue and convoys were arranged in order of arrival. This was the explanation given by our hosts for our being one of the last groups to leave for the inauguration grounds.

The ceremony was awe-inspiring from the traditional praise singer who heralded Madiba's entrance, to the choral groups that intermittently erupted into song. Mandela's address was a study in humility and forgiveness. He gave credit to all but himself. The audience was moved to tears and brought to its feet when he declared that:

> 'Never and never again shall it be that this beautiful land will again experience the oppression of one by another, and suffer the indignity of being the skunk of the world. Let freedom reign. The sun shall never set on so glorious a human achievement. God bless Africa.'

Then came the magnificent aerial display by the South African Air Force. It was colourful and impressive. It left no one in doubt about the country's military might.

As I sat waiting for our turn to leave the Amphitheater of the

Union Buildings, the venue of the inauguration, I could not help but wonder what the other Nigerian delegation members felt. I was very happy for South Africa, which had found its feet after 350 years of white domination and oppression. I felt sorry, though, that my country had squandered its promising future on the ignoble theatre of self-aggrandisement and ethnic divisions. However, my disappointment was tempered by a certain hopefulness that if South Africa could emerge from centuries of social and political oppression, so could Nigeria from its sisyphean politics of acrimony and ineptitude.

At the post-inaugural lunch, we were fed with a roast rack of veal, braised white asparagus and an assortment of South African wine. There was plenty of music and speeches from our hosts, many more handshakes and introductions. There was also a kiss on the hand from Jesse Jackson who constantly came over to confer with members of the Nigerian delegation.

With a last glance at the beautiful view of the cascading hills behind the Presidential residence, the Nigerian delegation departed, clearly impressed by the organisation of the events we had witnessed.

The World of Music Administration

There must be a reason why entertainment is called 'show business'. It has two sides – the 'show', also known as the 'creative' side, and the 'business' side. Many Nigerian artistes bury their heads in only the creative and allow record companies and managers to control everything else. Many are unaware that they are owed millions of naira by telecommunication companies and others who use and sell their music daily. The Copyright Society of Nigeria (COSON) was licensed as the sole Collective Management Organisation (CMO) in 2011, after many years of lobbying the Federal Government and our lawmakers.

Before then, artistes were deprived of our legitimate earnings from royalties due to us for the use of our intellectual property. Apart from the good fortune of a few, the Nigerian music industry has remained immobilised. It has grown in spurts and then stagnated, relying on artistes' individual efforts who are self-funded to bring gravitas to it.

The music industry has never been a model of collective effort with regards to its administration. This was primarily due to a lack of education and understanding of critical issues by stakeholders. Piracy, which diminished the industry, was categorised as a civil offence, not a criminal one. This was until we struck in 1986, banning all federal radio stations from playing our music unless royalties were paid and piracy criminalised.

Efforts to unite musicians had been made before 1981 when I began my musical career. However, a more dedicated attempt was made by Christy Essien, and her manager/husband, Edwin Igbokwe, in 1982. It led to the formation of the first serious musician's union called the Performing Musicians Employers Association of Nigeria (PMAN).

After an all-encompassing meeting at King Sunny Ade's Ariya Night Club in Lagos that year, he was designated as the first PMAN President. Other executive members were Sonny Okosuns, who was Vice President, Bala Milla, Gboyega Adelaja, Bobby Benson, Sir Victor Uwaifo, Chris Okotie, Commander Ebenezer Obey, Nelly Uchendu, Dan Maraya Jos, Prince Nico Mbarga, Emma Dorgu and Tony Grey. I was the Publicity Secretary.

After the King Sunny Ade presidency, Sonny Okosuns was elected, followed by Tony Okoroji during whose tenure I was also elected Vice President. After Mr Okoroji came Mustapha Amigo, and then Charles Oputa (Charly Boy). Things turned around to see King Sunny Ade elected President. His first time was an appointment. After him, Christy Essien-Igbokwe emerged as the first female President. There were many other presidents afterwards, too many to mention. Now nobody knows much about PMAN. Probably because not much is happening, except battles of supremacy between individuals claiming the presidency of it.

The problem with PMAN is a typical Nigerian problem; leaders who want to be in office forever, while remaining accountable only to themselves. They could not be called to order by anyone, and are gods unto themselves.

Once money began to pour in after our restorative efforts from 1986 to 1988, a period in which I served as the Vice President, I noticed that our focus shifted from the challenges besetting the music industry to building personality cults. I left PMAN soon after the sum of N20m was donated to the union by the Federal Government. I observed that I was no longer consulted or invited to meetings, whereas before then, I signed all PMAN letters since I was better known. I also paid the salary of PMAN officials for a period of one year from 1988 to 1989.

There is this perception that artistes who become engaged with unionism are those who have run out of creative juice and can no longer rely on their talent to earn a living. This is true in some cases. Others have devoted their time, energy, ideas and funds to drive the industry, through the mobilization of its practitioners. It has always been a mixed group.

During the Tony Okoroji-Onyeka Onwenu administration, we recorded huge successes at PMAN, such as the criminalisation of the offence of piracy with the copyright decree of 1988, and generally the protection of intellectual property. We glamourised and made popular the Nigerian Music Awards.

I took this verve to Lagos State PMAN when I won its election in 1991. We engaged our immediate environment through charitable outreaches and led advocacy for the growth of the arts, especially music at the community level.

The registration in 2011 of the Copyright Society of Nigeria (COSON) as a Copyright Management Organisation was designed to stimulate and ensure the proper distribution of royalties to their owners. It was a landmark achievement that had taken years of strategizing to achieve. An older copyright association, Musical Copyright Society of Nigeria (MCSN) headed by Mayo Ayilaran, had struggled along with us but was only approved in 2017 after it appeared that COSON, under Mr Tony Okoroji, had failed to represent the interest of the majority of its members.

In the period between 2011 when it was registered and 2020, COSON has reportedly – and by its own accounts – raked in over N1bn. I received less than N400,000 for my considerable repertoire of songs in use during the same period. Since 2013, I have been paid nothing for the licensing of my songs.

PMAN and COSON have failed irredeemably to safeguard its members' interests and fulfil the goals for which they were founded. Perhaps, we should have set them up with stricter rules, especially with regards to their administrative structures. A situation where one person is allowed unbridled access to the control of funds generated by others' creative output should have been prevented. It still can, if only the government agencies charged with an oversight function at COSON will do their duties. The Nigerian Copyright Commission (NCC) should tell the country why it has never ordered an audit of COSON, nor a proper investigation of its financial affairs. We must set up a more robust mechanism for accountability and prevent greed, recklessness and 'sit-tight' syndrome from taking centre stage. COSON and PMAN have become a microcosm of Nigerian dysfunction.

The Hunger Strike

The year was 2001; President Obasanjo was back on the seat as a civilian president and Nigerians were excited about the prospects of a new democracy, even if an ex-general led it. Ben Murray-Bruce had been appointed the Director-General of the Nigerian Television Authority (NTA).

The Nigerian entertainment industry was very happy about this development. Ben Bruce had been an astute player in the field. He had established Silverbird, an entertainment company which had brought many popular American groups such as Shalamar, Cool and the Gang, Evelyn King and many others for live performances in Nigeria. This gave us a chance to learn first hand from these international artistes. As far back as 1981, during my Youth Service at NTA, young Ben hung out with us, trying to push forward his vision for the entertainment industry.

Unfortunately, however, the new DG appeared arrogant and with the people surrounding him, decided that he had no use for Nigerian entertainers and would pay them no mind. We were flabbergasted.

It started with Charles Oputa aka 'Charly Boy' – a Content Producer and entertainment/social impresario. He had won a case against NTA's sale of his programme to an international network without compensation, but they would not pay up.

As concerned artistes, and with the involvement of Charly Boy's lawyer, Mr Bankole Shodipo, we began to strategize on ways to bring attention to the stalemate. The issue of the payment of copyright dues and the protection of intellectual property rights was gaining attention all over the world. Some of us in PMAN and in PMRS (a collective society and the precursor to COSON) had made sacrifices, even confronting a military government about its non-criminalization of piracy laws. Yet here we had a government agency, breaking the law of the country by refusing to obey a court ruling.

I dug into my file of grievances against NTA and decided to claim my residual fees for the repeated airing of my shows Contact and Who Is On by the network, and for the use of my song 'Iyogogo' in opening the working day for NTA for over eight years. I decided to write formally to the Director-General to look into my complaints. That, apparently, was what I did wrong.

Instead of acknowledging my letter and addressing the issues I raised, Mr Ben Bruce went into a tirade; I was told of how NTA did me a huge favour by using my works, even without my permission. He thereafter decided that he no longer wanted

to see my face at NTA. How dare I protest about the use of my works on the network? I was banned. A planned interview on the network was cancelled and I was declared persona non grata on the network

My colleagues and I were bewildered to say the least. It was double injury. NTA exploited my works for years without permission and without compensation, and when I spoke up, it slammed me with a banning order. Mba nu! No! Something had to give. This was my country Nigeria and not some foreign Banana Republic.

I decided to go on a public hunger strike - right in front of NTA Headquarters, in Victoria Island, until Mr Ben Bruce addressed the issues I had raised in my letter to him. Mr Charles Oputa joined me in the standoff, together with many others, until Mr Bruce was forced to address us. On the third day of the protest, he did when foreign news agencies had begun to report on the matter and it was becoming embarrassing for the Nigerian government.

With Mr Bruce's apology and the rescinding of the banning order, we vacated the front gate of NTA and went home. But not until the likes of Chief Gani Fawehinmi, the fearless human rights lawyer had made an appearance with hordes of followers to admonish Mr Ben Bruce and NTA that no harm must come to Onyeka Onwenu who is fighting for her rights.

It was a spectacular three days and though there were those who did not agree with our method or our vehemence on the matter, our point had been amply made.

Years later, in 2004, I was appointed a member of the NTA Board of Directors. God does have a sense of humour. I was immediately paid my residual fees for my programmes, but nothing for the use of 'Iyogogo' as a station opener for eight years. I considered that a sacrifice I had to make. The point had been made that the rule of law and due process had to be followed in the conduct of the affairs of national agencies.

Artistes have to protect their rights and demand for payment for the use of their intellectual property. Mr Ben Murray-Bruce, who later went on to a prolific career in the Nigerian Senate from 2015 to 2019, remains a friend. All is forgiven.

When Money Grew Wings

The Nigerian music industry is peopled by all manner of characters, some serious and some not so serious. Some of them are professional in their conduct and craft, while others are just out to make easy money. I believe that this is not peculiar to Nigeria. However, a situation where one artiste stole from another – not a song or part of the lyrics – but money from the other's bag, was a low point in my interaction with someone who must remain unnamed.

Envy, unhealthy competition and a shocking level of *bad- belle* among artistes meant that we all did not get along very well all the time. Everyone wanted to be the biggest star on the horizon. It took a lot of effort for many artistes to even talk to one another. With these rivalries, the idea of cooperating and coalescing our efforts towards the achievement of a common goal was rather alien to many. King Sunny Ade and I set an example with our collaborative efforts. But there was still work to be done.

It was not unusual for artistes to sabotage one another's act by tampering with the musical equipment to ensure that the other's performance fell below standard. I had an occasion where, clearly, my act was sabotaged by the engineer in charge of the equipment. We suspect he was paid by another artiste to do so. From then on, I employed my own technical crew, even if the equipment in use did not belong to me.

A few days after the demise of my friend, Tyna Onwudiwe aka 'African Oyibo' in South Africa, I had to perform at a wedding ceremony in Abuja. I had begun the day in a sullen mood; I was beset by grief. In the spirit of my profession, which dictates that, whatever the circumstances, the show had to go on, I went on stage to give one of my best performances. The audience showed its appreciation by showering me with high denominations of naira notes. The other two artistes on the bill were equally good and were appreciated, but not to the level that I was. One of them was not too happy with the situation, but how was that any of my business?

Flying back to Lagos, this artiste sat behind me, together with a woman whom I assumed was his girlfriend. I had a travelling bag into which I arranged the cash I was sprayed with (given) the night before, as well as other personal items. I stored it in the aircraft's overhead compartment, with the other artiste watching all the while. As we prepared to disembark, my colleague quickly got up to assist me. I reached for my cash bag, and he insisted on helping me with it. He then handed it over to his girlfriend, right behind him. In between the airplane and the tarmac, the cash was removed. I did not discover it until I got home. I immediately called him to inquire if he or his friend had taken the money. He thoroughly insulted me and let me know that his reaction would have been worse, if not for the 'respect' he had for me.

I was numb with disbelief. I knew that he had pilfered my money, N150,000 to be exact, but I had no proof. So, I swallowed my anger and forgot about the money. Six years later, I saw the same artiste on an Owerri-bound flight. We were both invited to an event there. He was very quiet throughout the journey. I said nothing more to him after our initial greeting, but my colleague could not look me in the eye. I knew that his conscience was bothering him.

As soon as we got into a common vehicle conveying us to the event, my colleague could no longer bear the guilt of the stolen money and the insults he had heaped on me. He quietly turned to one of our hosts who had come to pick us up and confessed that he had done something terrible to me and wanted my forgiveness. I did not allow him to disclose the fact that he had stolen my money and abused me on top of the vile act. I had forgiven him and moved on.

I have not seen this artiste since he made the public confession in 2010, but if he is reading this, he should know that he can still return my money, along with interest and then truly, all will be forgiven and forgotten. I am kidding, of course.

On a lighter note, I recall an incident during a concert at the Tafawa Balewa Square in Lagos hosted by Vice-President Augustus Aikhomu in 1993 to celebrate Nelson Mandela's release from prison. In the order of performances, I was asked to go first. Sonny Okosuns and Christy Essien-Igbokwe had insisted that they were my seniors; therefore, I should open the show for them. The moment I dropped the microphone, the satisfied audience began to leave the venue. My colleagues literally performed to an empty stadium. When the Mandelas visited a few months later, and another performance was held at the National Stadium Lagos, Sonny Okosuns insisted on performing first. Christy Essien- Igbokwe played next and I appeared last. They were afraid that the audience could desert the stadium and leave them playing to empty seats if I performed first. It was a supremacy battle I did not bother to engage in. So, again, I did not object and sang the song 'Winnie Mandela', which was the highlight of the event.

A *Taste of Nollywood*

The Nigerian film industry was not referred to as 'Nollywood' when I made my screen debut in 1998. It was just called videos. It was a trend started by Ken Nnebue, a businessman who had imported an excessive number of VHS tapes. He could not sell the whole consignment and wanted somehow to liquidate the stock. He took on a story of wizardry, *juju* and supernatural powers, in a video film called *Living In Bondage*. It sold like hotcakes. From this sprung a fully functional industry of quickly and cheaply made stories whose characters the people easily identified with. They told the peoples' story and created a mass appeal for Nigerian films.

Nollywood is now the third largest movie industry in the world behind Hollywood and Bollywood. At the time of this evolution, I was already a well-known singer/songwriter and I had no real desire or interest in the budding film industry. Everything changed, though, with my first attempt at professional acting in *Nightmare*, a movie by Zik Zulu. I had agreed to do it to raise money for orphans, to which the proceeds were given. Mr Zulu had effectively cajoled me into acting but I thought it was a one-off venture. Instead, it opened the door to more offers and pressure from movie makers. I turned down many but they would not stop coming.

One of my earliest successes was a film called *Conspiracy* with Larry Koldsweat. It was a tear-jerker in which I played a woman made insane by jealous in-laws and who tended to her twin boys at a garbage dump, until good Samaritans rescued them. The woman was healed and the family united in the end. It remains a favourite of many lovers of Nollywood. It also cemented my emergence as an actor of reckon, not a singer who fell into acting.

There were many more Nollywood films along the way for which I won awards. I won the African Movie Academy Award (AMAA) for films such as *Rising Moon* and *The Women's Cot*. Other notable ones were *Half of a Yellow Sun*, a film adaptation of Chimamanda Adichie's novel of the same title. In it, I played a troublesome and meddlesome mother of an only child, the main character, Odenigbo, played by Chiwetel Ejiofor. I 'channelled' my paternal grandmother, who was reputed to be quite troublesome. Anyone would need God's help if for some reason, she did not like them; it did not matter that they were guilty of nothing. In the end, though, I was happy that Mama, my character, did evolve into a loving and supportive mother-in-law to Odenigbo's original choice of wife.

Mama was a character I could sink my teeth into. I enjoyed her meanness when she needed to assert her will. An Igbo woman's tenacity knows no bounds when it comes to protecting her only son. Mama was also able to realise that she needed to work with her daughter-in-law to secure her son's happiness. She was a woman of strength and character, and she had my admiration.

I had a sneaky feeling that the novel's author first suggested that I be invited to read for the role. I do not know why. But I went to the audition in character, dressed like a 'Mama' would. After the first few lines, I caught the director smiling from the corner of my eye, and I knew that it was a pass.

I enjoyed the work process as the cast of *Half of a Yellow Sun* was filled with professionals. I particularly enjoyed working with Thandi Newton. She was gracious and friendly; down to earth and helpful. When I apologised to her about Mama's meanness, I said, 'Sorry that I have to be so mean.'

She replied, 'Yeah, but you enjoyed it.'

We both had a good laugh because she was right. More recently, I appeared in the film *Lion Heart* by Genevieve Nnaji and which was streamed on Netflix in 2019.

My romance with Nollywood has blossomed and I now absolutely love acting. I am excited by the opportunity to subsume my person in another's persona and deliver a performance that resonates with the audience. One has to have the ability to lose oneself in the role to become one with an adopted character.

On stage in 1985

A live performance on a college campus in 1987

With King Sunny Ade

On Stage With Sunny Ade in 1989

With Wole Soyinka and King Sunny Ade during a chance meeting at Daily Times office while promoting our duet Wait For Me

With Chief Emeka Odumegwu Ojukwu at My Album Launch in 1991

Mko at my album launch in 1992

Justice Eugene Ubezonu, my mum and aunt Dorothy at my album launch in 1992

With my friend and sister, Mrs Doyin Abiola.
At the press presentation of my album in 1992

Being sworn in as PMAN Chairman Lagos State

Singing happy birthday to Monsieur President

Dancing Iyogogo in Yamoussoukro

Getting ready for a video shoot with Zakki Azzi, Christy Essien-Igbokwe, Segun Adewale, Onyeka Onwenu and Sunny Okosuns

Onyeka with Chris Thomas King after performing a duet of "At Last" at the US National Day Celebrations in Abuja Feb 2009.

The making of the video - Dancing In The Sun By Charly Boy Oputa

Sonny Okosus with his back to camera cracking us up with his jokes just before a performance in Abuja. With us is Christy Essien-Igbokwe

Singing with Yvonne Chaka Chaka

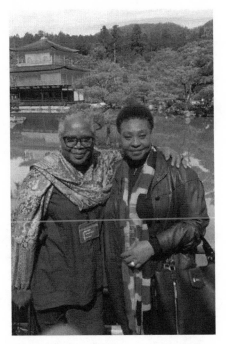

Visiting Japan with Yvonne Chaka Chaka
as members of Ashinaga (NGO) Board.

261

Singing for the IDPs

Monsieur President honored me by waving the handkerchief

With President of Liberia Ellen Johnson Sirleaf in the
company of other female artistes at an event in Monrovia

Hunger strike at NTA

Speaking with the American Press on my collaboration with King
Sunny Ade

Receiving my award from USAID in Washington DC. Standing with
King Sunny Ade - for the songs Choices and Wait For Me

With Geraldo Pino and Chris Okotie at a performance at Lords Nite Club

With my prodigies Chris Hanen(Ozigizaga) and Mike Okri. Both came from my Band Kabassa

On stage in 2019

On the day of the
election, after results
were announced. I
was seven months
pregnant with my
second son.

PART VI

Ties That Bind

My Marriage

'*Uzo eji nwa anaghi echi.*'
A relationship never ends in a marriage blessed with children.

All my adult life, I had resisted every attempt to discuss my marriage, or non-marriage, in the press. I had parried the question from journalists, refusing to address it at all and I had good reason. It was nobody's business if I were married or not. It had nothing to do with my career. I am a private person and I learned to keep my personal affairs away from public glare. My husband and I had an agreement from the onset of our relationship that our lives would remain private. That decision helped to shield our family from undue media exposure.

This was so successful that many Nigerians had no idea that I had been married, let alone, separated or divorced. Many did not know that I had children. The media was filled with lies. Some said I had a girl and not two boys. I just let people speculate. It was not as though there was any secrecy surrounding my life. Those close enough had the right information, yet I did not feel the need to divulge the same to everyone else.

I have refused to be defined by marriage or attachment to a man, which often seems to be the way a woman in Nigeria gains respect. She is considered a nobody unless she is identified with a husband. To be respectable, a woman has to have the appellation of 'Mrs'. I decided not to be an appendage to someone else. I knew that I had been given enough to be known by and respected for, other than being someone's wife. This is not to say that being a wife was not a most honourable and wonderful thing. But if you are not so inclined or opportuned, it should not be counted against you. Why then, one may ask, have I titled my book in a way that ties me closely to my father?

His love shaped my early years, and more than anything else, taught me about God's love. The love of my earthly father defined me, but only as much as it introduced me to the awesomeness of God's love, which ultimately surrounded my life with grace. It is interesting how Papa's love, however brief, continues to have a long-term effect on me.

In this book, I am, perhaps for the very first time, setting the records straight with respect to my connubial relationship. Yes, I was married. I married a man I fell in love with in 1984. We have two children: Tijani and Ibrahim. (Ibrahim later changed the first letter of his name from I to A, and thus became Abraham.) My husband is Yoruba, and was a Muslim when we met.

At the time, I was already a well-known singer, songwriter and television journalist. I had just concluded work on an album, *In The Morning Light*. I had written and presented the BBC/ NTA Documentary, *Nigeria, a Squandering of Riches* and released a single, 'Ekwe', with 'Trina 4' on the flip side, in the United Kingdom. I was an established artiste and I lacked nothing. My career was on the ascendance.

My husband, therefore, knew what he was getting into, associating with a famous woman. He was surprised though that no men were lining up to see me or beating a path to my door. My life was simple, rich and private. When he further inquired from his close friend, Chief Ephraim Faloughi, someone who had known me from when I was a child in Port Harcourt and who knew my family very well, my husband was told that he was dealing with a lady with impeccable character, and from a very respectable family.

I have heard it said that it is better to have loved and lost than not to have loved at all, and I agree. This love was passionate and committed. It was put to the test, time and time again, through life and death situations.

Eighteen months after we met and nine months after our first son was born, a serious challenge came up with some work; my husband had been given to do. Suddenly, he had to leave Nigeria for his safety and stayed away for five years. We lost everything and his businesses were destroyed. He was accused of something he did not do.

This was a very difficult time for me, as can be imagined. Only my family and close friends knew what I was going through. For the rest of the world, I had to keep up appearances of all being well. My faith in God and my love for my husband and son kept me going.

By the fifth year of my husband's 'exile', I had had enough. I did not care anymore if I lived or died. All I knew was that my husband could no longer be held down for something he did not do. I approached some people I thought could help us. I reached out to Chief MKO Abiola and my mentor, Alhaji Maitama Sule. I remember visiting the latter in Kano for three days. We sat in his modest living room against the backdrop of books and papers, talking for hours about politics and social issues. He gave me advice and he counselled. This kept my hopes up. Chief Abiola tried his best as well. However, I cannot but mention the extraordinary role played by Lieutenant Colonel Lawan Gwadabe, the Military Governor of

Niger State, who took it upon himself to raise my husband's matter with the authorities and he was exonerated. I am unable to pay back such people; only God can.

In 1990, my husband returned to Nigeria. My second son Ibrahim was born on 17 August 1991, on the Head of State's birthday, President Ibrahim Babangida, the very day he was leaving Lagos for Abuja permanently. My son, however, was not named after him. My husband's middle name is Ibrahim.

Now, my family was whole again and I could resume the semblance of being a wife, loved and protected by her husband who was also the father of her children. I could certainly appreciate why Winnie Mandela described herself as the 'most unmarried, married woman in the world'.

Six years after being back in Nigeria, my husband had to leave again. This time a health challenge had sadly come to him. I suspect that the years of undeserved punishment, of physical, mental, financial and emotional stress had taken their toll on him. The illness seemed as though it was destined to claim his life. Again, the Lord stepped in and stabilised him. He returned to Nigeria and we began efforts to resuscitate his businesses. God remained faithful and my husband began to thrive again. I give God all the glory for his resilience. Not many people would have survived the ordeal he went through. I have nothing but admiration for his courage and tenacity. Despite the constant physical pain that he has to live with, he never gave up.

I also thank God for my survival and that of my children. He alone knows how hard the going got taking care of everybody. He gave me the grace to do it all without complaining and without letting myself down. God did not disappoint, but showed Himself mighty on our behalf on a day-to-day basis. I grew in faith during this period.

Ndigbo Are Republicans: The Onwenu Family Meetings

I decided to discuss an aspect of Igbo republicanism here because tied to it, is the formalisation of my marriage. The worst thing that can happen to you in the Onwenu family is for the theme of the end-of-year family meeting to be built around you or your misdemeanour. The same thing applies to most families from the south-east geopolitical zone of Nigeria.

In our society, every individual has the right of self-expression no matter their status. Members of your immediate and extended family, even members of your community, have the right to question your behaviour and call you to order if deemed to be out of line with accepted norms.

In December 1990, a cousin of mine who worked in my office as a technician confronted me in the presence of the father of my son, demanding that I make myself available at an Onwenu family meeting called on my account. The Onwenus had been patient, trying to understand the delay in formalising a relationship that began in 1984 and had produced a son. They felt ignored and disrespected. My husband, however, was not happy with the way my cousin made his demands. Although he did not understand the Igbo language, he could sense that it had to do with him.

'How can he talk to you like that?' He asked.

Well, my cousin had the right to express himself on family matters, even though he was younger and an employee in my office. So, on December 26 that year, I had to appear before the combined Onwenu family meeting made up of my uncle's four wives, my mum, my brother Richard, as well as other cousins. They took turns asking me questions about my marital status. As far as they were concerned, I was a single woman who had a child with a man they knew and liked, but who had not deemed it necessary to explain to our family his presence in my life.

The Onwenus basically wanted me to either regularise my marriage, or leave it, with my son who was considered theirs anyway. Traditionally, the child of an unmarried mother becomes a member of her own family.

On 17 December 1991, just four months after our son Ibrahim was born, my husband with his cousin, Mr Dapo Elias, arrived in Obinetiti for a 'wine carrying ceremony'. He had given notice only a week earlier. I did not tell him about the discussion at the family meeting. However, being an intuitive person, he knew that he had to formalise the relationship or leave.

My family gave him a list of what was required, not a hard one to fill. It was mainly soap, drinks, gift items for the clan and a few others which he monetised. The bride price had been lowered to N5,000 (about $30) to make marriage more affordable for more people. What a shame, I thought. My husband should have been made to pay at least N100m. I was worth a whole lot more to him and that had been well demonstrated. When he said to my family that 'Your daughter will be well taken care of ', I chuckled. My family knew me well. I was the one taking care of everyone. They did not have expectations; they just wanted us to be happy in a formalised union.

The Onwenus were justified in their intervention. It was their right to protect the family name and they had given me enough time and hints to do the needful. I was humbled.

And It All Came Crashing Down

My husband is a good man, kind and generous to those around him. This was part of what attracted me to him. Every girl looks for a husband in a man who reminds her of her father. A few months after we met, we discovered that my father's cousin, Mrs Grace Kanu was dying of cancer and needed treatment abroad. My husband paid for the treatment which gave her another ten years of active living. This generosity towards others reminded me of my father. But people do change, and it would seem, my husband did.

It is pertinent to mention that as generous as he was, I was financially independent from the beginning to the end of the relationship. I have raised our two sons on my own. I paid their school fees, from kindergarten to graduate school in the US. I was responsible for everything they needed - food, medical bills, clothes, recreation and holidays. Everything. I also raised my nephew, my brother's son, DK III at the same time. I never received housekeeping allowance, yet we lacked nothing.

I did not complain. As a family, we had gone through so much disruption, separation and financial loss. I saw my role as a helper to the man I loved. No sacrifice was too much. I helped my husband through it all, even as he had helped me with some of my projects.

Eventually, when things began to improve for him, I still did not receive any financial support for the children. By this time, the young men were all in the university. A bit of assistance from my husband would have been very helpful.

To be fair to him, he had expressed to my siblings his disappointment in the fact that I was often the sole financier and caregiver to the Onwenu family. They were not pulling their weight, so I had to pull mine and theirs, he complained. He was right.

However, I had reasoned that even if I were an only child, I would have still taken care of my family, immediate and extended. I, therefore, refused to abandon my mother to accede to an unreasonable demand by my spouse.

My husband gave me an ultimatum: stop helping your family or you get no help from me. I continued and so I got none – not for myself and not for our children. He provided nothing except the accommodation of a house which we both built and owned together.

Leaving me as the sole financier of the immediate family was, therefore, a punishment for my refusal to stop helping my family, particularly my mother, who was completely dependent on me. I had come to accept that some men are like that. I may not have understood it, but I lived with it.

What I particularly had a hard time wrapping my head around was the silent treatment given to our children who did nothing but love and reach out to him. I was shocked at my husband's decision to distance himself from our children, sometimes for decades at a stretch. He would neither speak with them nor see them, not even at their invitation or suggestion.

After making so many failed efforts to communicate with their father, the boys and I came to terms with his penchant, and perhaps need to distance himself from us. There was also his inability to forgive a perceived wrong, but I never understood what I did wrong, except that I dared to rise above every emotional abuse and strive on. The boys and I have lived with the realisation that it was his choice to remain incommunicado, even though he had direct access to them.

The Jolting Lies

I n the five years that my husband was away, I understood what it meant to be a Nigerian woman, standing alone and exposed to a patriarchal society's hubris. A lot of negativity surrounded me and some of it came from family. Let me share one story that explains this experience.

I call it 'the jolting lies' because it made for conflicting conclusions if one were careless and did not appraise matters dispassionately. In this particular case, I had to dig deep into my arsenal of pre-existing convictions to come up with my own understanding. The people who advise you to go a certain route, are often the same ones who would laugh at you when the road leads to a regrettable end. There were also 'the jolting truths' which I will talk about later.

During my husband's absence from Nigeria, I vowed to God and him that I would not let him down. I promised to fight to clear his name, and I kept my promise. During this trying period, I was a young singer/songwriter left on my own to ward off suitors and wannabe 'sugar daddies'. I was, at the same time, taking care of my family all by myself. A close relative, someone whom I considered a second mother, gave me a piece of advice that I will never forget. There were three of us at this meeting – my mother, her sister Aunt Dorothy and I. My mother's sister wanted to know why I had chosen to wait for the father of my child, considering that we were not yet married. I had only one child then.

'Why are you wasting your life on him?' Aunt Dorothy queried.

I did not know how to respond to that kind of question, so I kept quiet. 'Look at you, such a beautiful girl. There is no man in this country that you cannot get. You can even go to Abuja, get a rich boyfriend and make a lot of money to make us happy.'

She went on to advise that I walk away from the father of my son in a time of difficulty, find a rich boyfriend and bring home loads of naira for her and her sister.

'After all, you are hot market,' she assured. 'You are famous and beautiful. Every rich Nigerian man would want you,' she concluded.

I was aghast. I could not believe the words that were being said to me. I glanced at my mother. I expected her to caution her sister, but my mum did not even look at me. She stared at the wall, stone-faced and uninvolved. My aunt was asking me to prostitute myself. The mother who raised me would not put up with such talk. I mean, it was the opposite of everything that she believed in and taught my siblings and I. Since she would not give her sister a suitable answer, I would.

What kind of control had my aunt now gained over my mother that she was allowed to give me such horrible advice, more so, in her presence? Was I being baited to see if I would fall for it? Perhaps I was being tested? I wondered as the words began forming inside me.

'Do you not think that it is too late for that? I was raised on certain principles and I do not think that I can change now.'

TIES THAT BIND

My aunt sat there, not knowing what to do with my words. I looked back at my mum, and she had a wry smile at the corners of her lips.

My mother never brought up the issue again. I assumed it was because it had not been her idea. But it made me think: Why was my aunt trying to do this to her sister's daughter? Surely, my mum would never give her nieces such sinister advice. I never forgot the incident. It reminded me of a Bible teaching from Proverbs 22:6: Bring up a child in the way they should go, when they grow up they will not depart from it.

My mother had raised her children to believe that we could survive, much like her, on the strength of our genuine endeavours, without having to latch onto others like leeches for easy money and assistance. Hope Onwenu epitomised the spirit of financial independence which became my survival mantra from my teen years right into adulthood. I am quite sure that my mother knew what my answer would be and would have warned her sister.

One of the greatest compliments I received from my husband was that I was a great mother. He told our first son in 2015, during their first conversation in over ten years, that he should know that his mother would go to the moon and back for her children.

My husband understood the power of words and how to wield them to mend or break someone. I do not remember it clearly, but he said something most revealing to me. It was along the lines of my aura being so powerful that when we entered a room together, he felt smaller and did not like it. If a wife was told that she was a bad cook for example, she could take lessons or go for training to improve her skills. Pray tell: How does one reduce one's aura so that it does not overshadow someone else's? I had no idea. I was not God who gave me the aura in the first place. By the way, was it not this same aura that helped my husband to be heard several times when he needed help? Why complain about it then? At some point, being married became like walking a tightrope. Nothing I did was right or good enough. When people have known each other for many years and they have been through so much together, they pretty much know the boundaries and lines not to cross, and the consequences of crossing them. For a woman though, these lines are not so clear. I was surprised at how much I could take, that I never knew I could. I accepted maltreatment, deliberate neglect and more. There were a set of rules of dos and don'ts that my husband compelled me to live by.

I was not allowed to employ a cook. This may be hard for some people to believe, but it is true. The closest I got to hiring one was my friend, Mama Ekaette, a caterer who would come to the house when the kids were in primary school, and help me cook. She would make *edikangikong* and *afang* soups, as well as stew which were packaged, dated and frozen for future use. They came in handy anytime I was too tired to cook. My husband found out about Mama Ekaette and stopped her from coming. I was not only to cook, but also had to serve my husband's food and clear up the dishes.

The housekeeper was not allowed to clean the master bedroom, except me. I was also obligated to wash his socks. If I could not cook and clean as quickly and as often as required, I was accused of giving my best to the outside world and not my family. It was petty, but I was expected to pick up the house phone, even if the caller was a habitual early morning, weekend caller, whom I suspected did it on purpose. If I complained about being woken up every Saturday and Sunday by 5 a.m just to pick up the phone and handover to my husband, it meant that I was not accepting of his friends.

All these were to 'keep me in my place' – whatever that meant – and not to allow my stardom to 'get into my head'. It was about control.

With all the rules and regulations to follow, and with so much time and effort expended on shopping, cooking, cleaning and taking care of the children, I still had to work to provide for my family, including my husband.

This had a negative effect on me. I was constantly on edge, overthinking everything. I spent the greater parts of my day in crippling anxiety. The abuse may not have been physical, but It was emotional and psychological and it took its toll on me. I lost interest in myself with a lot of weight gain. I was constantly depressed. I began to lose interest in my work; my creative spark was slowly ebbing away. It took my brother, Richard, to draw my attention to what I had allowed happen to me.

'You are losing yourself,' he told me one day in 2001. 'You should do something before it is too late,' he advised.

My depressive state, which I felt I had managed to conceal successfully, had become noticeable.

Someone else saw beyond the tired smile I struggled to wear on my face. It was my 17-year-old son, Tijani. On my fiftieth birthday in Lagos in 2002, when asked what he wished for his mum, simply said:

'I just want her to be happy.'

The arguments my husband and I had never took place in the children's presence. Hearing those words from my son compelled me to make a serious effort to help myself. No one was going to do it for me. I needed to have my children know that I was happy and content. My happiness and my fulfilment did not, and could not, depend on someone else.

When talking about marriage, my mother and I often shared a joke about Igbo men called 'Mama and Papa Ngozi'. When an Igbo suitor is wooing you, he will promise you heaven and earth. He would promise a professional musician like me a studio, with all kinds of sophisticated musical equipment. However, two or three years down the line, he would begin to pester the woman to wind it down, especially if their marriage had produced a kid or two. Papa Ngozi, our typical Igbo man, may even call a family meeting because of his wife. He would do this to enforce his rights (ownership rights) and the privileges they confer, such as the right to order his wife around.

The family, mostly his relatives, would hand down a judgment along with an ultimatum: obey your husband or get out of his house. The woman may have contributed to building the house, but it is still his house.

Jokes apart though, this was far from being a stereotype. There are true stories told by women who have encountered these peculiar types of Igbo men. It did not apply to all. I must quickly add that the majority of Igbo men are wonderful husbands and fathers. Their families hold a place of pride in their hearts, and in their pockets. I am convinced that the average Igbo man is proud of his wife.

I think that knowing how my freedom and liberty of mind were important to me; my mother was not surprised when I brought home a Yoruba man. There was no resistance to the idea whatsoever. The subject never even came up for discussion. But at the end of the marriage, it became obvious that in seeking to protect my independence, I had gone ahead and married a Yoruba man, who surprisingly imbibed the 'Papa Ngozi' syndrome more than Igbo men of a similar disposition.

One day in 2003, right in the middle of a very unsure period of my marriage, my mother invited my husband to a meeting. She did not tell me the reason, just that she needed to speak with the two of us. We obliged, of course, but were unprepared for what she had to say. I should have known, though. Mrs Hope Onwenu, the DK Onwenu Family matriarch had finally had enough of my absentee husband and she told him so.

'You have left this young woman by herself twice,' she started and went on a tirade. 'You have not helped her. Yet, she has been faithful to you and taken care of your children and business. You are back now but nothing has changed. It is not fair.'

Sister paused, turned and looked at me, then returned her gaze to my husband and said to him, 'Whatever it is you want to do; you should go ahead and do it.'

What? I thought. Did my mother not know that she had just signed my divorce papers? Yet, I was proud of her. She was no longer willing to watch her daughter go through so much pain and sacrifice, without appreciation. Typical Hope Onwenu! She meant every word she said, and no one was in doubt.

But then, she added another scene to the play. My mother turned back to me and dropped a bomb – which was a fake one – but my husband did not know it. She accused me of marrying a Yoruba man against her advice. I looked at my mum with disbelief. We never had such a conversation, not even once. She actually got on famously with my husband, the whole family did. The die was cast though, and my husband left. He never spoke to my mum again till she passed away. He did not attend her funeral and sent no condolences either. My husband did speak to me once on the phone during the period.

Even after my mother's performance, the marriage did not quite end immediately. The breakup had stretched on for years. The marriage was revived only if my husband needed some help from me. I would become an enemy as soon as the help was rendered.

In 2005, we had sold our house in Opebi, Lagos and invested the money in my husband's construction business. I moved into a flat nearby. However, the issue over the completion of the house my husband had given me in exchange for our Opebi home came up. The building of the house had been delayed and we – my mother, my children and I – needed to move in, but everything had gone wrong. The supervising engineer was careless and had made some structural mistakes.

When I raised concerns, they were ignored. Then one day, my husband, quite unprovoked, verbally abused me in the presence of my step-daughter-in-law, my staff and his, calling me all sorts of names. This had never happened before and it was shocking to me. I took it all in and walked away. That day, we both knew that it was all over, truly.

For some reason, my husband had always wanted to be the one to decide if and when our marriage would break up. It was very important to him, and he did break us up a good number of times. But the final break was my decision, and he has never forgiven me for that. I should have allowed myself to be trampled upon for as long as he wanted. I should have fallen apart and been unable to cope. However, much to his chagrin, I kept getting up and raising our family by myself.

As I shared my trepidation in writing such a personal history with my children, given our policy of leaving the family out of the press, they insisted that I should simply tell my story, since it was my life anyway.

My marriage taught me several of life's lessons. For instance, I learnt that forgiveness is even more beneficial to the forgiver than the forgiven, for the catharsis that comes with it. I have tried to pass this on to my children.

It has not been easy trying to work off the effects of a silent father on his children's lives, but it has been remarkable what the good Lord has extracted from the situation. It has strengthened our children. Our sons know and insist that they must rely on God and themselves to succeed in life. The idea of using my name to get ahead would not be a very helpful strategy, nor is it one that I would encourage. Each person must own their name and fashion their path. To reap a good harvest, they must sow their own seeds and nurture them. The world would have to take my children on their own terms and not because of their famous mother. I am quite proud of them, and I respect their independence and sense of self-worth.

I have learned that people come into our lives for a reason and a season, and sometimes for no more. The important thing is to focus on that greater reason. I do believe that doing my best to help my husband survive the situations we had to contend with and that could have taken his life, was the reason God brought us together. While doing what I was meant to do, our relationship brought into the world two wonderful human beings, to whom being a mother has been a rare privilege. My children were born in love, and they have been raised in love as well – a lot of love.

When asked if they have any regrets in life, some often say that they do not, whereas they do. I have a few regrets, I admit, but not my marriage and family.

I can state with every molecule of my being that my children are my greatest achievements. I am fulfiled as a person because of them, and I shudder to think about what my life would have been like without them. Through this situation, I have come to appreciate the beauty of The Serenity Prayer:

God, grant me the serenity to accept the things I cannot change, the courage to change the things I can and the wisdom to know the difference.

All My Children

Tijani Charles

On 9 November 1985, a fine Saturday morning, my child arrived by cesarean section. I had 'placenta previa', a condition where the placenta lies low in the uterus and partially or completely covers the cervix. During labour, the placenta may separate from the uterine wall as the cervix begins to dilate. The doctors did not want to take any chances. Therefore, I had to have a caesarian section. When he was delivered, I saw the placenta wound around the baby's neck. This could have suffocated him if I had tried a natural delivery. With epidural anaesthesia, I was fully awake and could see and hear everything happening around me. 'All his fingers and toes are complete,' my friend, Judith Higher, a photographer who came to record the birth, whispered into my ears. Then, Tijani was put into my arms; a perfect little thing.

Is this really happening? I thought to myself.

There I was, holding this being whom I had spoken to for nine months, but whom I was meeting for the first time. He was just looking into my eyes and crying. At the time my first son came, I was 33 years old and not entirely sure I wanted to have children. To stop my mother from constantly harassing me about my ticking biological clock, I told her that my doctor said that I may not be able to have children, and so it would not be fair to inflict that on an innocent husband. It was a lie. I am not sure that she believed me, but she did ease up on the pressure for a while.

Here I was, transformed from the one who was unsure about childbearing to this new mother at Portland Hospital, London, holding a baby boy, a spitting image of his father. It was such a surreal moment. As my husband popped a bottle of champagne for my mother and aunt who had arrived from Lagos the day before, a nurse whispered to me that my son had been born in the same hospital as Prince Harry. A few days later, the same doctor who had circumcised Prince Harry, performed the same function on my son.

There is a way motherhood changes a woman. It teaches patience, which I began to learn even before I left the hospital. My personality usually did not suffer fools gladly and like my mother, I had little patience with people who could not keep up with my fast-paced, get-it-at-first-attempt attitude to life. As we prepared to leave the hospital, I eagerly changed his diapers and dressed him up for our first outing. I was still learning to do the breastfeeding and diaper thing, having been a mother for only three days and still recovering from surgery. I was excited and looked forward to being in my own accommodation. We had rented a house at Golders Green, London, and I had plenty of help: my mother, though ill from Greaves' disease, my aunt Dorothy and her daughter Chinyelu, as well as a housekeeper.

As I put on the baby's clothes, I heard a slight thud at his buttocks. Then, a slightly pungent smell followed. My baby had 'pooed' all over his newly changed diaper and clothes. I had to wash, clean and dress him up all over again. That day, I learned patience. I continue to learn it every day on this motherhood journey that never comes to an end.

Our son was christened Tijani Charles Obianozie. Obianozie came from my mother. It means that 'My household is now in order'.

As a new mother, there were changes taking place in my body.

Emotional and mental adjustments were all happening at the same time. Yet, it was a wondrous event and a huge milestone. A whole human being had been entrusted into my inexperienced hands, into my care. My life was no longer mine to do as I wished. TC owned me and not the other way around. I stayed awake to watch him sleep and he would not sleep unless he was lying on my chest. I ensured that he had everything that he needed and more. TC and I spent six months in London before returning to Nigeria in 1986. While there, I completed work on my album *One Love*, one of my most successful yet. It seemed that motherhood had also rejuvenated me.

Tijani was an extraordinary child, handsome, thoughtful and precocious. He was a carbon copy of his father and my Yoruba in-laws would say '*O ti poju*', meaning 'it is too much'. The only things he got from me were my skinny legs.

TC developed an early interest in drawing, mainly cartoon characters, having watched a lot of those, which I had to watch with him. He was an only child for the first four years of his life but he found many friends to fill in the gap. One of them was a little girl in Okupe Estate, Maryland, Lagos where we lived. Her name was Ibiere, but we fondly called her IB. We often bumped into her on our daily walks in the neighbourhood and they formed a friendship that lasted into adulthood. This continued until Tijani got another brother from another mother, Dixon Kanu (DK III), my brother's son.

Dixon Kanu III

In 1988, my brother Richard, desirous of having a male child, had his wish met when Dixon Kanu Onwenu III, was born. He intended to raise his child in Nigeria, so he asked me to do so on his behalf. I had no choice in the matter as that was my mother's heart's desire. Four years earlier, she had given Tijani the Igbo name of 'Obianozie', which attests to continuity. But DK lll was her true successor.

When she also asked me to raise DK III, there was no hesitation on my part. It would have been a fruitless exercise anyway. Richard was still residing in Cote d'Ivoire and DK's mother, Margareta, a lovely, gentle lady of Ivorian extraction, had agreed that I should raise her only child. She had not met me, but knew of me. I was touched by her vote of confidence.

The only condition I gave was to my brother. I asked him not to leave the child's upbringing and financial obligations entirely to me. He promised not to. Regrettably, he did not make good on his promise. From the moment DK III was handed over to me until he graduated from University, he was completely my responsibility.

It was a long trip for father and son the day the 18-month-old DK lll arrived. He was wet, hungry and cranky. He was in a strange land, surrounded by strange faces. Having done his job of bringing home an heir to the family name, my brother left the heirloom with my mum and I, to manage. We had to acclimatise the little boy to his new reality, while Richard took a well-deserved rest.

My mother took charge immediately. DK was bathed, changed and fed. His father could be seen moving around, so that was reassuring, but the boy would not sleep, no matter what we did. My mother and I took turns carrying him and singing him lullabies until, very tired, he fell asleep.

DK quickly latched on to me, which was good but also problematic, as he would not allow anyone else, not even my own son TC to come close. We all understood his need to monopolise my attention for the first three days but we had to break it. I belonged to all and we had to make that clear. When this was done, TC and DK became brothers, friends, and cousins at the same time. The relationship was so strong that my brother and I had to step in at times to ask for the inclusion of their younger brother, Abraham, in their games and hangouts. It was futile. They just did not consider him worthy of their company. He was too small, but he kept wanting to belong, unsurprisingly.

Raising DK lll was not an easy task. Apart from the huge financial responsibility, the hidden and perhaps the most difficult part, must not be neglected. For me, it was important not to lie to DK about who I was. I was an aunt who loved him with the love of a mother and raised him as such.

DK's mother had not been able to visit us in Lagos despite several invitations from me. When her son was three years old, we all went to Abidjan Cote d'Ivoire for a show and to see her. It was wonderful to watch mother and son reunite. After that, we lost touch again for twelve years, until an opportunity came in 2009. During DK's final year in the university, he had to travel to Cote d'Ivoire for a class project. We encouraged DK to look for his mother, and Richard provided all the mutual connections that he shared with Margareta. She was eventually found.

I cried tears of joy when the story of the reunion of mother and son was relayed to me. It was only then that I felt satisfied that I had done my job, and relatively well. DK had been an emotionally tasking child to raise, and I must add that my brother did warn me from the beginning. Understandably, and perhaps because of his separation from his birth mother, he was distant. DK was not physically demonstrable of emotions by nature and was not a great talker. It, therefore, took a long time to build a special relationship with him. But I did and it was one which my mother reinforced while she was alive. I began to school him in all things Onwenu, hoping that he would take up the responsibility and honour of being the head of the family.

My mother had a special place in her heart for her grandson. I believe that one of the things that helped prolong her years was the fact that the Onwenu heir apparent was growing up right in front of her, and she was making her own contributions with counselling, storytelling, special food, and nanny care. One of my mother's most memorable dishes was called Grandma's vegetable yam. This was a wonderful way to get the kids to eat vegetables. It had a variety of those, such as *ugu* (fluted pumpkin leaves), *kenkere* or *ewedu*, spinach and *ukpaka* (fermented oil bean seed). This dish was usually devoured in minutes with everybody asking for seconds. If you had leftovers, it tasted even better the next day.

Abraham Chukwuemelie

All my children are special gifts from God. Although I had wanted a second child, my husband had been away from Nigeria for about five years, and I had given up on the idea. I was 38 years old. Then he came back to the country in 1990 and Ibrahim was born the following year. He looked like my father, DK Onwenu. I had given my father an ultimatum to return. I said, 'This is your last chance because I am not having another after this.' Abraham was a child of my middle age, cute and adorable but not as pampered as Tijani.

Abrahim was a quiet baby. He did not cry much. He was not as demanding of my attention as there were many people in the house, but he could smell me from afar. I guess it was the breast milk that he was drawn to. When he was three years old, he held my head to his chest, patted it and called me 'baby'.

That was how I became the proud mother of three young men: Tijani Charles (TC), DK III and Abraham.

Considering our situation, my devotion to my role as an effective mother was non-negotiable. It was also one for which no sacrifice was too much. I owed my children and wards a safe and loving home, where their rights as people were respected. They were more than adequately provided for and given access to the best education and social amenities as were necessary for their upbringing. My children were raised as caring men who appreciated and respected everyone, both male and female.

One of the best decisions the boys made was to return to Nigeria after their studies abroad. They took after their mother in that. Living together again, and having more time to talk face to face has been immensely helpful to me, on my second leg of the mothering business. Living with them as adults, also aroused questions about stories long forgotten, questions not easily answered, but answered over and over again. They needed to know exactly what happened between their dad and I.

In our family, everyone is free to ask questions and expect straight answers. My children could rely on this. They know that I have too much respect for them to lie. Trust had been built up from the time they were born; I worked very hard never to break that trust. The children decided to reaffirm a decision they had taken individually, which was to forgive their father and move on. It was not difficult, however, to share with them what I knew about him when he was a compassionate, caring and generous man who empathised with others and took on their needs as though they were his.

I had often said to them that in moving on with their lives, they must not forget to reach out to other young people who may have had to deal with abandonment issues. I have seen them do that. It is something that pushes their determination to succeed. Let me share a story that captures this, and how Abraham gained his university admission.

One day in 2008, Abraham came home very upset about something his father said to him on his way to school. It was his last year at Dowen College in Victoria Island, Lagos.

'Do not imagine that your mother will be able to send you to school in America, she is barely managing with your brother,' his father had said.

Even if this were true, why taunt our son with it? What joy did it give him? By the way, was it not his responsibility to pay his children's school fees? I rose in righteous anger. In all my life, a few things had upset me as much as this one.

'Get ready, you are going to college in America next year,' I told Abraham.

When he left my room, I went down on my knees and cried. Then I prayed. I made a deal with God and I handed over all my children to Him, again.

Three months later, there was a knock on my door. It was my Abraham and he burst into my room, waving a printed email in his hand. There was no way I could have expected him to utter the next words I heard.

'I got in, mum, I got in.' His face shone as he spoke.

The University of Pittsburgh, top on our list, had accepted him into the freshman class of 2009 based on his application and SAT scores. They did not wait for the result of his West African School Certificate examination and this had been a late college application.

Abraham and his brother Tijani have both finished graduate school and are working for themselves. DK III has finished university and is doing very well for himself as well.

Blood is Thicker Than Water

W hen I began this memoir, I planned to write solely about my experiences. Yet, I found trends in my life that I had not imagined were there. A lot of it is centred around relationships and how they affected me. My life had so many other people's lives intertwined with it. By telling my story, I also tell theirs to some extent. Some of the names have been mentioned in different parts of this book, and some will be mentioned here.

Azunna Ononye, nee Obionwu

'*Nwa Ogalanya tijie odu, ewelu odu kwuo ugwo.*' When the child of a rich man breaks an elephant tusk (or an expensive item), it is simply replaced with another. This was Mama Nnukwu's praise name for Azunna.

Azunna was the product of my mother's first marriage to Davis Obionwu, who died eight days before his daughter and only child was born. The name Azunna means 'born after her father's departure'. My mother refused to remain in her deceased husband's family, either in celibacy or married to her brother-in-law as Igbo tradition allowed. She chose to leave with Azunna, who was only a few weeks old. Sister went back to her parent's home on the other side of Obosi town.

The Obionwu family retaliated by forcefully taking the child away from her after she was weaned. Azunna grew up with her paternal grandmother in an environment of great wealth. She was indulged and spoilt to no end. Her aunts, afraid that she could become irreversibly so, conspired to move her away from her doting grandmother's care and into her uncle's. She stayed there until she was 17 years old and returned to us voluntarily. Azunna's story only emerged bit by bit as we grew older. At no point were we made to feel that she was any less a sibling because we only shared the same mother, and not the same father. It just never mattered.

Being the eldest child in the family, Azunna had a very special place in it. After my mother, she was next in the hierarchy. She was disciplined and taught by example. She was physically dark and lovely, very much like Sister, from whom she inherited her impeccable dress sense. When I had my first period, it was Azunna who explained the facts of life to me. I guess by the time it was my turn; my mother was tired of explaining the stuff, so she got Azunna to take over. She was also given the power to discipline us and she did so with a fair hand.

My eldest sister's education stopped at secondary school. She chose to get married during the Biafran War, to the love of her life, Mr Chris Ononye. They were blessed with a surviving child, Chinyelu, her husband, and many grandchildren.

Azunna told the poignant story of how our maternal grandmother, Mama Nnukwu saw her as a child of three in the care of a nanny and grabbed her. Mama Nnukwu had attended a meeting near the Obionwu part of the town. The bewildered nanny ran after them, pleading with everything in her to have Azunna back, as the Obionwus would 'kill' her if she returned home without the child.

My grandmother loved Azunna like her own. It may be fair to suggest that the circumstances of her birth, 'born behind her father' endeared her to Mama Nnukwu. But Margaret Nwokoye was also a wise and reasonable woman. If she had succeeded in kidnapping

Azunna, the Obionwus would have been back swiftly to claim her. The back and forth would have been unending and the child would have suffered more. She, therefore, decided to let go, and my mother had to do the same. How painful it must have been, how utterly empty my mum must have felt. She lost her young husband just a year after marriage, gave birth to their only child eight days later, and now had to let go of that child as well. She never spoke about the pain, except in passing, but the pain was there.

After leaving her husband's family, Sister had gone back to her teaching profession at Central School Obosi. Azunna would tag along like her shadow. Headmaster Ahamba had a problem on his hands: what to do with my mother's 'mini-me' to keep her out of the way. Mama Nnukwu suggested a solution and it was a brilliant one. Why not start a class for small children, where they could play and be engaged during school hours? For good measure, and as an added attraction, she volunteered to supply her *akara* balls to all the children every day. That was how the first kindergarten school in Obosi was founded. In fact, this special class was referred to as *Nta akala,* which means 'those that eat akara'. It was highly successful and nearby towns followed suit.

Mazi Chukwudum Richard Onwenu
a.k.a 'Omekannaya' (One who acts like his father)

Chukwudum Richard Onwenu was born in 1944. He was the first child of my parents. Growing up as the only son of Honorable DK Onwenu meant that great things were expected of him, particularly of the scholastic kind. He was just 12 years old in 1956 when Papa died, but he had begun to feel the weight of the expectations planted on his small shoulders. He told many stories of how Papa would always compare him to William Aniche, a close family friend's son. William was a brilliant student but a few years older than Richard. Yet, Papa expected his only son to be a genius from the womb.

While growing up, I do not remember having a close relationship with my brother. Being seven years older and with two siblings in between, he was somewhat distant. As an only son in an Igbo family, he expectedly got more attention from our mother. He was given more pocket money than the rest of us and was better dressed than most of his peers. My brother was sociable and had many friends who usually filled the house with good cheer. Our home in Port Harcourt was always a beehive of activities with Richard at the centre of it all.

He was a renowned goalkeeper who attended St Augustine Grammar School Nkwerre, and Dennis Memorial Grammar School (DMGS) Onitsha, for higher school. He later had a teaching stint at Enitonia High School in Port Harcourt, in honour of our father, Hon. DK Onwenu, who was the school's principal at the time of his death in 1956. Richard was respected and admired, a promising scion of an illustrious family. We were all very proud of him.

Throughout our growing up years, Chukwudum as he was then known, was very protective of his sisters. His friends knew where the boundaries were with regards to us. The two junior ones, Ijeoma and I, were not even allowed to attend parties, certainly not the same ones he attended. Even the Students' Union parties in Obosi which were safe and provided a lot of fun, were off-limits. He was a very good enforcer. If he spotted you at such a gathering, he would stop whatever he was doing and chase you out. It was worse when he could not secure a female interest for himself; he took it out on us.

To be honest, I didn't quite like him growing up. I thought he was a tyrant.

And then, in 1980, having just returned from my studies in the United States, a sassy, opinionated, independent-minded feminist ready to take on the world, my brother who returned a year earlier, was most respectful and accommodating. He treated me like an equal. He encouraged me and was proud of my work as a reporter at the NTA. That meant a lot to me.

Dr Dibugwu Zoe Onwenu

My sister Dibugwunwanyi Zoe Onwenu was born in Aba, now Abia State in 1946. She started her primary school education at St Andrew's Anglican School Obosi in 1950, but had to transfer to another St Andrew's Anglican School at Obinetiti, Arondizuogu, when our father came back from his sojourn at Durham University, England.

Done with her elementary school education, Ogidi Girls Secondary School was her choice for O' Levels or the West African School Certificate programme. She easily scaled through the scholarship screening exercise and finished the programme as a scholarship student. In 1965, she passed out with distinction, and while trying to get a job in the United Bank of Africa (UBA) as a clerk, she ran into an American lady, Estelle, who eventually took her to the United States for the rest of her education.

While growing up, Zoe was my tutor. She taught me music and poetry. She made me recite poems and take up debates on topical issues to polish my speaking skills. She made it a habit with my brother to correct my English, whether written or spoken and introduced me to *The Sound of Music*, even before I saw the film. Zoe always admonished me to never tarnish the good name our father left behind. She always went on about preserving the DK Onwenu name.

In 1973, Dibby as she was sometimes known, returned to Nigeria having obtained a Masters degree in Economics from Harvard University. She worked at Mobil Plc for a year before leaving to take up a lectureship position at the University of Lagos in 1974. She remained there until 1988. Before calling it quits, she took a sabbatical leave in 1979 to study for a doctorate in Economics at the Smithsonian Institute of the University of Glasgow, Scotland.

Zoe and I had a lot in common but she was far more intelligent and much more beautiful, with great legs. She was also hardworking and tenacious, and would not quit midway but take things to their logical conclusion. Zoe was stubborn and often stuck to her convictions until a superior argument could be provided. My elder sister was a disciplinarian to the core. She would not brook disobedience.

Dibby was fond of apportioning roles and careers to every member of the family. One day, she reasoned that it would be nice to have a medical doctor among us and picked me to study for that role. Richard interrupted and asked why she could not take that one up herself. She was six years older than me, my brother reasoned, so we would have a medical doctor in the family sooner. Failing to come up with a counter-argument to my brother's rebuttal, the matter ended there and never came up again.

Zoe-Dibugwu was my hero and role model. With her meagre savings as a student, she financed the coming over to the United States of America of myself, Ijeoma and our cousin Ifeoma Ejindu. She loved Papa and took care of the family he left behind. She never got over his death.

Interestingly, with a name like Dibugwu, which means 'a husband is the crowning glory of a woman', Zoe-Dibugwu never got married and never had children of her own.

The last time I saw her was on 11 December 2004. She had been rushed to the hospital in Obosi a day earlier and nearly died on December 10, the same date that we had lost our father in 1956. I flew in from Lagos to see her. She was slipping in and out of consciousness as she lay on her hospital bed. When I walked into the room, my mother was at the foot of the bed, trying not to look so sorrowful. I began calling out my sister's praise names, what the Yoruba call *oriki*:

Ada Onwenu,
Ada DK,
Ada eji je mba,
Ada agba olu Nwanne ma nwanne,
Nwanne na anu ogu nwanne,
Ezigbo ada, Ada ukwu,
Ada ka ibeya, Ada Mazi,
Ada Izuogu na Iheme,
Ada aba olu.
Ada mara nma,
Ada onye ukwu,
Ada obi oma,
Ada Ogbufo

It brought her out of her unconscious state, but she kept slipping in and out of it. At every attempt I made to leave the room, she would protest with a muffled sound, and I would stay back. At the doctor's advice, we took her home, to my grandparent's compound, where she spent some of her childhood years. She was made comfortable and passed away on 12 December 2004.

'Papa, papa, papa,' were her last words.

Professor Ijeoma Onwenu-Otigbuo

Ijeoma is my immediate elder sister and one in whose hands I suffered the kind of 'oppression' that senior siblings dish out to their younger ones. There was the 'knock' on the head when no one was looking, and the 'stud' which was delivered to my limb to make me fall on my face when no seniors were at home. I suffered all that from Ijeoma.

Of all my siblings, my relationship with Ijeoma was the most difficult, perhaps because she was an immediate elder sister. The sibling rivalry was inevitable. It is called *otolu onye n'onye,* meaning one who is the immediate elder sibling. As she was closer to me in age than the others, we had life's experiences that were peculiar to us, such as the story of the BIG THREE – the singing group we formed with our cousin Ifeoma Ejindu, during the Nigeria-Biafra civil war in 1968. Ijeoma and I share a lot of interests, memories and perspectives on things as well.

Despite our inability to get along most of the time, our children are the closest of friends and cousins. They generally ignore us and would not be drawn into our on and off relationship. Perhaps we had done a better job in raising them than we did in relating to each other.

When we do get along, however, we thoroughly enjoy each other's company. My sister Ijeoma is funny and fun to be with. She is gregarious and entertaining; a perfect host who made sure that you felt welcomed and pampered in her home. Being closer in age, we shared a lot of interests, memories and perspectives.

Growing up, there was no doubt in my mind that Ijeoma and brother Richard were my mother's favourites. She bent over backwards for them and was perhaps more protective of the two than she was of the rest of us. I did not mind at all; I had my Papa's love to a degree that was astonishing. Surely I could afford not to have that special treatment from my mum who really saw me as a representative of my father. Ijeoma often calls me *'Nwunye Papa'* – Papa's wife.

There are so many anecdotes and stories about Ijeoma that if I should write all of them, they would take up a whole book. I will share just one more here.

Running Away From Home

Most children dream of running away from home at some point in search of freedom to do whatever they want, or as a punishment to their parents who would become anxious for their safety, and therefore spend time and effort searching for them.

They would often threaten to do so to blackmail their parents to ease up on punishing them for a misdeed.

In my family, if you threatened my mother with talk of running away, she would ask you to do so immediately, and if there was something she could do to help. That was vintage Hope Onwenu. She would call your bluff anytime. I guess she knew deep down that it was all blackmail.

But there was once my sister Ijeoma and I actually ran away.

This is how it happened...

I cannot quite remember what the offence was; we probably came home later than the curfew at 6 p.m and our 'knotted grass' trick failed to save us.

Behind our house at 1 Degema Street, is a place we called the backyard. It was an empty patch behind each building where you grew a garden or did chores like washing and drying clothes. There was a myth about the tall grass that grew there: If you were returning home late, past your curfew, you tied knots on three of the leaves and then walked away without looking back.

It sometimes worked, by chance I think, but not always as was the case on this occasion when we got into trouble. It was the Christmas period and we were grounded. The most painful part was that our holiday in Obosi with our beloved maternal grandparents was cancelled. This was the highlight of the year for us, something we always looked forward to.

Ijeoma and I considered that this was cruel and unusual punishment. We needed a break from Sister and we wanted to be with the usual crowd of friends in Obosi attending parties, 'Sunday Jump', we called them. We also wanted to experience semi-rural life with our Uncle Njio, who was ready to spoil us at the drop of a hat. How could Sister be so mean?

Something had to give, we thought. Consequently, we plotted our escape, very quietly. We needed big brother's connivance and so we did chores for him for three days. We also sold bottles and tin cans for recycling, and raised a bit of money for transport. But it was not enough.

Enter Peter Ajagu.

Peter worked as a transport dispatcher at the motor park. The Ajagus were close family friends, so we were safe. We managed to convince him to provide free seats for us on one of the buses plying the Port Harcourt-Onitsha route. The bus would have discharged us at the Idemili junction, about 3km from Obosi before proceeding to nearby Onitsha, but Peter Ajagu arranged for us to be dropped off at the gate of our maternal home. That way, he could be sure that we got there safely.

On D-day, we got up early, did all our chores and then some. Sister was pleasantly surprised and with a smile which said 'Okay, the punishment has sobered them up', set out for a meeting at St Peters Church. As soon as brother Richard gave the all clear, Ijeoma and I took off to the park where an already loaded bus with just two seats left was waiting for us. We departed for Obosi with bated breath.

We only felt out of reach when we turned into Obosi village and began to see the all familiar mud walls covered with ogbeji — dried palm branches, along the route. We breathed in that earthy smell of all things natural and with a slight harmattan in the air, wondered what adventures the visit would bring. The closer we got to our maternal home in Ire-Obosi, the more our excitement grew.

Great were the expectations of happy times- the sensation of being there during the Christmas season.

Word would quickly spread as to who was already there among our friends — Pearl Amobi and her cousins, the Iwekas – those in our age group, Onuorah Ibezue, the Justice Nkemena crew – Uju and Peter who were our mates, our cousin Ifeoma Ejindu as well. They were all there. We decided that we had taken the right decision. Our grandparents were delighted to have us and promised to deal with their daughter, our mother, should she come barging into Obosi to retrieve us. And barged in she did, the very next day.

Sister took one look at Papa Nnukwu's mien as her car drove in, and beat a fast retreat. Apparently, she had returned from her meeting and met a near-empty house. She knew something was up when Richard showed no sign of worry, even after she persistently asked for our whereabouts. Peter Ajagu then confirmed that he had seen us boarding an Obosi-bound vehicle. He assured her that we were safe, but Sister did not like the fact that her orders were flaunted. She came after us anyway.

With our mum back in Port Harcourt, we were then free to enjoy our holidays and we did, but some of us, far too much. With the fireworks, bangers, knockout and bisco made available by

Uncle Njio, my sister Ijeoma threw caution to the wind. She began 'terrorising' our grandparents by displaying them all over the place, throwing some onto the roof, particularly the kitchen, which was made of mud and thatch. My sister was having fun, protected by Uncle Njio, who was a rascal himself.

Finally, Mama Nnukwu had had enough of Ijeoma's shenanigans. She called us to a meeting one morning after the usual family prayer. There was a new protocol in place, she warned. Before any of the grandchildren would come for Christmas holidays the following year, we would have to wait for a formal invitation. If you did not receive yours by the end of November, know that you are not welcome back, she added.

That was a huge mistake, going by my sister's response. 'Well, I know that this is about me – I shall not be expecting an invitation – so I might as well enjoy myself to the full'.

Much to Mama Nnukwu's chagrin, the fireworks continued.

But we were all back in Obosi the following Christmas.

Everyone had their usefulness and there were services that only they could provide. In between dancing and singing for my grandparents, I sold my boiled groundnuts in front of Mama Nnukwu's Provision Store. I like my groundnuts crunchy and not too soft. I cooked them that way, so that if I did not sell all, I ate the rest. I found out that many people liked crunchy boiled groundnuts too, so I made some pocket money from my little enterprise.

My sister took care of shaving Papa Nnukwu's hair and his pedicure. Even though my grandmother would wonder why her husband would allow the often-distracted Ijeoma to take a razor to his head, for some reason, he always did. But you often heard his screams of '*Nwata a egbuo nu* Nwokoye – *o gbue nu mu o*' meaning, 'This child has killed me', to which his wife would turn a deaf ear.

Very early in the morning, fresh palm wine – nmanya nkwu – sweet and slightly intoxicating would be brought in for my grandparents. Mama Nnukwu always had a bottle beside her bed lamp, which she enjoyed with her guests now and then. Ifeoma, Ijeoma and I would take turns drinking out of it, in secret. But in hindsight, I believe my grandmother knew. How could she not know? With the three of us having a go at the bottle several times during the day, who would not notice?

Occasionally, while Papa Nnukwu served this drink to a visitor, we gathered around him, hoping to be given a sip. The palm wine was served in a calabash cup. Papa Nnukwu said it tasted better that way. He would offer a cup to any of his son's wives who were present, Njio's wife, for example, and only then would we be given small sips.

When you are a wife in the family and such courtesy is extended to you by your father-in-law, tradition and respect demand that you kneel down to accept and drink from the cup. One day, my younger cousin Ngozi Ejindu, fancying herself as the in-house comedian asked: 'Papa Nnukwu, *o mu sekpulu ani wee nnuo ya?* Should I kneel while drinking?'

The replay came, followed by general laughter from all present.

'If you like, stand on your head, just drink and give me back my cup.'

Dr. Ijeoma Onwenu-Otigbuo is a Professor of Microbiology at Montgomery College Maryland, complete with many important publications and awards in her field. I admire her for her industry, tenacity and the ability to weather the storms of life. She also had a great sense of humour, with an ability to mimic people with near accuracy. This made me believe that she is the greatest actor Nigeria is yet to have. I hope that she would take up that challenge. Ijeoma raised five children, Kanu (Jnr), Ucheoma (late), Emeka, Ndidi and Chichi.

I had another sister born after me in 1955. She died in infancy. Her name was Nnenna.

My favourite dress a gift from big sister
Udeaku Obioha in 1971

My sister Dr Ijeoma Onwenu-Otigbuo in 1971

Àzunna. My Eldest Sister

Zoe - Dibugwu

Richard Onwenu

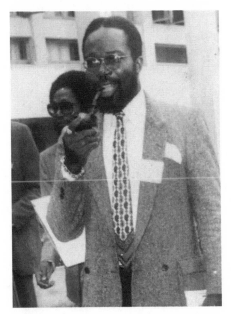

Richard Onwenu

Richard's Football Experience

My brother's football experience meant a lot to him and I always hoped for an opportunity to republish it for a much wider audience. I am happy to do so here.

RELIEVING MY EXPERIENCE AS A MEMBER OF THE EASTERN REGION OF NIGERIA SQUAD TO THE 1963 SIR SAMUEL MANUWA CUP FINALS
by Richard K. Onwenu

This submission is my first ever to any newspaper in the country, not only on the above subject matter, but on any other as well. I assume that many would wonder what motivated me into writing on a topic that perhaps belongs to the dusty recess of history, and what exactly I intend to achieve by so doing.

Before I state what the immediate propelling motive is, let me mention that since my re-entry into the country in 1994, I had had it in my mind to write a report of some sort about my experience as a former member of Sir Manuwa Cup.

The write-up would serve as a documentary testimony not only for myself, but for other members who may have inadvertently committed everything to memory, and now find that they either have difficulty in recalling certain details of the tournament or had only a blurred memory of them.

I have so bandied about the impact that I made as a member of the squad that my sister, Onyeka Onwenu, who is ever willing to listen, suggested that I make a report of it.

When Segun Odegbami paid a fleeting visit to the house last month, my sister made a formal introduction and I immediately seized the opportunity to inform him that I was once a good footballer in the sixties who played up to the level of the junior academicals. The subsequent discussions that ensued, after all the entreaties, was quite refreshing, especially when I knew that I was talking to somebody whose breath for soccer was deep and wide. In my discussion with Segun, I could not help but reel-off names like Dr. Johnny Egbonu (London Boy), Ernest Ufele, Luke Opara (Jazz Bukana) –all of whom subsequently played for Rangers International, Rtd. Air Commodore Ikazoboh (Member of the Northern Region Squad), Senator Empire Kanu, Mr. Akinwunmi (Pele), Asiodu, Oranye - all belonging to the Lagos Squad.

Segun was not disposed to talk for long because he had an engagement to attend to but what our encounter did was to fire me up to begin to consider more seriously about writing periodically on soccer. Having come to this decision, I figured that there could not be a better point to start than my experience at the Sir Manuwa Cup Tournament of 1963.

The Sir Manuwa Cup tournament was organised and held in memory of an illustrious son of Nigeria, Dr. Manuwa, a pre-eminent medical doctor who worked for the World Health Organisation before he died.

Before 1963, the best school teams from each of the four existing regions (North, West, East, and Midwest) plus the Capital, Lagos would assemble in Lagos to determine, through the tournament, the best team in the country. By 1963, this method of determining the champions was considered not the most appropriate, in the sense that the country was being denied the opportunity of discovering budding talents who might happen not to be attending any of the schools that emerged as the regional representatives. Therefore, regional representatives were henceforth determined by inviting players from as many schools as possible, in a particular region, to be coached and screened before the selection of the squad that would eventually represent a region. This task squarely rested on the shoulders of the regional coach. During my time, our regional coach was Late Dan Anyiam - once the Captain of the Nigerian National Team in the fifties.

I will digress a little at this point to touch on what it meant to be a member of the regional squad, because it meant a whole lot! As a member of the squad, one brought instant recognition, if not prestige to their family. It was such an honor to be photographed and mentioned on the pages of our newspapers. The recognition that came with the membership of the squad spilled-over to affect the squad member's secondary school's reputation, members of his family and friends. It also afforded him the ability to make new friends (be they male or female). The social standing of a squad member increased both inside and outside the confines of his school. The Squad member was treated with so much dignity and respect. Some of us were elevated a step further by getting invited to play for the Challenge Cup. I recall vividly that Bob Cole (our first-choice goalkeeper) and Dr. Johnny Egbonu made the Port Harcourt Red Devils Team for 1963. That team went on to win the Challenge Cup for that year against Plateau United. An encounter that ended in a 1-0 win in favour of Port Harcourt.

I have so far not stated the pecuniary rewards that went

to the football players. They received very little or nothing in terms of remunerations. At times allowances would be provided but this occurred at the discretion of the local football association. Footballers were expected to be active in other areas of endeavour through which they earned money for their subsistence. Playing football was considered a mere side attraction or a disposable hobby. Whoever attempted to accord it undeserved seriousness as it were, was considered extremely unserious and might be treated with contempt. As a matter of fact, playing too much football in my days was practically tantamount to heading towards becoming a wayward scholar. One would need to be an outstanding student to escape this stigma.

Back to the Sir Manuwa Squad selection process. As I mentioned earlier, it was the sole responsibility of the regional coach to screen and select the squad. Eighteen of us from different schools made the squad. I attended St. Augustine's Grammar School, Nkwerre, and three players were invited from my school.

It was only I that made the final squad as a substitute goal-tender to the first goal-tender Bob Cole (Tragedy). Although I subsequently played for a third division team in Britain, being a member of the regional squad defined my development as a footballer while in Nigeria. Other members of the Squad who had made a significant impact on the Nigerian football scene were Ernest Ufele, Luke Opara (Jazz Bukana) - all starred for Rangers International Football Club once they were done with school and were still very much relevant in the present Nigerian Football Scene - at least, at the Club level.

We took off from Enugu on the night of the 9th of August, 1963 at around 11 p.m. and arrived Ibadan at about 8 a.m.

on the 10th August. The Dick Tiger versus Gene Fullmer World MiddleWeight Championship fight had been slated for 8 p.m. the same day. We therefore had ample time to have both breakfast and lunch and had some leisure time inside Ibadan Town. The fight lasted for seven rounds with Gene Fullmer throwing in the towel just as the 8th round was about to commence.

Nigerians went wild with celebrations as Dick Tiger was announced the winner. We (the members of the Eastern Squad) were hilarious and felt that it was a positive sign that we were going to win and take back the Cup to the Eastern Region. Just as Ibadan was agog with the celebrations, it turned out that everything consumable was in terribly short supply in the entire Ibadan metropolis. Even drinking water could not be found anywhere in Ibadan. In view of this, we were compelled to leave for Lagos immediately after the fight. We got to Lagos at about 10.30 pm and checked into the King's College compound, where provisions had been made for us to camp. Our first match came up at 4 p.m. on the 12th of August, against the Northern Region. Dick Tiger was the guest of honour and the players were elated. We felt privileged to be presented to shake hands with the World Middleweight Champion who had just defended his title for the second time.

The North had a formidable team with a redoubtable Rtd. Air Commodore Anthony Ikazobor (former NFA Chairman) and a few others whose names I cannot readily recall. The match was a keenly contested one. Both teams played not only to win but to impress the spectators – more especially the Middleweight Champion of the world. At the final blast of the whistle, the Eastern Regional (my team) had edged out the Northern Regional team by two goals to one.

An interesting aspect of football at this level, at the time, was that the game plan was almost always never adhered to once the game started. There was a lot of chasing of the ball to the detriment of the formation that the Coach had prescribed on paper. The Lagos team overcame the Mid-Western team by a slim margin. The tournament ran on a knock-out basis and finally Eastern Region and Lagos emerged as the finalists. The duel between these two teams ended at four goals to one in favour of Lagos. They simply handed us a thumping loss that left us shell- shocked. We had taken a beating that did not, in the least, reflect the star-studded nature of our team.

We paraded stars like Ernest Ufele, Nwokedi (our Captain), Christian Eze, Bob Cole (Tragedy) (all from Zixton Grammar School, Ozubulu). We also had in our fold Onyenso (Government College, Afikpo), James Ezenwa (Government College, Owerri), Mushei (New Bethel College, Onitsha), Alex Onugha (Birabi Memorial Grammar School, Bori, Ogoni), Ozuah, Briggs (both from Trinity College, Oguta), and Luke Opara (Notre Dame, Abatete). The Lagos team, in turn, had stars like Empire Kanu (Senator Kanu), Akinwunmi (Pele from St. Finbarrs), Asiodu (Igbobi) and Oranye.

Let me quickly add that before the clash of these two teams, the players from one squad were hardly on speaking terms with those from the opposing one. We hardly exchanged greetings with ourselves although we were all sharing the same camp facilities. This would show how seriously we viewed the ultimate showdown between us. With hindsight this typically depicted what was missing in the tournament as a sport at this time.

Despite the fact that as the defending champions we

were mercilessly beaten, we received a warm welcome when we got back to the Eastern Region. When I arrived at Port Harcourt, I was treated to a hero's welcome and the warmth that permeated the atmosphere would make anyone think that we were the Cup winners. My parents' house became an instant bee-hive of friends and well-wishers. Some wanted to know why we did not emerge victorious at the tournament, while others just came to be told new stories about Lagos.

I took great pride in showing off my Sir Manuwa Cup Tournament outfit. And in my very first match at St. Augustine's Grammar School Nkwerre, it was time to advertise my sizzling soccer outfit which was beyond the reach of the rest of the school players who were not fortunate to make the squad. I was doubly blessed by gifts from Prince Arthur Eze who was my boy at school. Arthur handed me about five sets of football jerseys which his late uncle (Dr. Walter Eze of Toronto Hospital, Onitsha), had brought back after his sojourn at McGill University, Canada. So, as a goaltender, I was extremely flamboyant and at the risk of sounding immodest, I believe I was a good one too. My goal-tending name was "Shehu Usman."

When I arrived at Dennis Memorial Grammar School (DMGS) for my Higher School Certificate programme, my entry was heralded even before I could kick a ball. The news of my arrival spread like bush fire in the harmattan season. It was as though all the soccer inadequacies at DMGS had been corrected by my presence. It is best, perhaps, to let the appraisal or magnitude of my contribution be told by others. I will let D.M.G.S. old boys who recall my stay make the assessment themselves. But I must not hesitate to say that I introduced a lot of glamour and showmanship into goal-keeping while I was there. All of which was enhanced as a result of making the Sir Manuwa Cup Squad, of Eastern Nigeria.

I grew in poise and self-confidence whenever I was at the goal post. When I got invited a second time in 1964 for the Sir Manuwa Cup Squad selection, I turned it down in the belief that my books deserved more attention and that there was very little to be gained in devoting time and energy towards soccer adventures. What I gained from making the squad went beyond being photographed and mentioned in the newspapers. Each member of the squad received the sum of £200 every four days. That was a lot of money for most of us, especially when weighed against my miserly college stipend which was a paltry one pound and ten shillings per term. With the savings that I made, I was able to buy my first Parker pen with which I wrote my West African School Certificate Examinations in 1963. I also bought presents for my mother, sisters, and other relations.

The joy that I received from being part of this tournament was indelible. I still relish that small chance to distinguish myself and by the same token, the prestige of my family and school. The monetary reward was quite secondary at this time of the country's soccer evolutionary process because it was not uncommon for a player's photograph or name not to ever feature on the pages of any of our dailies throughout his playing career.

My only regret to date is that apart from Rtd. Air Commodore Anthony Ikhazobor and Mr. Alex Onugha (resident at Obosi), I had not been opportuned to meet any of the other members of the 1963 Sir Manuwa Cup Tournament. God willing, I hope this will soon come to pass.

With the boys at the National Assembly - on a holiday trip to Abuja

The graduation of my nephew , DK Onwenu 111 from University

The boys - Abraham, TC and I

With my sister Ijeoma and our children in 2002 my late niece Ucheoma stands
right behind me.

With TC, DK 111 and Abraham at his Art Exhibition in 2019

Ma Hope Nnenna Kawa - Onwenu.
Richard's daughter

PART VII

Politics

The Bumpy Road of Politics

The way and manner in which my father passed away left a sour
taste in my mother's mouth. As far as she was concerned,
politics was to blame. Ever since, she looked upon it as a
profession reserved, not for noble people, but for gladiators. The
Onwenu family believed that whatever the Ozis did towards Papa's
untimely death, they did not do alone. The popular feeling in our
home was that some very influential people who had become alarmed
at my father's meteoric rise in politics, may have found the hardened
jealousy of the Ozis as an opportunity to cut down Papa's life.

According to my mum, Arondizuogu people asked for her
permission to retaliate but she rejected the idea and instead, handed
everything over to the One to whom vengeance belonged – God.
That is how my father would have wanted it, and most importantly,
what Christianity preaches.

Sister's abhorrence for all things political made sense. Taking
our cue from her, no child of my father's had the stomach for the
Nigerian brand of deadly politics. Certainly not me, or so I thought.

All my siblings – Azunna, Richard, Zoe and Ijeoma – turned out to
be great teachers. But not me. I had no patience – a crucial attribute
if one were to be effective in the profession. If I were not inclined to
politics and did not possess the temperament of a teacher, what then
of my father did I inherit? As I tried to figure this out, it occurred to

me that if I could excel in whatever I did, my work would still bring honour to my dad.

I continued with my indifference to Nigerian politics for over 20 years. I even convinced myself that I was not interested. Yet, as a social commentator and critic, I was politically engaged.

As the years went by, I became increasingly dissatisfied with the degree of help I could render to those who were dependent on it. I thought about the ones who had no voice and no power. I felt the need to expand my platform of operation, as it was impossible to change or contribute positively to a situation if you kept standing outside of it.

One day, just months before my 50th birthday, I had an idea. Why not run for the Chairmanship of my local government Ideato North in Imo State? The idea seemed to drop into my head from nowhere, but it made sense. The local government is the closest to the people I wanted to help, those my father loved, in the place where he is buried. I could give them the best of me, by being responsible, responsive, innovative and creative in handling matters at the local government level.

But how do I convince my mum, who is diametrically opposed to politics? What about my husband, would he allow me to take up a political office? Would his ego be threatened by having as his wife, a Chairman of a local government?

I had a feeling that if I shared my interest in Nigerian politics, my mum would wash my mouth with soap. I took the chance anyway, and her response, surprisingly, was positive. And so was my husband's.

Many wondered why I chose to run for political office at the most local level, with all my qualifications. And I asked, 'Why not?' Apart from the fact that all politics is local, I reasoned that if we got our policies right by making them sensitive to the needs at that level, then perhaps we would also get it right at the State and Federal levels.

Good local government is the foundation of our success as a nation. We, therefore, have to engage politically at the grassroots level. I wanted to be a part of that process.

For the eight years that I spent pursuing this dream, I got to know my people better, and in the process, myself. I became acutely aware of their needs and challenges. I had to be their voice on issues of development and the provision of amenities. On one particular occasion, I had the opportunity to confront the Minister for Works on television and challenged him about the deplorable state of Federal roads in my Local Government Area. Attention was immediately drawn to the roads.

By the time the Presidential elections were held in 2015, we had secured the commitment of that Ministry and Sure-P (the programme that managed the Federal Government's savings from fuel subsidy removal), to build the very important road from which other minor roads in my area branched off.

Had President Goodluck Jonathan been allowed to continue for a second term in office – and I believe the outcome of the election could have been legally challenged given the unlawful use of multitudes of underaged voters in Buhari's strongholds – the Orlu/Uga/Akokwa/Ndizuogu/Umunze/Okigwe federal road, would have been properly rehabilitated.

I was never the Local Government Chairman; had I been, I would have ensured that funds were judiciously used. My administration would have ensured the timely payment of teachers' salaries, and the repair of over 60% of the roads that fall under local jurisdiction.

We would have also created an investment-friendly environment as it used to be. Ideato North had been host to the automobile assemblage industry; palm produce export (NIPROC owned by Mazi LN Obioha) and Hercules Breweries owned by Raphael Obioha, amongst many others. But at least the local government had the first telephone exchange in the area.

I was told that Nigerian politics was a cesspool, and how dare I insert myself into the muddy waters that was local politics. I recall that Lagbaja, the famous Nigerian masked musician, made this comment at my 50th birthday celebration in 2002. But I had carefully thought about the problem before making my decision. I had the best intentions of serving my people and the timing was right for me. My children were grown up, and I was well established in my career. I had mapped out my financial stability through diversification and the creation of multiple streams of income.

To those who recommended that I run for more prestigious titles, I had this to say: It was not about prestige. It was about positively affecting the lives of everyday people who had been forgotten by their constituency heads.

Politics in Nigeria seems to be about money. Every four years when the politicians came around to ask for votes, the poor would provide them in exchange for money, thereby sentencing themselves to four more years of misery and grinding poverty. That is the prevailing practice in which community leaders and influencers had a stake. Even traditional rulers had to be settled. Usually, by the time the campaigns roll in, people are so hungry and can only think of how to meet their most pressing needs. Certainly, a politician who has had to buy votes would attempt to recoup his investment as soon as he is sworn into office.

Politics is the largest industry in Nigeria. For the majority, it is a succulent gravy train that guarantees a return on investment. There are people who are in it, not to serve but to feather their nest. They are the political mercenaries whose desperation for the returns of power can cause them to shed blood to achieve their aim.

Although my campaign did not try to bribe anyone, buy votes or throw about promises that we knew we could not redeem, we did have to call meetings with various groups and associations. When we did, we had to provide food, drinks and transport fares. Sometimes, we offered stipends for the poorest among our people to meet their personal expenses. It was essential to visit traditional rulers, community leaders and heads of town unions to acquaint them of my political programme. If you did not do this, it would be construed as a slight, which was a risk one could not take. You were not expected to go to any of these courtesy visits empty-handed.

My political campaigns for the two consecutive attempts I made were self-funded.

If you have not played politics at the Local Government level, you have not played politics. It is the rawest form of it and it comes with deceit, lies and treachery. I found that some of my closest campaign staff were eating with the enemy, my opponents. But in local politics, there can also be found kindness, love and shared values. I always had a local music group, *Igba,* to accompany me on the campaign trail. We sang and danced with their rhythmic drums, gongs and *ichaka,* the local calabash rattle. We shared food and drinks and spoke about our hopes and aspirations for the future.

For years after my return from the United States, I struggled to understand why poverty seemed to have become entrenched in our society. I found that there was a sense of entitlement to any assistance from those who were expected to offer it. It seemed many people did not want to learn to fish but wanted fish placed on their dining table at regular intervals. If the intermittent break between the handouts were too long, then you would be asked: 'What have you done for us recently?'

This has to change.

People often ask how I can combine various aspects of my artistic career with politics and more mundane responsibilities. I can say that it all comes quite naturally. For a given assignment, I may need to bring together two or more of those attributes to bear.

I have had to use my skills as a singer/songwriter in politics to connect better with constituents. My skills and experience as a journalist also gave me the ability to communicate with them, while some of my other activities, such as home management and entrepreneurship, gave me necessary managerial skills. My ability to succeed and thrive under challenging circumstances came in handy as well.

Interestingly, I quickly discovered that in politics, anything goes. You can lie, cheat, steal, blackmail, denigrate and assassinate the character of others, all in the name of politics. It is in fact, accepted as a natural fallout, and that even if offended by it, you had a duty to let it go.

When I made my decision to run for office at age 50, I had reached an internal resolution with my God as to how I would pursue the political dreams He gave me. A covenant was made and God has been faithful. After eight years of trying unsuccessfully in the political field, I went back to ask if I had heard from Him correctly; after all, I believed He had told me to go into it. I came to the realisation that He hadn't actually told me that I would succeed. However, my venture into local politics did open doors of opportunities for me.

The Fear Of Women

O f the three major ethnic groups in Nigeria, the Igbo come a dismal last in terms of the acceptance of the participation of women in politics. Yet, Igbo women are some of the most focused, hardworking and committed people in Nigeria. When appointed to high offices in the land, they have recorded the best performances yet. I am reminded of women like Ngozi Okonjo-Iweala, Dora Akunyili, Kema Chikwe, Oby Ezekwesili, Princess Stella Oduah, Chinwe Obaji, Joy Ugwu, Arunmah Oteh, and Chinelo Anohu-Amazu, to name a few.

What then is the source of this nervous fear of women, and the penchant to limit their participation in politics? These are people who have shown themselves to be as competent as their menfolk and who inherited the spirit of fearlessness from their ancestors. If we find the answer, I have no doubt it would give us a better understanding of why Ndigbo are willing to sacrifice all for that male child but not the female one. I am told things are improving for the better in this regard, but I assume, not fast enough.

A woman's place in Nigerian politics is largely decided by the men who would determine how much power they are willing to cede to women at any given time. These men are in charge of the party machinery. Power is intoxicating, and most people will not give it up without a battle. The men would gladly have women doing all the work; mobilising supporters for the Party programme, singing and dancing, standing in line for hours to do the voting and even defending the votes.

But as soon as the election is won, they share the spoils of office with perhaps a few crumbs for the women. We liken it to helping push a broken-down vehicle up the hill, which then leaves us behind with smoke in our faces once it starts-up again. This is, by and large, the lot of Nigerian women. I admit that the experience may differ in intensity from one group to the other.

As a woman in politics, one must be prepared for the barrage of sexual harassments and propositions everywhere one turns. There is no running away from it, so you might as well face it squarely when a man proposes sex, whether, in a transactional or non-transactional arrangement, it is either because he genuinely fancies you or he wants you as a trophy.

Some men are frightened of powerful women with brains and grit. In the light of that, they take it upon themselves to get you into the bedroom, where they think you should exclusively belong. After that, you are no longer a threat as they would have gained bragging rights which you can be sure they will use.

Imagine standing up to debate a serious matter of great importance, and you have slept with half of the men in the room. Of course, this is an exaggeration, but a woman's ability to pull her weight in political circles would be whittled down if she had slept her way to the top.

It is a long-held belief, at least within the Nigerian socio-political space, that only men are cut out for politics. To perpetuate such a myth and continue to keep women out, the men who are invariably in charge of party mechanisms do everything they can to

limit women's participation in the day-to-day running of the Party.
Meetings are called for late in the day and can go on till the early
morning hours, often in a hotel where supposedly, decent women
should not be seen. I would be at those crucial meetings, even if I
had to check-in and stay in the same hotel where they were held. I
would be there with my own people for protection. If women are
called prostitutes because of their gender and because they are in
politics, they should not be offended; rather they should see through
the obnoxious labelling and remain resolute to stake their claim to
power like everyone else. If you must date someone, do so because
you want to, but not for political or financial reward.

I have often wondered why political parties in Nigeria all have
Women Wings. They are redundant and ineffective in championing
the cause of those whom they represent. They are used as a rallying
point for keeping the women useful during campaigns, after which
they are forgotten.

Why can't we have women as chairmen, secretaries and treasurers
of political parties? A party that allows women to occupy such high
offices sets an example that says that it is willing to take women on as
equal partners in politics and development.

It can sometimes be irritating to hear women who are
accomplished, independent, and living lives of purpose, say 'I am not
a feminist' when in actuality, they are. They dissociate from feminism
out of fear of the negative connotations that have been dubiously
ascribed to that word. Men have led us to believe that feminism is
akin to aggression, extreme assertiveness, lack of femininity and a
desire to be a man. Nothing can be further from the truth.

I am a feminist because I am a woman who is blessed. I am
talented, hardworking and imbued with a strong sense of self - a
belief that I can contribute my quota to make the world a better place

I have the drive and focus to be successful in whatever I chose to do. I have the conviction, confidence and passion to succeed. I do not allow rejection to weigh me down. I love the person I was created to be, and I am grateful to God, Who made it so.

Being a woman does not make me the weaker sex. I do not have to apologise for my strength of character and my ability to rise from every fall. As mothers and nurturers, breadwinners and bread-bakers, we have the capacity to take on multiple roles.

Do I believe that a woman's place is in the home? Yes, I do. I also believe that her place is everywhere and anywhere she wants to be – at home, in the office, at the marketplace or on a public podium. Was Deborah not a judge and a warrior in the Bible? Did Queen Amina of the ancient city of Zazzau in north-west Nigeria not conquer territories for her people? God can and does use women for whatever role He chooses and when. Why should I allow myself to be restricted because society says so? Both I and my country would be the ultimate losers for it. Consider how much Nigeria has lost by limiting women to certain roles. Would this country not have benefitted if we had many more Okonjo Iwealas, Dora Akunyilis, Grace Alele-Williams, Mabel Seguns, and Chimamanda Adichies? Margaret Ekpos, Sambo Sawabas, Kuforiji Olubis, Mrs Ransome Kutis, Stella Okolis, to mention only a few. By our actions, we say to little girls that they cannot dream, that all they are good for is being used as sexual objects. They are abused physically, sexually, emotionally and in every other way. We traffic them into prostitution and slavery. Or we marry them off at 10 years old. What a shame!

Although women make up more than half of Nigeria's population, they are disproportionately represented among its poor and uneducated. It does not matter what part of the country you look at; women face immense social and political challenges. In south-eastern Nigeria, until 2016, when a judgement of the Supreme Court made it possible, women were excluded from family inheritance. In other words, a girl child had, until then, no share in her parent's estate, only the male children.

My mother, afraid that this custom would negatively impact me, ensured that I was not disenfranchised after her death. While she lived, she was in charge of the DK Onwenu Estate, and in the event of her death, everything was to go to my brother Richard, her only male child. She decided to sell, not give me, a piece of land near the family home in Obinetiti, so that if I had to leave the family, I would not go too far. This proximity would ensure that I could still take care of the maintenance of the main house. The piece of land sold to me was hers, not my fathers and though she would have preferred to have made it a gift, as a payback for all that God had used me to do in the Onwenu family, she preferred to sell it to me for a profit so that it does not breed a sense of envy against me.

As events eventually revealed, my mother's fears were not misplaced. My brother Richard asked me to leave the family house as soon as my mother passed away. He also confiscated three other pieces of land that I had purchased on my own with the false excuse that women are not allowed to own land. It is obvious that I would not have gone through such an ordeal if I were a man.

The National Centre For Women Development (NCWD)

Onye ndiro gbara gburugburu na-eche ndu ya nche mgbe nile.
A person surrounded by enemies guards their life at all times.
- Igbo proverb

This saying was often heard on Radio Biafra during the civil war. We were reminded of the need to be vigilant every minute of the day, as we were surrounded by 'enemies' – Nigerian troops. We also had to be alert to the fact that while we prayed for God's protection, we needed to pay every attention to self-preservation. This admonition remains indelible in my heart. It has proven to be a wise counsel in every situation that I have been tested.

A politician once told me that life could change quite drastically in a moment, with just a phone call. This was before my appointment to public service in 2013. The irony of it was that it was the same 'wise man' who made the phone call himself, in his capacity as Secretary to the Federal Government of Nigeria. It was Rt. Hon. Anyim Pius Anyim, who was the former President of the Senate. He called to inform me of my appointment as the Director-General of the National Centre for Women Development (NCWD), a parastatal under the supervision of the Ministry of Women Affairs.

It was only after that phone call that I remembered visiting the NCWD complex years ago, an edifice situated right opposite the headquarters of the Central Bank of Nigeria in Abuja. I cannot remember what prompted the visit, but I never heard anything more about the place until my appointment.

The National Centre for Women Development was founded in 1992 on the principle of providing the conditions for a better life for Nigerian women. As a public body, it emerged from the Better Life for Rural Women Campaign, a brainchild of the former First Lady, Dr Maryam Babangida. As most First Ladies are, she was heavily criticised for her fashion, but mostly for her audacity to have a vision and the courage to pursue it.

Our attitude towards First Ladies who aspire to carve out a niche for themselves using the strength of their position can be sometimes appalling. The public reaction is usually, 'How dare they aspire to distinguish themselves when they can just look good and enjoy their husband's position? What do they want to prove?'

It was a tall order emerging as a trendsetter for women during a military era, but Mrs Babangida gave Nigerian women and our issues potent visibility. She was keen on involving women in every aspect of the Nigerian social experience, and she did so with elegance. Maryam Babangida was a tall, dark beauty who had a great sense of style. She was blessed with a model's silhouette and possessed a combination of beauty and brains that is so compelling, and at the same time intimidating for insecure minds.

As it was popularly called, the Women Centre was set up as a national centre for excellence dedicated to the pursuit of gender equity through research, data bank development, training, documentation, advocacy, and women's empowerment. The Centre provides training in skills development and income generating activities. It facilitates the formulation of policies affecting women in all sectors and promotes international cooperation for the attainment of its objectives.

The Women Centre building was funded by donations from women, non-governmental organisations, and individuals across Nigeria. Thereafter It was designed to be self-funding and self-sustaining. The edifice was constructed by Julius Berger, the foremost construction company in Nigeria. It consists of several buildings – the administrative block of offices which also houses the Hall of Fame for eminent women, the 65-room Dora Akunyili Guest House, a 100-bed space hostel, a shopping mall, crèche, a 1000-person capacity multi-purpose hall with meeting rooms, training and demonstration rooms, as well as the Bola Ige ICT Training Centre.

I do not know how my name came up for this appointment. I do recall that at an event in Lagos in 2013, I met the First Lady, Dame Patience Jonathan and she inquired after my plans for the 'future'. I mentioned that I had heard rumours of an appointment as Director-General, Nigerian Television Authority (NTA). She then asked a vital question: 'So, if it is not NTA, you will not serve your country?'

'I go wherever the Lord sends me,' I answered.

It was the right answer because, a few months later, I was appointed Director-General, NCWD by the President of the Federal Republic of Nigeria, Dr Goodluck Jonathan.

I reported to work in Abuja ten days later. But I had begun to acquaint myself with the scope of my responsibilities at the Centre.

The Centre was a rundown facility which needed rehabilitation both in spirit and in structure. I needed to inject a refreshing sense of purpose in achieving the Centre's mission. I had the feeling that most Nigerian women, like me, were unaware of the Centre's existence or its purpose.

The NCWD when I took over, was a place with lax rules, corrupt practices and wholesale thievery. Employees came to work and left at their own discretion. Not much was getting done. There was a lack of commitment on the part of many members of staff.

I was a political appointee, not a career civil servant; therefore, I was received with scepticism. I was derided as a common musician who knew nothing about administration. To make matters worse, some thought that as an Igbo woman, I should not head an organisation which rightfully belonged to the Hausa/Fulani. I had to prove from the onset that I was not anti-North but pro-women.

One of the first things noticeable about the Management Board of the NCWD was that there were only two women Directors: the Director of Training and myself. There were perhaps two others, who served as Assistant Directors among twelve men. 80% of the Directors were from the northern part of the country, as well as 90% of the Deputy Directors.

Surprisingly, the male Directors saw nothing wrong with the fact that women were not allowed to run the affairs of an organisation set up for them. However, we were always an object of ridicule everywhere we went. It was embarrassing for me. Wherever we introduced ourselves, at large meetings or events, Nigerians sneered at our delegation, mostly populated by men.

These were the Director of Finance (DFA) and his deputy; the Director of Policy, Research and Statistics (DPRS) and his deputy; the Legal Adviser and his deputy; the Director of Human Resources (DHRM) and his deputy; the Head of Estate Management and his deputy, as well as the General Manager of the facilities (the guest house, hostel and multi-purpose hall). The Director of Medical Services and the Head of the Procurement Unit (HPU) were also men. The Acting Director-General who handed the office over to me was a man. He was also the Director of Estate Management.

He, it was, who took over from me when I was disengaged. I did not leave the situation the way I found it, though. By the time I left the NCWD, four more women were added to the Management Board. The ratio became 5:6, still in favour of the men but the lopsidedness had been significantly reduced. There was also a more national spread.

I sensed from my consultations with women across the country that there was disappointment at the nominal and ineffective existence of such a well-conceived idea as the National Center for Women Development. The parastatal had never really represented the ideas and principles that informed its creation. The onus was on my administration, therefore, to set the organisation on its proper course.

I realised this, even more, when I met with the First Lady, Dame Patience Jonathan after my appointment. She exhorted that I clean up the place and set it going on the right path. She was aware of the rot which had begun before she became First Lady, but she was confident that I could get the job done. Mrs Jonathan advised me to be steadfast and focused, no matter the criticisms and efforts to derail me. Opposition, she cautioned, was something that I should expect, but must not allow to dampen my zeal for progress.

The First Lady, Mrs Patience Jonathan, was a pillar of support for me and a huge source of encouragement throughout her stay in office. I am most grateful for that. But the extent and level of deterioration at the Women Centre was beyond belief and there were no funds to fix things. We were underfunded but with much expected of us.

The unease that greeted my appointment was derived from the fear of some 'powerful stakeholders' who had an interest in the Centre being badly managed. They had their proxies on the Management Board who reported back to them and protected those interests. When I set about closing the many wasteful areas through which the Centre was defrauded, they were not happy with me. But they were shocked at how quickly we transformed the place.

I have always believed that it was a good thing to be underestimated. It leaves one's doubters awestruck when God begins to unfold His agenda through one. My detractors had not looked into my background, or they would have found out that I had ample experiences under my belt. For instance, I had served as a Chairman of the Imo State Council of Arts and Culture in 2010, with an impressive record of achievements.

In 1996, I acquired a lease on a property on Isaac John Street, formerly known as Sea Gardens, a zoo in the middle of Ikeja, that housed alligators, birds, monkeys and such like. It was previously a thriving venture but had fallen on hard times. There were still cages filled with monkeys and birds, and a large alligator in a pond in the middle of a makeshift driveway when I took it over.

This decaying property was converted into a 300-people multi-purpose hall. I built my office at the back of the large hall and ran my business from there.

A little digging would have helped those who looked down on me as an undeserved recipient of the position of DG of the Women Centre. Throughout my career, I have never shied away from women's issues, whose advocacy found expression in both my music and my public interventions. I understood, however, that no achievements were enough to deter jealous and blind opposition.

A Culture of Indiscipline

Work at the Women Centre started at 9 a.m for most workers, except for the cleaners, security personnel and crèche attendants who had to start earlier. However, most staff - junior or senior – would saunter into their offices at 11 a.m or 12 noon, only to leave by 4 p.m or even earlier. They took days-off with no care about the terms of service or what normal procedure mandated. Some were known to stay away for long periods. I recall a particular middle-level officer who had travelled with me to Morocco and Senegal, but could not write a report on the meetings we attended. I wrote them for her. She also stayed away from work for half a year, all the while collecting her monthly salary. She was not the only one.

These absentee staffs were usually shielded by their Heads of Department, who themselves were often delinquent and took time off whenever it suited them. A senior staff member told me that I should not expect him to be at work before 11 a.m because his young son often kept him awake at night. So, he slept late in the mornings. I was expected to understand his predicament and accept this as normal behaviour. This staff worked in my office. I quickly removed him.

There was not much in terms of a security arrangement around the Centre when I arrived. People loitered around. I had no idea who was a lodger at our guesthouse or hostel and who was a visitor. There were rumours of a prostitution ring being operated right under our noses at the lodgings. I had no proof of this, but I took note of the many scantily clad ladies waiting on men with flashy cars around our premises every evening.

More worrisome was the fact that there seemed to be a general lack of accountability at the NCWD. At the handover meeting a few days after my assumption of duties, notes and documentations were scant, verbal explanations were not forthcoming either. Without real and actionable handover notes to take off with, I was left on my own to fumble and make mistakes. I insisted that minutes of management meetings be published to enable us follow through with decisions taken.

Asking too many questions as I did was considered too probing; insisting that staff do the work for which they were paid, was being high-handed. Whatever good I brought to the table was going to be resisted, and nothing I wanted to achieve was going to receive any support from some senior and middle-level staff.

Barely one month after I assumed duties, the wonderful and much-admired Senator Helen Esuene of Akwa Ibom State came to visit as part of her oversight function. She was Head of the Senate Committee on Women Affairs. It was found that the 250KVA power generating set for the whole complex had been cannibalised and sold off, just the night before. As I was receiving the Senators, many of whom were meeting me for the first time, I was also coordinating with our Legal Advisor and the police to have the suspects arrested and prosecuted.

I quietly led the Senators into my office and briefed them on the situation. I was grateful for the support, advice, and encouragement I received from them. By the time they left the Women Centre, I was convinced that they were on board with the kind of discipline and commitment that had begun to permeate the new administration.

Fortunately for me on the day of this visitation, there was no power outage in the Abuja Central Business District. The vandalisation of our main power generator may have been timed to disgrace me, to show that I was incapable of handling the affairs of the parastatal, but the plan failed woefully. It was, however, the first of many trials to come.

My conduct of a successful tenure as DG of the NCWD was non-negotiable. Failure was not an option for me.

The Agency was not well funded and most times, funds were late in coming in or they did not come at all. However, that was not going to stop me; neither was opposition, subtle or overt from the staff members. I had to develop creative ways to kick off the important programmes that we needed to carry out.

We suspected these acts of destruction and sabotage came mostly from the Estate Manager, headed by the former Acting DG who wanted his position back. I, therefore, took a leaf out of the Anyim Pius Anyim 'Book of Senate Presidency'. In 2002, he deftly retired a troublesome Arthur Nzeribe from the Senate by suspending him for the period. When it became clear that the Estate Manager would not give up his attempts to embarrass me at any given opportunity, I decided to remove him from his post as Head of Estate Management and took over his duties myself.

I began looking into the affairs of the department, and it was an eyesore. Not only did the staff not show up for work, but we also could not count on the cleanliness of the premises, and there were litanies of complaints about the non-provision of essential amenities such as light and water.

I took to conducting daily inspections to ensure that we cleaned up before and after every event. Even the toilets did not escape my attention. I also reassigned the incompetent General Manager of Facilities, who could never account for how much money we made. Things immediately took a turn for the better. The Women Centre came alive in physical beauty, cleanliness and orderliness. We stopped the loitering around by strangers who had no business being there and sacked the *suya* (roasted beef) and provision sellers who were not licensed.

Security

At the height of the Boko Haram bombing rampage in Abuja in 2014, we realised that we were vulnerable. We were in a very strategic location in the capital city of Nigeria. As a matter of priority, we began to secure the premises. By law, we were a hospitality outfit, among other things and were expected to make daily reports of our lodgers' names and details to the police. None of that was being done until I got there. We were also leaking funds from the non-reportage of income from our guest house and hostel. We had non-paying 'permanent guests' whose identities were not known. They often locked up the rooms and went away with the keys for weeks.

It turned out that one of them was a Malam who had been brought to the Centre to make incantations and bury live animals on the grounds. This individual suddenly left the Centre and never came back for his personal belongings. But not before he was reported to have threatened to unleash Boko Haram terrorists on us. The threat was overheard and reported by another lodger. We forwarded it to the police and investigations were made. Nothing came out of it, but we had done our job.

In order to secure the Centre, even more, we changed security providers and built barricades in front of the edifice to separate us from the main road. Our staff, consultants and resource persons were issued new identity cards and had to show them at the gate to be let in.

Another major challenge for us, however, was the lack of proper lighting in the whole complex. PHCN, the national power company, was not reliable and our generators were expensive to fuel, maintain and salvage when cannibalised. A service company and a hospitality outfit like ours could not function in Abuja without steady power supply. We decided to install solar energy to power the guest house, hostel and multi-purpose hall, as well as the internal driveways. The challenge, however, was that with all our beautiful ideas, we had no funds.

In the end, we pulled it off. We were able to do it, and within the timeframe we gave ourselves. A power company, Omatek, led by the late Florence Seriki was most helpful in this regard. She gave us a good discount and a staggered payment plan which made it possible to take immediate possession of that renewable energy source.

Our Achievements

The first success story we recorded was the joint hosting of a seminar on the issue of Gender Mainstreaming - raising the percentage of women in politics in Nigeria. We were invited by the National Orientation Agency (NOA) to partner with them on a highly topical issue engaging the minds of Nigerian policy influencers.

Calls for the reservation of 35% of all political appointments and elective offices for women began to gain ground. Some of us provocatively advocated for 50% of positions to be set aside for Nigerian women. And why not? This was followed by the first celebration of the International Day of the Girl Child on 11 October 2014. It was such a great success that it became institutionalised as a yearly event. It gave us the opportunity to reaffirm the agenda for the girl child.

From its establishment in 1992 until September 2013 when I joined, the Women Centre structures had not received any serious attention in terms of renovation, repairs or rehabilitation. The structures had stood the test of time, but they needed immediate attention. After decades of damage and neglect, they were showing signs of decay.

The Dora Akunyili Guest House, our cash cow, had a fire outbreak in 2009 and was not properly rehabilitated. Water seeped through the walls of the 65-room two-story building, emptying into the parking lot below. The hostel, the cheaper accommodation, had parts of it rendered uninhabitable due to malfunctions and issues of water leakages.

We began our renovation work by giving our multi-purpose hall an immediate lift. We resumed the installation of a new cooling system on which much money had been expended without results. The payment had not been completed and neither was the work. With our renewed efforts, payments were staggered and the new air-conditioning units became fully functional. That was a remarkable improvement for the 1,000-capacity hall and there was an upsurge in rentals.

The same thing happened with the completely renovated and re-furnished Dora Akunyili Guest House. It was reopened after an 18-month spell.

I had put everything in place to commence the main renovation work required at the hostel, before news of my disengagement came in February 2016. We had, however, cleaned it up and began to observe the best industry practices.

The shopping mall, strategically placed in the middle of Abuja, a lucrative space, had been shared among 'stakeholders'. Some people, like the erstwhile Estate Manager, had three shops allocated to himself and members of his family. The beneficiaries simply collected high rents from their tenants and paid nothing to the Centre. We sanitised that situation as well. The Centre improved its crèche, known to be well run, and raised its fees for the Central Bank Staff who were our main customers. They had it too cheap for far too long.

By my sixth month at the NCWD, I began to receive very positive comments about the dramatic changes there. The renovation work had begun to yield results with increased patronage. The grass was mowed, hedges were trimmed, and flowers bloomed. We cleared the pathways and disposed of our rubbish on time.

After the first tumultuous months, I began to notice changes in staff attitude at all levels. As we registered one successful execution after the other, they began to develop greater interest in their work. I took to briefing them regularly on important issues and seeking their input. I never took decisions on my own; everyone was always carried along. I ensured that the interests of the junior staff were well protected and their entitlements paid on time.

When our ad-hoc staff's salary, drawn from the Centre's revenue, was late in coming, I often stepped in with personal funds. The cleaners needed to be able to show up for work until their salaries were paid, and it is in knowing that we will take care of them in that regard that their commitment was strengthened. These advance payments were never recovered. I knew the risks but I took them anyway, and I will do it all over again given the same circumstances.

Low Salaries

One of the first things that struck me about the Nigerian Civil Service was how poorly our workers were paid. My salary after taxes was approximately N450,000 per month (about $1,730). There were, of course, other emoluments such as rent allowance which was N3m. That was rather low for Abuja. For a two-bedroom flat in Jabi, a decent and safe area, not far from the Central Business District, I paid N4m. For my second flat, a three-bedroom in the same area, I coughed up N6m.

There were reports that some of the richest homeowners in Abuja were civil servants, some of whom were secretaries or clerks who rose through the ranks. That may be true. However, and without excusing the corruption behind their material acquisitions, their actions might have stemmed from a desperate need to augment their miserly salaries.

You may then wonder how I coped with the poor remuneration my job offered. During my tenure, I virtually emptied my savings account. To augment my income, I also continued to work in the entertainment industry whenever possible. That was the only way I survived financially.

Barely two weeks after I left the NCWD, I began receiving calls from someone purporting to represent the Economic and Financial Crimes Commission (EFCC) Chairman, using his phone number.

He claimed that he had received petitions against me. When he threatened to arrest me if I did not provide money for the 'boys', I asked him to go ahead and make my day. Even if they had held a gun to my head, they would have had to shoot because I had no money to give anyone. In any case, I never succumb to blackmail. They left me alone. Not long afterwards, I read in the newspapers that the EFCC Chairman's number had been cloned.

Innovations

Apart from the physical renovations we made at the Women Centre, there were perhaps some non-tangible achievements which were equally important, if not more so. One of the outstanding and innovative trends we started was the celebration of the International Day of the Girl Child on October 11 of every year. This day was set aside to focus on the girl child and the challenges she is confronted with.

I had been very concerned about the daily reports in the media of rape, sexual and physical abuse, kidnapping, baby factories and the trafficking of young girls in Nigeria. There was sexual abuse at the Internally Displaced Persons' (IDP) camps around the country, where it was alleged that sex was being traded for food. Young girls were being taken advantage of by those who had been charged with their protection, and there was an alarming upsurge of teenage pregnancies within the camps.

There was also the deteriorating state of our educational system. Primary, secondary and tertiary institutions were derelict with little attention paid to the girl child's peculiar needs, especially in areas of security, sanitation and the provision of qualified teachers.

When my friend, Dr Akudo Anyanwu of Friends Africa, an NGO, suggested that our two Agencies organise a seminar in celebration of the Day of the Girl Child in 2014, I jumped at the idea. We went a step further by involving the Office of the First Lady of Nigeria as a co-convener giving us a wider scope, and we took advantage of the advice and direction which were of immense help.

As usual, we had no money, just hope and faith. However, we were determined not to fail. It had to be a world-class event that would serve as a rallying point for a new onslaught on critical issues surrounding the girl child.

We brought all these together in a two-day seminar titled, *Women and Girls Summit 2014: Reinforcing the Agenda for Girl Child Education.* In attendance, the Summit had the President of the Federal Republic of Nigeria, Dr Goodluck Ebele Jonathan (GCFR), as Special Guest. He was represented by the Minister for Women Affairs, Hajiya Zainab Maina (CON).

The Office of the First Lady was a co-convener of the Summit; thus Her Excellency Dr (Mrs) Patience Faka Jonathan was at the event, as well as the following people: The Senate President, David Mark, represented by Senator Helen Esuene, Chairman of the Senate Committee on Women Affairs; The Chief Justice of the Federation, Justice Maryam Aloma Muktar represented by Justice Mary Odili of the Supreme Court of Nigeria; the Ambassador of Finland; Representatives of Bill and Melinda Gates Foundation; family health organisations; UNESCO; the United Nations; Dr Grace Ongile of UN Women; the Deputy Head of Mission, United States Consulate Abuja, Mrs Maria Brewer; Hasfat Abiola, as well as Dr Uche Amazigo, retired from the World Health Organisation and very active with her NGO in school feeding programmes.

In attendance, we also had retired Judge Dr Vicky Okobi; former President of National Council for Women Societies Hajiya Ramatu Bala Usman; Hajiya Hajo Sani for the Ministry for Women Affairs; Hajiya Bola Shagaya; Rt. Hon. Anyim Pius Anyim, the SGF who was represented by the Permanent Secretary, Mrs. Binta Adamu Bello, and Barrister Danladi Kifasi.

There was the Ambassador of Finland, Ms. Pingo Suommela-Chowdhury; SA to Mr President on Women Affairs Dr Asmau Abdulkadir; SA to Mr. President on Social Development and Special Duties, Mrs Sara Pane; Hajiya Bilkisu Yusuf (now late); Dr Salma Abassi and other social activists, Mrs Bolade Akin- Kolapo, Mrs Funmi Roberts, Mrs Martha Omoekpen Alade, Dr Moji Odeku, Mrs Amy Oyekunle. Also present were the Project Manager of Exxon Mobil Nigeria Mrs Constance Nwokejiobi; TV personality Violet Arene; Chairman of the NCWD Board Mrs Becky Igwe and the other board members.

Between our two Agencies, Dr Akudo and I were quite confident that we could raise the amount needed for a worthy cause, such as the one we were undertaking. It turned out that we had been overly optimistic. We were able to get some branding but no one was prepared to dig deep into their pockets for us. We got some international Agencies to brand sections of the event and pay directly to vendors for publicity materials, food, water and such.

At an event in Lagos, I had approached Alhaji Aliko Dangote for assistance, also Femi Otedola and a few other tycoons in the oil industry. They made promises, but only Aliko Dangote came through with N2m. Stella Okoli of Emzor Pharmaceuticals, in her characteristic manner, threw in her support with N1m. There were also anonymous contributors whose donations amounted to N1.2m.

I recall that the Central Bank of Nigeria made a donation of N500,000 ($1,923). I sent a 'Thank You' note to the CBN Governor Mr Godwin Emefiele, despite my disappointment with the miserly amount of money the apex Nigerian bank gave us. When I met him in person, I was curious to know why he sent us such a paltry sum for the branding of our meeting hall, having received great publicity from the event.

'But you sent me a nice thank you letter,' he responded.

I replied that it was the polite thing to do, but added that I would make the donation public. He pleaded with me not to and promised to make amends at the next opportunity. He never did. The worst disappointments came from the Ministries of Health and Education. They had encouraged us to go ahead and use their names as co-sponsors of the event, claiming that they strongly identified with the ideals of the Summit. The Minister for Health had pledged N5m to secure the branding for the main auditorium but never paid up. Unbeknownst to us, the man was leaving the Ministry only weeks later to contest the gubernatorial election in his native Ebonyi State.

Once he left, no official there was willing to expend a millisecond to listen to stories related to the money he promised for the Summit. They had enjoyed the publicity and goodwill that came with associating with our winning idea. Nothing else mattered to them. I suspected that they were never serious about redeeming their pledge. Even worse was the case of the Minister for Education. He was a no-show and did not bother to send a representative to the event.

The communique that emanated from the first Women and Girl Child Summit was circulated to all participating agencies, groups and associations. It was made available to the offices of the President and the First Lady, as well as related Federal Ministries and Embassies.

One big takeaway for me from the event was the contributions and full participation of the girl child in it. Girls and boys from schools around Abuja held a pre-summit event where they came up with resolutions that met their expectations. It was heartening and enlightening to hear their concerns in their own words, some of which were dire and pressing.

In 2015, my administration held another successful Seminar. It has since become an annual event.

All in all, I must confess that my time at the Women Centre was not all work and no play. There was fun, enjoyment and camaraderie. There was fellowship and friendships that have endured. Gradually but surely, the senior cadre staff began warming up to me, and some decidedly worked and sacrificed their time and ideas to improve our performance. They knew that the commitment I demanded from them was not to punish anyone but to pool together our efforts towards a successful end. In taking their responsibilities in the Agency seriously, they achieved self-development as well.

As is customary in Government, some positions at the Women Centre were filled with experts who were seconded to us from other Ministries. It was usually a hit-or-miss with those. Sometimes they were good and sometimes, they were dreadful.

A Deputy Director of Accounts sent to us from the Auditor General's Office was sent back because of his rudeness and refusal to take instructions from my office. He would lean over with his hands on my table while talking to me, or perhaps to put it more correctly, while talking at me. Once, when he was asked to leave my office, he stood at the door staring at me with a smirk on his face. I had to instruct that he not be allowed into my office unaccompanied. This gentleman was of no value to the Women Centre, as he often came to work after 11 a.m and sometimes would not show up at all. Even with all the evidence of his misbehaviour, his original ministry insisted that I keep him. I refused to accept such an attitude from a deputy director or anyone for that matter, lest it became contagious.

The Office of the Auditor-General from whence he came insisted that he stay with us until his retirement in a few years. But we did not need his nuisance and insisted that he left. I was warned by my Director of Finance that I had incurred the wrath of 'some very powerful people' by sending him back. I believed him, but I also had to do my job.

We had a Legal Adviser from the Office of the Attorney General, whom we suspected had thrown away all our cases by not showing up in court and not keeping us informed about the court processes. We found out that he was advising the 'enemy' as well. One of the instances that tested and proved the staff's solidarity and unity was when he threw away one of our cases that we had no legal reason to lose. He simply did not show up in court and then kept us in the dark. We only found out that we lost the case when a Court bailiff arrived to remove our only functioning staff bus. Staff members trooped out to try and delay the action until we could raise the money to pay the court fine and retain our only bus. We did that successfully and to the credit of everyone present at work that day. This act of solidarity included drivers, cleaners, trainers, instructors, directors, managers and the DG.

After this wonderful show of support, I was convinced that we had truly turned the corner at the Women Centre. We not only had a real commitment to work; we had also acquired a genuine sense of belonging. The inclusiveness of our administration had united us under the common cause of promoting the wellbeing of Nigerian women. This was generally the case, but I was equally aware that the entrenched opposition was determined to trip me into an untimely and disgraceful exit by implicating me in some illegality. Or at the very least, prevent a successful tenure for me.

The Fatwa

As we worked hard to improve the functioning of the NCWD, and perhaps as a sign of desperation on the part of those who did not want us to succeed, word came that the erstwhile Estate Manager had used his position as a most senior officer to declare a Fatwa against me. It was alarming and most disturbing that at a time when Boko Haram was making incursions into Abuja and there was a general sense of insecurity, someone would exhibit such recklessness in calling for the killing of another person. The Management Board took the decision to make it public. We called a general meeting of the Staff to openly address the issue. In the end, the opposition cowered and could not justify their scheme to their supporters. The story fizzled out and work at the Centre continued at an even faster pace. They had energised me.

After this incident, there was greater cooperation amongst senior and middle-level staff. Suggestions, complaints, and even jokes were shared when appropriate; gifts too, especially books, health supplements and food which mostly came from me. There was great solidarity among the female members of the management. They knew that they had an advocate in me and that I would fight to protect their rights, which I did. I fought for their delayed promotions to take effect and ensured they were given their due respect. Some of them have remained my friends. I recall this with profound gratitude.

Surprisingly to me, some members of management staff, including the Director of Finance, with whom I did not always agree, turned out to be people of ideas. We shared a passion for programmes that would positively impact Nigerian women. We had a plan to set up a farm and a housing estate built by the owners - low and middle-income women. We planned to do this in conjunction with some NGOs and international Agencies, through a loan scheme with socially responsible banks.

This shared passion enabled us to pry back from the Ministry of Women Affairs the sum of N214m (about $823,077) designated for constituency projects in Alimosho LGA, Lagos State and in Abia State. It was 'mistakenly' misappropriated by the Ministry of Women Affairs.

The projects were not executed and the Ministry refused to return the funds. The Ministry of Finance, I must say, fought for us and decided to return the funds from the Ministry of Women Affairs Budget. Finally, on the last day of 2016, just before the stroke of midnight and after spending the entire New Year's Eve at the office of the Accountant General hunched over computers, the Director of Finance (DFA) and I were able to confirm that the money had been returned to the Centre's account for the projects. One of the projects, the construction of a Women Development Center at Alimosho, fell under the constituency of a Member of the House of Representatives, Hon. Femi Gbajabiamila. He worked closely with us to ensure that the funds were retrieved and injected back into the project. He later became the Speaker of the House of Representatives in 2019.

Disengagement from NCWD

Barely six weeks after the project funds were returned to us, I was disengaged as Director-General of the NCWD.

When it was time to leave, I expressed my preference to present my handover notes to the most senior Director active on the Board. It fell on the Director, Planning, Research and Statistics (DPRS). My choice was logical, since the perpetual 'Acting DG' was not an active member, having been replaced as the head of the Department of Estate Management. The DPRS, was a competent and knowledgeable officer, albeit a reluctant contributor and a non-supporter of mine. I was convinced, however, that he would rise to the occasion in my absence.

The conduct displayed by the erstwhile Estate Manager at my disengagement, however, was disgraceful. He organised a mob of some junior and middle-level staff, along with hired thugs to harass and embarrass me at the point of my leaving.

'She must carry her load on her head and leave the premises,' the crowd ordered.

This had happened before to some former DGs. I was leaving office on the ninth month after President Muhammadu Buhari assumed office, and the events leading to my disengagement became an issue of national discourse.

The Implication

The ugly plan that was hatched to humiliate and harm me was audacious, but perhaps, and thankfully so, it did not play out the way it was designed to by its dubious architects. Things might have escalated out of control and many people would have been hurt. I was alarmed that we had created an atmosphere in which certain groups in Nigeria felt that they could visit acts of violence on the person of the Director-General of a Federal Government Agency, and get away with it.

I thought it wise to document and protest what took place, hoping that the relevant Agencies would look into the situation at the Women Centre and stop future occurrences of such crass lawlessness. Of all the people we petitioned - the Ministry of Women Affairs, the Head of Service, Office of the Secretary to the Federal Government, the Inspector General of Police, as well as the Presidency - only the Head of Service took action. After its investigations, some of the Directors connected were queried.

In the course of the investigations, it was found out that the erstwhile Estate Manager who had now taken over as the Acting DG after me, did not tender any certificate or evidence of any kind that he attended the schools he claimed in his job application. He was therefore asked to produce them. That may have unsettled him. The lack of certifiable evidence of his educational qualifications had been an ongoing issue since a staff audit was ordered by the Centre's supervising Ministry and Governing Council in 2006. The Acting DG appeared untouchable, however. He was said to have some very powerful backers, but he was not alone in the questionable certificate situation. There were others whose educational and professional qualifications were adjudged dubious.

The results and recommendations of the panel charged with this audit were never implemented. Unfortunately, the Acting DG died of a suspected heart attack on his way back from an official assignment. May his soul rest in peace. With his death, the DPRS whom I had chosen initially, was confirmed as the Acting DG. He stayed in office for one year.

We had earlier managed to secure funding to complete a study of the Involvement of Women in Nigerian politics since 1999, the inception of the Fourth Republic. There is always a need for statistical data to be made available in the system, and for it to be accessible to all who may wish to use the materials from there. On the last occasion that I spoke with the DPRS turned Acting DG, months after taking over my office, he confessed that hitherto he did not fully appreciate the demands of the office. He had come to see everything in a different light. I chuckled, remembering his total lack of cooperation and support for me. I thought that he would adopt a more supportive attitude if he had it to do all over again. I wished him well.

In early 2018, a substantive Director-General was appointed and the DPRS went back to his job. He retired shortly after. The Director of Finance was moved to the Ministry of Women Affairs, where he served as the Deputy to the DFA.

News of my coming disengagement had been made available to me by two people on two occasions. One of them, a Member of the House of Representatives, had promised to help take my name off the Disengagement List.

With the Center's DFA by his side, nodding in agreement, the House Member proceeded to present me with a bottle of perfume. I accepted the gift – it was the polite thing to do. I noticed that this unusual present had been tampered with. The seals on the package and the bottle had been broken. Nonetheless, I opened it and sprayed a bit of the heady scent on my wrist and thanked the bearer. He still did not get his request of influencing the award of the contract for his constituency projects as I was determined that in the awarding of contracts, we went by the book and did not bend the rules.

In any case, as I explained to this person that I was not even on the Tender's Board. My role was to ensure that due process was followed. I was being removed because I was appointed by the previous Government and considered an outsider who was shaking things up quite a bit. It did not matter that I was doing a decent job. The way I saw it, I was giving my all to the office, so much so that my health was beginning to suffer. I was underpaid, unappreciated and not supported by my supervising Ministry.

Why would I want to pay anyone to keep a job like that? I was happy to let the chips fall where they may, and I said so to anyone who cared to ask. The chips did come falling, not long after the perfume presentation. I did nothing to aid the removal of my name from the Disengagement List. I lobbied no one. I chose to stay focused on the job till the very end.

My Freedom

On Friday, 14 February 2016, I went to the Abuja Airport to catch a flight to Asaba, and from there to Nnewi by road. I had a function there the following day. After waiting for hours, the flight was cancelled. I booked another to Enugu, further away from my final destination. However, as I could not reach my pick-up to inform them of my change in travel plans, I decided to cancel the trip altogether.

I headed back to the office to get more work done. No sooner had I sat down on my desk than a bee buzzed in.

This was around 4 p.m. Suddenly, there were many more and soon the entire office was swarming with bees.

I quickly ran out and called the attention of my secretary who brought in some insecticide and sprayed the room. The bees had been attracted to an opening in the wall behind a small refrigerator where a sticky substance had been smeared. My office security locks had been changed a few times, but someone seemed to be able to get in and out at will.

My safe was broken into, but there was no money in it to be stolen. I spent the entire weekend in a state of disquiet. I could not put my finger on what was wrong, but definitely, something was. There was a sense of foreboding which I could not shake off, no matter how hard I tried.

On my way to the office on Monday, the newspaper headlines

revealed the source of my agitation. There was an announcement of a disengagement exercise, but no names were mentioned. I quietly prepared for what I knew was coming. I had conducted myself in office as if I expected to leave any day. Nothing was left undone that should have been done. I quietened my spirit and thanked God for His protection and the courage He furnished me to lead such a tasking Agency. I settled down for work, starting with the first management meeting of the week.

I noticed at the meeting that the DFA (Director of Finance) was absent. His Department had a report to present. He sauntered in halfway through, with the excuse that he had gone to the Office of the Accountant General to process some files. I also noticed that he was unusually pleased with himself, and gave the cold-faced DPRS a very warm greeting. As they whispered in low tones, I jokingly asked the DPRS why he gave such a special greeting to a latecomer, especially as he was not wearing his 'Maharaji' headdress.

The joke had a bit of history to it. Months earlier the NCWD had celebrated the 'Week of Ending Violence Against Women' in which we organised a walk around our expansive premises, in a candlelight procession. Our guests were the head of UN Women, Dr Grace Ongile and Mrs Bisi Fayemi, a technocrat of repute and wife of a two-time Governor of Ekiti State. Everyone was mandated to wear something orange, the colour of this international event. Mr DFA had us all laughing when he appeared in an orange 'Maharaji' headdress.

My joke was intended to douse the tension in the room, as the news the DFA brought was quickly passed around. They were now in the know, albeit unofficially that their DG was on the Disengagement List. The DFA had connections in the State House, Office of the

Secretary to the Government and the Accountant General's Office, from where he was seconded to the Women Centre. He always claimed to have the ears of very powerful people in government, especially with the ascendance of President Buhari. I believed him.

Two hours later, I heard an uproar outside my office window. There had been an announcement on the radio and my name had been mentioned for disengagement. The loud celebration had begun from the office of the Acting DG in waiting. From then on, he began a frantic effort to arrange a disgraceful exit for me.

Suddenly, three glum faces showed up at my office. They belonged to the Deputy Legal Adviser, the ICT consultant and the Director of Human Resources Management (DHRM). All were hard-working members of the Management Board who were loyal to the ideals of the Women Centre and committed to its excellence. They had come to ensure that I got the confirmation of my leaving from them and not from my detractors. They looked so sad, perhaps, given the persecution that we all knew would come. It was up to me then, to help them regain their balance. I started by praising and thanking God for His grace. I reassured them that I was strong and resolute and that 'all things will always work together for good, for those who love the Lord and are called according to his purpose', as written in the Bible. We had worked and delivered to the best of our abilities, with fairness to all. I assured them that based on these, no one had cause to fear.

At this point, the mood in the room changed and became refreshingly celebratory. We were all encouraged. I began to pack my belongings and prepare my handover notes, even before an official letter arrived from the Secretary to the Government's Office.

By the following day, Tuesday morning, everywhere at the Centre, was charged. Some members of the Management Board did not even bother to show up. One of them was the head of the Training Unit who had just returned from Ethiopia with the Minister for Women Affairs. It was a trip that was made without the Centre's authorisation.

The Honourable Minister had sowed a seed of indiscipline and insubordination in the Women Centre and like the one before her, she had her spies and allies to report on every activity and every decision taken at management meetings. Some of these reports were entirely made up to tarnish my administration.

I finished packing at about 5 p.m and we began loading my belongings into my official car. It was then that I realised the enormity of what was planned for me. The crowd of protesters booed each time an item was put into my car. Some of them had positioned themselves to do me bodily harm and others to spit at me.

I put a call through to our police contacts, but they did not pick my calls. I called the Special Advisor to the Minister for Women Affairs to inform him about the brewing trouble and the need for the Minister to step in before irreparable damage was done. He, in turn, called the DFA, DPRS and other Senior Directors and warned them to diffuse the situation. He advised them not to leave my side until I was safely out of the Women Centre. I understand that he also called the Acting DG in waiting to impress upon him the implications of any harm coming to me under his watch.

On my part, I reached out to individuals whom I felt should be aware of what was going on. Eventually, I managed to speak to the House Member who had given me the perfume gift. He ensured that police were sent to the Centre to protect me.

Word had quickly spread among some Igbo people, mostly traders, about the situation. They began to assemble nearby, hoping to offer their protection, if need be. I was very grateful for this show of solidarity from people I did not know. However, I did not want the altercation that probably would have ensued if the two divergent and emotionally-charged crowds were to lock horns. I made haste to leave the Centre before any further escalation.

By 8 p.m on the day of my disengagement, five mobile policemen had arrived at the Centre and took up positions. Two were in my office. I was assured that ten more were on their way to us. The DFA, DPRS, Assistant Legal Advisor, HPU, ICT Consultant, and a few others followed me to the car.

As we walked out of my office, heading towards the ground floor of the administrative building, I decided to stop by the office of the Acting DG-in-waiting. This move was not in the least expected. There, I met one of the wives who was also a middle-level staff at the Centre and the Union Leader, taking instructions from him about what to do to me. My appearance left them startled and confused, both quickly left.

I addressed the Acting DG-in-waiting. I let him know that I was aware of his plans and machinations to return the Centre to the mess it was before I came, but that he would fail. I wished him the best of luck otherwise. As we stepped down to the ground floor, approaching the exit, we were surprised to see the rude, arrogant and incompetent finance officer whom we had sent back to the office of the Accountant General. I asked him what he was doing at the Women Centre. He replied that he had come to 'congratulate' me.

We noticed that he had one hand behind his back, as if he was hiding something - perhaps a knife, I thought.

His former boss, the DFA, pleaded that we proceed to the car immediately. He was a bit nervous, but I was not. The two armed policemen gave me protective cover as I calmly proceeded to my car, not in a hurry, but at my own pace, blowing kisses to the crowd as I left. Finally, the drivers had agreed that my official car could be used to take me home, but they chose a stranger to drive it. My official driver refused to release the car keys, insisting that he would drive me home, which he did.

As soon as my car pulled out of the riotous situation amidst hisses and boos, the only Igbo person – the ICT Consultant, who was accompanying me to the car – was set upon. He managed to escape unharmed, but he was threatened and had to stay away from the office for weeks. He petitioned the Office of the Minister for Women Affairs. Shortly afterwards, his contract fell due for renewal, and it was not.

Just days after I left the National Centre for Women Development, I began hearing news about a drastic return to the old ways. The wife of the Acting DG, now 'The First Lady of the Centre' with her coterie of aides, including her brother, were deployed to strategic areas of the Centre's revenue streams. Months later, the high standard of maintenance which we had meticulously set up, began to crumble. I was not surprised to hear that the generator house got burnt down. I suspect that the generators themselves may have been cannibalised before the skeletal remains were set ablaze.

NCWD And The Mother Ministry

The National Centre for Women Development is under the supervision of the Ministry of Women Affairs. The relationship between the two is competitive, and not always in a positive way. The Ministry, which, as a matter of duty, should support the NCWD chose to remain indignantly opposed to its progress. It seemed to me that it wanted the Women Centre to remain a dull appendage of its mother ministry.

The Minister at the time of my appointment was opposed to it. She had her own candidate whom she wanted to get the job.

Her reception was cold, uncooperative and reeked of unspoken disdain. The height of this hostility was the very toxic words she said to me along the corridors of the House of Representatives.

We had gone there a few months after my appointment to defend the 2014 budget. I had no experience in such matters and so was all eyes and ears to absorb whatever knowledge I could. After the presentation, I congratulated the Honourable Minister for her deft handling of the questions from the House Members. I told her that I looked forward to learning from her and was delighted to be a daughter to her Ministry.

She looked at me with a cold stare, and then with a piercingly clear voice, said: 'But you are the type of child that when you were coming out, I should have closed my legs and crushed your head.'

'What?'

Her words had landed with a heavy thud in my chest. Other members of my management team were nearby, and so was the Permanent Secretary of the Ministry who had never bothered to speak to me or return my greetings.

After what seemed to me like an eternity and in slow motion, I heard myself say, 'Well, I just wanted to congratulate you for a job well done. May God bless you.'

I walked away still in a state of shock. I was so alarmed by this statement that I took the time to report it to some influential women in politics. I could not understand the Honourable Minister's extreme dislike for me. I had a feeling that it had to do with the positive changes being made at the Centre within a short period. Also, the Office of the First Lady had taken to sending me to represent her at events, which I did effectively.

The Minister was someone I considered an old soldier in the battle for Nigerian women's social and political advancement. I remain respectful of her credentials. On the day that President Goodluck Jonathan left office and some of us who had been appointed by his Government had the opportunity to escort him home to Bayelsa, we flew in the same airplane.

I got in first and reserved a Business Class seat for the Minister. We enjoyed a long conversation about the wonderful ways God had blessed us. In the course of that discussion, it seemed that the anger, jealousy and mistrust slowly melted away. I remember thinking that we could have had this understanding a lot earlier. We could have achieved a lot more together if we had a more cooperative relationship.

Having stayed on as the Director-General of the NCWD nine months after the change of government, I witnessed the coming of another Minister for Women Affairs. In between though, I was blessed with the opportunity of working with a fair-minded and progressive Permanent Secretary, Mr Ezekiel Oyemomi. He had the self-assurance to appreciate my result-oriented administration. In fact, he gave every support and advice that we needed to achieve more.

On the day of the new minister's swearing-in, I was at her office to receive her. There, I also met a new Permanent Secretary, Oyemomi, having been unexpectedly retired. The new Permanent Secretary followed the tradition of the one before Oyemomi and refused to speak to me.

It is important to note that my ranking as a Director-General was equal to that of a Permanent Secretary. But perhaps being the head of a parastatal under her Ministry, she felt that I was in an inferior position relative to her. Two of the three Permanent Secretaries I worked with treated me with determined scorn. However, I never complained, choosing to direct my attention instead to the demands of my job. Often, underserved opposition is a sign that one is doing something right.

Soon after her swearing-in, events began to unfold that portrayed the Minister's attitude towards me and the NCWD as downright hostile. The Centre extended every courtesy to the Hon. Minister, bending over backwards to accommodate her wishes, but nothing seemed to please her.

On one occasion, she made a strange official request of us, for funds to travel to an African Union (AU) meeting in Ethiopia. This was a huge amount of money and I was at a loss where to pull it out of. I realised that I had been put in a terrible dilemma. I was damned if I did, and damned if I did not. In the end, I resolved to do the right thing, and stand by it, no matter what. I would not give away money that had been budgeted for other programmes. Three weeks before my disengagement and just two weeks before the AU Ethiopian trip, the Ministry and the NCWD were invited to defend their 2016 Budget at a hearing by the Senate Oversight Committee on Women Affairs. It was the practice that both organisations shared the same budget 'envelope'. One lump sum was approved for the two and from there, our Mother Ministry would fund our non-capital expenses as it pleased.

The new Minister made a hasty presentation of her budget and took off for another meeting at the State House. After her exit, I was left alone to present the Centre's budget to a committee chaired by the former First Lady of Lagos State, Senator Oluremi Tinubu.

The Committee members were initially sceptical, but they soon began to warm up to the Centre's vision and achievements. Before long, we were receiving nods of approval and promises of support, even as they challenged us to step things up a notch or two.

Reports of our pleasant outing at the Senate Chambers soon reached the Minister's ears. In our next joint outing, she came with a temperament typical of one with an axe to grind. This time, we were at the National Assembly Chambers. The Centre's report came first and the Minister was there. It was a well-received presentation, though not without critical appraisal and input from the Committee members. When it was time for the Minister to make her own presentation, she opened up with a tirade against the way I was running the Women Centre. She accused me of not consulting her and carrying her Ministry along in my activities.

The Minister tore into me as one would an old foe. When she

was done, I asked for a chance to defend myself, which was granted. I calmly reminded the Honourable Minister of how I had received her in the office on the first day and even paid a visit to her home. I subsequently consulted her and received letters of approval for every activity at the Centre, at which she was always represented.

She became visibly uncomfortable. But I went further. I drew the attention of the panel to her strange financial request to fund the Ministry's participation at the AU meeting. At this point, I was persuaded to stop by the members of the House Committee. The Honourable Minister and I were called aside and advised to make greater efforts to work together for improved results. I hugged the Minister and reassured her that I held her in high esteem and I looked forward to her guidance. She gave me the cold shoulder, and I knew the die was cast.

Partnerships

One of the areas of strength we had at the Women Centre was the fact that we were allowed to work with or partner with international Agencies and foreign governments in our common areas of interest. The Japanese International Cooperation Agency (JICA) was one of such Agencies. It had worked with the NCWD since 2007 in establishing Women Development Centres (WDC) in several states across the country. This was to help drive rural development.

By 2016, when they began to wind down the programme we ran together, 24 WDCs had been established or reactivated in six States. Since 2010, the NCWD had on its own resuscitated the WDCs in 22 States. Many, however, were not functioning to capacity.

Some of the work required in the resuscitation of women centres involved the training of the trainers. To adequately address this challenge, JICA and NCWD jointly produced a three-volume training manual on the establishment and reactivation of WDCs. We were presented with a daunting task.

A lot of research had to be done, data collected and analysed. It needed to be correlated and properly presented in a readable manner. The DPRS was in charge. He had been particularly forthcoming in running the JICA Partnership. I gave him every support he asked for and more. It fell under his department, so also did the supervision of the American Corner, an initiative of the United States. It supported five core programmes: English language learning, educational advising, alumni activities, cultural programmes and information about the USA. The mini- information centre was housed by the Bola Ige ICT building within the premises.

However, putting together the Women Development Manual was particularly challenging for him. The first editorial effort was not up to par with the desired quality. I made corrections and ordered a second one. Surprisingly, it turned out to be worse than the first. It was written in Japanese-English; by that, I mean that it was presented in a manner that borrowed heavily from the way the Japanese would present the English language to themselves. I understood the point being relayed because of my familiarity with the subject matter, but I was not sure the average trainer would understand it. I intervened and we set a new deadline for the manual to be reconstructed. The DPRS was only too happy to dump the project on my table.

For the next six weeks, I stayed up late at night and in-between other equally important assignments, to complete the rewriting and editing of the manual. It was done pro bono. Everyone was proud and happy to be associated with the success story.

I had a policy of reading every correspondence emanating from my organisation to the outside world. English, spoken and written, was a huge challenge for many members of staff at all levels. To have insisted on vetting all external correspondence was to take on additional burden. I preferred the rigours of editing to the shame of appalling correspondence.

The accomplishments we registered at the National Centre for Women Development could not have been possible without the partnership of some international Agencies within the UN fold.

These were The United Nations High Commissioner for Refugees (UNHCR), UN Women, UNICEF and of course, the Japanese Aid Agency (JICA) as mentioned above, all sustained close working relationships with us. They assisted us in areas such as computer literacy and training programmes for skills acquisition and empowerment. For example, the UN Women, conducted numerous computer training program that benefited rural women from all over Nigeria and the trainers who ensured that many more people benefited from the knowledge.

I found the attitude of the Japanese Government towards providing aid to Africa most honourable. They were never noisy or condescending about the assistance they rendered but showed respect for their hosts' cultural sensibilities.

The UNHCR successfully executed a training programme with the Women Centre to benefit the Internally Displaced Persons (IDPs) from the northeast of Nigeria. My concern for the plight of the women IDPs had inspired me to write and produce the song 'Not Alone' for advocacy work. It was done at my own expense. UNHCR came on board the project, to help with the duplication and distribution of it, as well as the making of a video recording. Together, the two Agencies commenced on 9 December 2015, the training of 350 women IDPs in various skills acquisition programmes. This was an on-going project. The trainees were equipped and empowered to become employers themselves. Earlier, both Agencies, as well as the National Emergency Management Agency (NEMA), had visited IDPs in Yola, Adamawa State.

NCWD: Lessons Learned

One must never succumb to blackmail no matter the intensity of the pressure. The imperative is to stand strong, for truth can only be followed by vindication. In my case, we were targeted for blackmail by a group drawn from other Agencies but working in tandem with some of the Centre's key staff. Their mission was to embezzle the N20m lifeline extended to us by the Ministry of Finance to complete our renovation work at the Dora Akunyili Guest House. This group knew about the release of the funds even before I did.

A serious battle ensued to keep the money away from their scavenging efforts and direct it towards the project for which it was given. In retaliation, I was accused of extorting funds from a contractor whose work at the Guest House had been so shoddy that I had to fire him. I dealt with their distractions and baseless allegations, even while I focused on completing the work which I did successfully.

Upon finding out what my salary scale and emoluments were as DG of the NCWD, I inadvertently let out a small whelp. The SGF to whose office I had gone to collect my appointment letter, asked me what the matter was.

'How does one survive on such a small salary?' I asked.

The SGF looked at me and without batting an eyelid declared: 'That is why it is called service.'

Thus, I knew that I had to downsize my expectations and make personal sacrifices on the job from the very beginning. As a government administrator, you are not expected to spend your money on the job. There are times, however, when you have no choice. Some of my expenses were not covered by your salary and entitlements, but they had to be made anyway.

For a woman who had to represent her country around the world, I had to look the part and bear its cost. Sometimes, my travel expenses were borne by me because my Agency was not fully funded. It was a risk I took knowing the consequences, which was that I would not be reimbursed. But work simply had to go on.

Government officials are seen as corrupt, and despised as such. However, it is family and friends who would put pressure on you for the 'spoils of office' to be extended to them. I lost a few friends who felt that I did not 'carry them along' in my 'enjoyment' of my position's financial rewards. Any assistance that I did render to them was just not enough in their view.

Years after leaving my appointment and knowing I came out of it poorer than I when I went in, these friends and relatives have still not forgiven me.

Therefore, I resolved to continue to be true to myself and my principles, to remain answerable to God only and no one else.

Finally, people appointed to offices must never hold on to anything that does not belong to them. They should take a bow and leave the stage once their part is done. The message is this: Take nothing but your dignity and your sense of honour with no regrets. Give everything, nothing missing, and nothing held back. The chance may come but once.

PART VIII

Encounters

Gani Fawehinmi

I cannot quite recall the first time I met Chief Gani Fawehinmi. I remember protesting with Alao Aka-Bashorun, the incessant incarceration of the irrepressible character that was Gani. Aka-Bashorun was a lawyer and human rights activist whose integrity was his calling card. I met him through my husband, and he was a good friend who stood by my family at a time of difficulty. He took me to Gani's office where I signed a petition in Gani's defence during one of his spells in jail, under Gen. Ibrahim Babangida's military regime.

This singular act, I believe, led to my friendship with Gani Fawehinmi. He gave me his unwavering and undiluted support at critical times.

In 2001, I embarked on a hunger strike to protest my ban on Nigerian Television by Mr Ben Bruce, the all-conquering Director-General of the government-owned Nigerian Television Authority (NTA). The ban was imposed because of my demand for my residual fees on work done for NTA and copyright dues for using my song 'Iyogogo' on the network for over 8 years.

During my protest outside their headquarters where I had camped out with my supporters and the press, Chief Gani Fawehinmi showed up with a crowd of his followers – the man in the street – who surrounded him everywhere he went. They blocked Ahmadu Bello Way where NTA is situated. Gani stood on top of his car and in a loud voice declared, 'Mr Ben Bruce, we are watching you. Nothing must happen to Onyeka Onwenu'.

Gani proceeded to extol my qualities, if not virtues, recounting as it were, both those I deserved and those I never knew I had. Such was the force he deployed to any cause he found worthy.

In 2007, I was asked by the Chinua Achebe Foundation to conduct personal conversations with some iconic names for its 'Interview Series'. I spoke with Chief Gani Fawehinmi and Margaret Ekpo. She was a notable politician of the pre-independence and post-war era.

My conversation with Gani Fawehinmi turned out to be one of his most enjoyable, according to him, much like Chinua Achebe himself in the documentary *Nigeria a Squandering of Riches*.

Gani's interview brought out a side of him not well known to Nigerians. There was a gentle caring soul beneath the hard-hitting activist with a huge social conscience. When it came to matters concerning his mother, Gani was like red clay in water. He revealed a vulnerability and tenderness that was at once serenely human and touching. His love for his mum was palpable and he shed tears talking about her.

In 2007, I needed the best legal representation in a case where a powerful lawyer had joined forces with his client and friend who is my first cousin, to try to dispossess me of a property I had leased and developed. The politically well-connected lawyer had threatened to run me out of Lagos because he just did not like my personality. I had never met him before and would not recognize him if I saw him in person. I had never seen the photograph of this camera-shy senior lawyer.

Gani Fawehinmi was incensed on my behalf and ordered his law firm to defend me pro-bono. By this time, my friend had fallen ill, the fallout of the conditions he had to endure in and out of jail by oppressive Nigerian military regimes. I therefore insisted and did pay a fair share of my legal fees, unknown to him. Gani Fawehinmi had watched me struggle to develop the Unity Center Events Place in Ikeja from 1996 to its opening in 2002. .

Gani Fawehinmi, a senior advocate and defender of the oppressed, was my friend and a friend to the common man. He was a man who cared little about his own life and comfort, choosing to sacrifice it all for what he believed in. He loved Nigeria, and agonised over her avoidable failings. He died in the service of his country.

Gani stood resolutely against corruption and maladministration in the country. There will never be another like him.

Alhaji Shehu Shagari
(former President of Nigeria)

'**Y**ou this Squandering of Riches woman.'
I heard a voice from behind me. It was as if the owner just could not wait to unburden his mind and so shouted it out from afar, in a manner that would stop me in my tracks. I turned around and met the stern glare of Alhaji Shehu Shagari. His government was sacked in 1983 by a military coup led by Major General Muhammadu Buhari. Who himself became an elected President three decades later.

Alhaji Shehu Shagari was a soft-spoken and humble man. A relatively small-framed person, he was rarely given to bellicose statements. I was startled by his sternness.

Wahala dey o, I thought to myself as I braced up for the verbal onslaught that I knew was coming. I had faced several confrontations and even threats to my wellbeing, regarding my presentation of the documentary *Nigeria, A Squandering of Riches* in 1984. It centred around the massive corruption in government at the time.

The occasion of my encounter with the former President was at Nelson Mandela's inauguration, precisely ten years after my documentary was aired in Europe and Nigeria.

There were a few witnesses to this event, the most prominent being General Sani Abacha. I looked at him to say something to ameliorate the tension in the air, but he kept a straight face and showed no interest at all. President Abacha must have said to himself, 'Woman carry on your head the trouble you caused.'

I asked President Shagari if I could speak. He said nothing, so I took that as a yes, and I spoke.

Seemingly from nowhere, I found my voice and the courage to say this: 'I did not lie, sir. It was my country as I saw it. You are a good man, it was nothing personal, but I did not lie.'

There was silence. It was clear to me that my words had sunk in and the unassuming confidence with which I spoke had disarmed the former President. I quietly eased myself out of our shared space and went looking for my friend, Winnie Mandela, who was also at the inauguration.

When I met President Shagari a few months later at a function in Abuja, he was friendlier and quite considerate. He spent time talking with me and was delighted when I complimented him on the exemplary conduct of some of his sons who were serving their State and country in various capacities. Thereafter, he would stop and chat with me anywhere we met.

President Shehu Shagari passed away on 28 December 2018 at the age of 93. May he find peace with his creator.

Chief Martin Agbaso (Ochudo)

While campaigning for my local government's Chairmanship in 2003, I came in contact with Chief Martin Agbaso, a businessman, philanthropist, and politician. He was engaged in the gubernatorial race in Imo State that year.

Sometimes, you may not know that there are people who repose confidence in you, where others are striving to pull you down. In politics and public service, it was often the case. You would come across people that felt intimidated by your credentials or were angry that as a woman, you did not cower and tremble at their presence.

Ochudo (seeker of peace), harboured no such insecurities. I was pleasantly surprised when he reached out to me to be his running mate in the coming election. It did not work out because I was reluctant to leave my party, the People's Democratic Party (PDP), to join his All Progressives Grand Alliance (APGA).

It is believed by many in Imo State that the first held gubernatorial election there was won by Chief Martin Agbaso and his party APGA. However, it was cancelled by the Independent National Electoral Commission (INEC). Another election was held but it did not favour Ochudo.

The story of Imo State would have been starkly different from the wholesale brigandage and pillaging of public funds that has since been the case, particularly during the 'reign' of Governor Rochas Okorocha (2011 - 2019).

It is sometimes said that in politics, there are no saints, that politicians wheel and deal, and all is fair in love and war. Ochudo, however, remains a man of integrity and a lover of all that is fair and just. I am convinced that he is the best Governor Imo State should have had.

Chief Sam Mbakwe

Chief Sam Mbakwe was the Governor of Imo State in 1980 when I returned to Nigeria from my sojourn in the United States. From all accounts and evidence, he was a very good governor who had the interest of his people as his priority. Sam Mbakwe was called 'The Crying Governor' for always lamenting the lot of Ndigbo in post-war Nigeria, and demanding treatment as equal partners in the Nigeria project.

He built infrastructure in Imo State, some of which are still being enjoyed today. On many occasions, I visited his Government House, attending State functions and command performances. I met Chief Mbakwe on those occasions, but he never told me of his special relationship with my father or that he knew my family at all.

It turned out that not only did Sam Mbakwe know my father but that he was also trained by the 'Old Teacher'. He even lived with us for many years as a young man.

There existed a photograph of my parents, Aunt Dorothy and Sam Mbakwe. When he was told about the photograph, he requested for it, ostensibly to make copies for his collection. He promised to return it, but he never did, once he got hold of it.

Surprisingly, when the man Mbakwe referred to as 'Nnam Ukwu' (Big Daddy) – my father – died, Mbakwe neither showed up for his funeral nor sent condolences to his family. Then one day, in 1988, long after he had ceased to be Governor, he came to Arondizuogu to visit my mother, whom he had heard was in Imo State. My mother would not receive him. In a true Hope Onwenu fashion, she told him off for not asking after his principal's family since 1956 when he died. An embarrassed Sam Mbakwe had nothing to say. There were no excuses.

I was, therefore, doubly surprised when years later, the same man showed up at my house in Ikeja, Lagos. I welcomed him. We spent the next two hours talking about my father. We were both in tears in the end. I believe that he came to me to unburden his spirit, and put down the baggage of guilt which must have weighed heavily on him.

Sometimes, there are lapses in human relations and unless you have an understanding spirit, you may walk away with an unforgiving one.

The first thing that Chief Sam Mbakwe said to me was: 'I used to carry you in my arms when you were a baby.' Though we missed many decades of not knowing each other, I was happy that we reconnected before his death. When he passed away, my mother asked me to go ahead and represent the family at his burial. I did.

Ken Saro-Wiwa

Let me state here an irrevocable truth, the acceptance of which should prompt an apology from the Nigerian state. The killing of the writer, environmental and human rights activist, Ken Saro-Wiwa, was a crime against humanity, worthy of every condemnation possible.

Ken Saro-Wiwa died in the pursuit of his people's best interest, the Ogoni of the Niger Delta. He was a martyr, along with all who have died in the pursuit of justice in Ogoniland and Nigeria.

My encounter with him many years before his death was public knowledge. Our disagreement centred on the role he assigned to Ndigbo before, during and after the Nigeria-Biafra war. His feelings about Ndigbo were tainted, I believe, by the lies and conspiracies of a government whose main interest was to seize control of his region and the national wealth.

In 1989, Ken Saro-Wiwa published a book entitled *On A Darkling Plain*. In it, he accused Ndigbo and their leader, Emeka Ojukwu, and the Biafran Army of atrocities against the Ogoni people during the three-year conflict. These lies were perpetuated by people like Ken Saro-Wiwa who were either totally deceived or in denial of the truth. The atrocities they referred to were carried out by others but blamed on Ndigbo.

Emeka Odumegwu-Ojukwu did not start the Nigerian Civil War. It was foisted on him and the people of Biafra. They had to defend themselves or be annihilated. The war, a tragedy well documented, began with a pogrom and then turned into a full-scale genocidal onslaught against a virtually unarmed people. The intensity of this war had not been seen since World War II. It was modern-day genocide aided by four world powers - the US, UK, the Soviet Union and China - while much of the world looked away.

To blame Ojukwu and Ndigbo for atrocities committed by others would simply not go unchallenged anymore. I stood up to Mr Saro-Wiwa's unsubstantiated claims in defence of the Igbo cause.

I let Mr Saro-Wiwa know that what Emeka Odumegwu-Ojukwu did was to lead Ndigbo in their fight for survival. Biafra needed a leader and Odumegwu-Ojukwu was there. He could have done nothing but lead. I asked Ken Saro-Wiwa why my mother was beaten into a coma in Port Harcourt immediately after the war, for daring to reclaim her house. Talking about the seizure of all Igbo-owned properties in Port Harcourt in the 'Abandoned Property' saga, Mr Ken Saro-Wiwa cared very little about the legacy of people like my father, who died in active service as a member of the Federal House of Assembly and the Principal of Enitonia High School.

He did not give a hoot about the men and women who built the foundations of Port Harcourt, which came to be known as the Garden City, a progressive community of people from different backgrounds and ethnicities. I reminded Saro-Wiwa that the war never ended for these families affected by the 'Abandoned Property' policy.

In 1995, Ken Saro-Wiwa and eight others were condemned to death, accused of killing their kinsmen with whom they differed on the tactics of their agitation. Ken Saro-Wiwa and those accused with him were hanged to death in Nigeria despite a worldwide appeal for their pardon. It exemplified to me how easily anyone could become a victim of the Nigerian state. Ken Saro-Wiwa was a thorn in the flesh of the Nigerian government for seeking the rights of the Ogoni people and the protection of their environment.

My disagreement with him over the villainous role he ascribed to Ndigbo and his continued demonisation of Odumegwu-Ojukwu, notwithstanding, I acknowledge his sacrifice. He fought for and died for a just cause, the survival of the Ogoni people of southern Nigeria. May his gallant soul rest in peace.

Margaret Onyema Orakwusi

Margaret Orakwusi is an enigma. People like her are a rarity; you only meet them once in a lifetime. When this happens, there is eternal gratitude to God that such people still exist. With an intimidating profile of business interests in law, maritime, fish trawling and farming, Margaret Onyema Orakwusi runs where men fear to walk.

I met her in 2006, at a time when I was at a low point in my life. I was about to be thrown out of my flat in GRA Ikeja, and the house I was to move into in Lekki was not ready. My husband and I built a house in Opebi, Ikeja in 1992. However, in 2004, we needed to sell it to raise funds to restart his construction business following years of inactivity due to illness.

Quite the business-minded person, my husband drew up a contract that sold the house and in exchange, gave me another house in Lekki to be ready in two years. It was a fair deal and we both signed on the dotted lines. However, close to the completion of the house, I had problems securing access to it. When I did, much had gone wrong with the wiring, plumbing and other important finishing details. Eventually, after much protest, I moved into the house, unfinished. I had no choice. During this period, I had with me my 89-year-old mother, my 14-year-old second son and 17-year-old nephew, Dixon Kanu III. Tijani was at school in the US.

Following a threat by the landlord to evict me in two days, I quickly moved my family into the new house and the consequences were nearly disastrous. The change-over switch blew up in the middle of our first night there; we had to put out the small fire that ensued. Pipes were bursting inside the walls, we had leakages everywhere. Some toilets had no doors and bathroom tubs were cement encrusted. Electrical pipes were used for water and water pipes for electrical conduits. It took a lot of money to repair all the misconstructions that were made.

In my effort to secure the rights to my property and the apprehension that followed the explosion and water leakages, I met an angel in the person of Margaret Orakwusi. At a reception that we both attended, she introduced herself. Her simplicity and humility were evident.

I found myself drawn to her gentle nature and convivial demeanour. Soon, I was telling her about my current challenge, which was how to secure the papers to my house. I had learned that my husband had no plans to spend any more money on finishing it and would not hand over the papers to me.

Margaret came to my rescue. She got my husband to process the house papers even though it ended up not just in my name but also in that of our two children. That, he said, was all he would ever give them. He asked me to sign an agreement that my children and I should expect nothing further from him. I asked my lawyer to sign it on my behalf immediately.

All the work that my lawyer did, she did pro bono. But she was more than my lawyer; she became my friend and sister.

Margaret Onyema Orakwusi is the first daughter of His Royal Highness, Igwe Onyema of Ogwu Ikpele in Ogbaru, Anambra State. This very down to earth princess is blessed with some very successful siblings, including the Director-General of the Nigerian Stock

Exchange, Oscar Onyema, a Member of the House of Assembly, Prince Chu Chu Onyema, Kate Emuchay, Dr Emeka Onyema and several others. Every sibling is accomplished in their own right and in their own fields. One thing that stands out about this family is the love they have for one another. It is obvious when they are together or speak about each other. It is admirable to see. Any friend of an Onyema automatically earns the friendship of all the Onyemas. What a pleasant family!

Dr Goodluck Ebele Jonathan
(Former President of Nigeria)

I met President Goodluck Ebele Jonathan and his wife, Dame Patience Jonathan in 2004 when as Governor of Bayelsa State, he hosted the Africa Movie Academy Awards (AMAA). They were wonderful hosts throughout our stay in Yenagoa, their State capital. I remember the very first thing that Dame Patience said to me: 'You and I are sisters, you know.' I was touched as she went on to treat me as a sister indeed. Her mother was from Umuahia in Abia State and she spoke the old Igbo dialect of the area. It was delightful to hear her speak her Igbo and it endeared her to me.

I interacted with the Jonathans while they were in Bayelsa, and also while Goodluck Jonathan served as Vice President, Acting President and eventually, President of Nigeria. What an incredible journey. I wrote the song titled 'Run Goodluck Run' to encourage the Acting President to run for the substantive position when the opportunity presented itself. I am not sure if it was the song that he had expected to hear, as he had not made up his mind to run for the Presidency in 2009, but it was the song that God sent. I would like to believe that it gave him the confidence to declare his ambition.

I found President Goodluck Jonathan to be the quiet, brooding type, not loud and not given to small talk; a highly intelligent, peace-loving and hardworking man. I was surprised that he was quite knowledgeable about music and music video productions. The first video production of 'This Land', the theme song for Nigeria's Centenary Celebration, was lacking in many details about the Nigerian Military, Police, Youth Service Corps and other depictions of the Nigerian life, including the image of past-Presidents and the current one. I had been advised to leave them out of the compilation. After a meeting with Mr President, he constructively critiqued the production by one of Nigeria's best videographers, Mr Clarence Peters. The President was right.

The second rendition was a much better production. Even in areas, he was least expected to have one, this kind of input was quite often what happened each time I brought an issue to his attention.

In September 2013, President Goodluck Jonathan appointed me as the Director-General of the National Centre for Women Development, an office I held for two and a half years to the glory of God.

Mrs Patience Faka Jonathan

(former First Lady of Nigeria)

H er sense of humour is guaranteed to leave you in stitches whenever she unleashed it. She could laugh at herself with depreciating candour, which only the truly self-confident possess. This former First Lady of Nigeria is one filled with 'street' wisdom and a discerning mind. When she presented her analysis of Boko Haram activities in the country, many laughed at her appraisal of the violence. They have since stopped laughing. She was right.

As the Director-General of the National Center for Women Development, I worked closely with the Office of the First Lady, and was often called upon to represent her at national and international fora. I am a proud beneficiary of her unrelenting support for the upliftment of Nigerian women. She was passionate about their cause and we had a President who was not afraid to champion that cause as well.

I had written three songs inspired by her husband, Mr President, and she was very appreciative of my support. Dame Patience Jonathan never requested that I write one about her. But then, I found myself at the helm of the NCWD, an organisation that was spearheading advocacy for women issues, and Dame Patience Jonathan was launching a National Peace Youth Concert. This was in response to the insecurity spreading in the northeast and spilling onto the streets of Abuja; a campaign of terror which was a huge source of concern as it tended to destabilise the country.

Just a few months into my tenure, I watched the First Lady put aside her prepared speech on 'Reducing Infant and Maternal Mortality' to say these words instead:

'Don't call me Patience; call me Mama Peace.'

Mrs Jonathan lamented the senseless killings going on in the country. I was moved. When I attempted to put together a song to power the Youth Peace conference which my Agency was involved in organising, those words rang in my ears. Here, are the lyrics:

Don't call me Patience
Call me Mama Peace
My heart is breaking
For the bloodshed on the streets
How can we stand by
When the world is on fire?

I chose to love
And I chose to care
Don't call me Patience
Call me Mama Peace

Chorus:
Let there be peace
All over the world
Let there be love
In your heart and mine
Speak peace
Try love
Hold on to hope
Let there be peace
All over the world

From the day the song was released to the public in February 2014, Dame Patience Goodluck Jonathan came to be known as 'Mama Peace'. I hasten to add that this song and video were produced at my own expense and not the Agency I headed.

I thank President Jonathan for believing in my abilities, and giving me the opportunity to serve my country.

I equally thank Dame Patience Jonathan for the encouragement without which, I would not have made as much impact.

Alhaji Atiku Abubakar

I met Alhaji Atiku Abubakar for the first time in 1999, on the day that he was elected Vice President of Nigeria under Chief Olusegun Obasanjo's presidency.

I was in Yola for a musical ministration. That visit on its own was a miraculous story. Yola was far away, so when the invitation came, I was very excited but burdened. It came at a time when I was quite ill. I had an 8lbs fibroid growing in me and taking away much of my body nutrients.

Four days before leaving for Yola, I had gone to the Blessed Sacrament of St. Agnes Catholic Church, Maryland, Ikeja, to quietly meditate and pray for healing. Then I felt a prompting in my spirit.

'You are asking me to heal you, but you will not go to Yola for me,' was what I heard.

I went home immediately, called Yola and asked my hosts to book my flight. I told God that I would know if it was His prompting, if He would do the impossible by returning me to Lagos right after the event, which was the day after the Presidential election. No airplanes would be flying that day but I dared God to do the impossible.

It happened that my being part of the church programme was a 'spirit lifter'. A small bus carrying a band from Kano to the event had been involved in a ghastly accident and lives were lost. The programme had gone on, but spirits were low. My coming made a difference as the audience really felt uplifted.

Late in the afternoon of the day after the elections, I asked my hosts to take me to the airport. They knew about my challenge to God, and they simply laughed but decided to humour me. They also knew that there were no planes flying. As we approached the airport, it was quite clear that there were no activities there. I was being consoled with promises of more dry fish to take back to Lagos with me if I waited till the following day, but I would not be discouraged.

Lo and behold (as my maternal grandfather Papa Nnukwu would say), there was a small, private jet revving up on one side of the tarmac as we drove in. I turned to my hosts and said, 'God has sent a private jet to take me home.'

Truly, He had. I was ill and had planned to report to the hospital for a scheduled operation in a matter of days. It turned out that the aircraft was there to fly Alhaji Atiku Abubakar and his family back to Abuja. There was at this time, every indication that he would be the next Vice President of Nigeria. Earlier on, he had won the gubernatorial race in Adamawa, with Boni Haruna as his running mate. I spoke to one of his wives, who permitted me to approach the future Vice President. I was given the only remaining seat on the aircraft, and it took me all the way to Lagos, after dropping off the Atikus in Abuja.

I did bring back some delicious dry fish such as *Asa* and catfish. My hosts had placed them in a secured carton, tightly sealed for the journey.

I shared some of it with my mother, knowing it would end up in her steaming pot of *ofe onugbu*. I gave some to my closest friends who found it hard to believe that I had the presence of mind and absence of shame to carry a big box of dry fish on a 'Presidential' aircraft, all the way from Adamawa to Lagos.

'Are you kidding? What shame?' I responded, noting that I was too busy thinking about the different dishes I could prepare with the fish, than worry about any embarrassment.

Adamawa is blessed with some of the finest species of freshwater fish, chicken, meat and produce. I made it a point of duty to bring back some, whenever I visited.

Throughout Atiku Abubakar's first term as Vice President, I barely had any contact with him, until 2002 when I joined the election campaign of the Obasanjo/Atiku second term bid. Together with other well-meaning members of our party, the PDP, we traversed the country's length and breadth to drum up support for the ticket.

Many of us moved to Abuja, the centre of the campaign effort, at our own cost. I lived at the Petra Hotel in Area II Garki for months, and only went back to Lagos for the weekend and for my musical performances.

After the second term elections were won in 2003, only Alhaji Abubakar Atiku called to thank me for my support. He provided airline tickets for my boys and me to travel to the United States for a well-deserved vacation. It was a heartwarming gesture and I appreciated it very much.

God glorified Himself on my trip to Yola, and I knew that my healing was assured. I had a successful operation by Dr Ohieri at his First Consultants Hospital in Lagos. I was walking around a day after my surgery, to the marvel of my doctors. My God is indeed a promise and covenant keeper.

Captain Issa Bayero

I encountered Captain Issa Bayero on the political trail of the Obasanjo/Atiku second term bid for the presidency. We were both members of the campaign team. Bearing in mind that I was in Abuja at my own expense, Captain Issa would pick me to and from the Nnamdi Azikiwe Airport Abuja, from where we took off every day to various places around the country. That saved me a good amount of money in transportation costs, and a friendship was formed.

Captain Bayero, a seasoned pilot who flew Presidents and dignitaries around the world, is a prince of the Kano Royal Family, but you would not know it. He is humble, gentle and self-respecting. He was also good company and a great conversationalist. Thank you, sir, for your friendship.

Prof. Jerry Gana

A s Minister For Information in 1988, under the General Ibrahim Babangida administration, Prof. Jerry Gana led the public enlightenment campaign, called MAMSER. He had the gift of the garb and coined the phrase, 'If you are a leader, lead well', to which you can add all manner of callings. If you are a teacher, for example, teach well. In essence, the philosophy was: be your best at whatever you set out to do. It resonated across the land.

However, it is not for his communication skills nor for his statesmanship that he is recognised here, but for his kindness and consideration for others.

In my opinion, Professor Jerry Gana is a Christian who lives by the dictates of his faith, to love and help others, no matter who they were and where they came from.

During the 2003 campaign for the Obasanjo/Atiku second term Presidential ticket, few people knew that those of us in the campaign effort were there at great costs to ourselves. Coming from Lagos, I had to fund every bit of my participation, including flights to and from my base every week, hotel accommodation, feeding as well as local transportation in Abuja. But we trudged on because we believed in the cause we were supporting. There were no expectations of a reward and none was extended.

I did not realise that Prof. Gana took note of our sacrifice and one day, midway into the campaign, he asked me to see him early the following morning for an urgent message. I respectfully obliged. I imagined that he was probably going to give me a special assignment to get done. I was in his home office as early as 7 a.m, where I met at least five other people already waiting to see him on various matters.

Coming out of a prayer session, Prof. Jerry Gana quickly pressed an envelope into my hand, in it was the sum of N200,000 (about $1,200). I was utterly stunned by his thoughtfulness and kindness. I never expected it, I did not ask for it, but I was touched beyond words. I am sure that Prof. Gana may have forgotten this incidence but not me. It spoke volumes of who he is as a Christian and a fellow Nigeria. He has a reputation of being his brother's keeper with the demonstrated ability to love and relate to all, without prejudice.

President Muhammadu Buhari

I first met Major General Muhammadu Buhari in 1980, just weeks after returning from the United States to commence the obligatory National Youth Service Scheme (NYSC).

My relative by marriage, Dr Alex Eneli, whose uncle, Sammy Ejindu, was married to my Aunt, Dorothy, lived next door to a business tycoon, Chief Sunny Odogwu (Ide Ahaba). It was he who offered to help ensure that my Youth Service Deployment be in a place where my services could best benefit my country. The best place for me, given my talent and exposure, was at the Nigerian Television Authority which had its headquarters in Lagos.

It was in Chief Odogwu's house, just days after my return from the United States, that I met Mohammadu Buhari days after returning, who was then a Brigadier General. He was quiet and acetic in demeanour but was willing to meet with me. Looking back, nothing told me that the taciturn gentleman sitting across me would play a central role in the political tides of my country, or that I would end up justifying the coup that brought him to power in 1983.

In the end, I did not need Brigadier General Buhari's help in securing an NYSC placement with NTA Lagos. I was hired on my own credentials and through the recommendation of my mentor Alhaji Aminu Wali.

Not long after his second coming as a civilian president, I had the opportunity of being part of the team to brief him on the affairs of our mother ministry, and the National Centre for Women Development, as its Director-General. The other team members were the entire Management Board of the Ministry for Women Affairs, led by its Permanent Secretary, Mr Ezekiel Oyemomi.

I had a good and productive relationship with the Permanent Secretary, who was supportive of my programme while in office. Mr Oyemomi took pride in the modest achievements we recorded under him and identified with them, never feeling threatened by the accomplishments of the NCWD. May God bless him for his critical support and fairness to me.

However, some of the Directors of the Ministry were not as favourably disposed towards me. Whenever we had a joint outing, the mother Ministry treated the NCWD as a poor relative. We had to insist on being heard; otherwise, we were ignored. I was told, however, that this was usually the case. My parastatal was looked upon as an interloper. This was made worse by the fact that my administration was fast-paced and highly productive.

On the morning of the Presidential briefing, I came alone to Aso Rock, none of the NCWD Directors were invited. I arrived to the cold stares of all but a few of the Ministry's Directors. One was kind enough to share the report which had been prepared without any input from my parastatal. In fact, we were only given five lines in it. Well, at least, we were mentioned at all and I was present at the meeting, I tried to comfort myself.

The Permanent Secretary delivered a strong presentation. However, I was not given a chance to speak at all. But I sensed that the President wanted to hear from me. My Agency had been vocal about the Internally Displaced Persons (IDPs). Mr President repeatedly asked what we were doing to assist them. When it became clear that the Ministry had no programmes or plans for that sector,

I sought to rescue the situation. When the President repeated the question the third time, I leaned over and asked the Permanent Secretary for permission to speak. As it were, the Women Centre had been conducting training and advocacy programmes for the welfare of the IDPs. I had little awareness that President Buhari was looking in my direction. He then asked me to speak up.

'Mr President,' I began, 'With the kind permission of the Permanent Secretary, I would like to brief you on what my parastatal, the National Centre for Women Development, with the support and supervision of the Ministry for Women Affairs, has done for the IDPs.'

I proceeded to give him a succinct account of our training programmes in skills acquisition and empowerment, as well as the privately financed production of the song, 'Not Alone' in support of Nigeria's IDPs.

Mr President seemed quite pleased with my brief and the meeting was brought to a close on that positive note. However, the Directors of the Ministry of Women Affairs were livid and indignant with my intervention. If looks could kill, I would have died on the spot. There were unpleasant stares trained at me that communicated their deep and seething displeasure.

I had stolen the show; I heard someone say. It had not been my intention, of course, but the President wanted a bit of good news and he knew that I had something to say at the meeting. As we plunged out of the Meeting Room for a group photograph, there was a lot of jostling among the Directors to ensure that they positioned themselves closest to President Buhari.

I quietly waited on the wings until a protocol officer took charge and created room for me and the Permanent Secretary, with space in-between us for the President. He took turns shaking hands but was interrupted twice when it was my turn until finally, I was the last to be so greeted. I bent my knees to greet the new President of the Federal Republic of Nigeria, as I had been taught by my mother to do when greeting elders, and went back to my office immediately after.

The following morning, three major national newspapers, Thisday, The Guardian and the Daily Sun, all had photographs of President Buhari, the Permanent Secretary of the Ministry of Women Affairs and me on their front pages. I was quite convinced that it was by design, not coincidence. Whatever it was, it had the singular effect of dousing the 'blackmail' of my office by elements drawn from other Agencies, who wanted money and control of the Women Centre. But then, another storm began to brew thereafter.

Some misguided elements among Ndigbo took up a campaign to disparage me in the traditional and social media space. For bowing my knees when greeting President Buhari, I was abused, called names and insulted. It was a vicious campaign by people who had been unhappy about my rising profile. Characters who felt they did not benefit personally from my being the DG of NCWD, joined in mocking me. They claimed that the reason I greeted the 72-year-old President of my country on bended knees was so that he could retain me in my position as Director-General.

However, the inconvenient truth was that I was known for bowing in greeting to older persons or even younger ones, in respect of the position they occupied. I was raised to respect my elders and people in authority.

My reaction was one of great amusement. I promised that when next I met President Buhari, I would go down on my knees, completely, to greet him. My detractors could then go and hang themselves. But, of course, all that was before the senseless bloodletting that has continued in many parts of Nigeria under his watch. I have felt that not enough was being done to protect Nigerians from marauding militias and terrorists.

Tony Elumelu

Most people will, at least once in their lifetime, find themselves in a position where they are in desperate need of rescue. Sometimes, and quite surprisingly, that rescue may come from a quarter one never expected. It may happen that the help comes in swiftly, and is seamlessly rendered in a manner that is dignifying to the receiver.

That was precisely the help that came to me when my husband and I needed some debt relief. This assistance immensely helped us towards a much-needed recovery after a sustained period of challenges that upended our lives.

Battered by the crushing blow of debt we had run into, my husband and I had a meeting with Mr Tony Elumelu to see what could be done to reduce the magnitude of it. He was the MD of UBA at that time, and handed over the matter to Mr Kennedy Uzoka, who succeeded him in that position.

In a matter of days, we reached an understanding that was beyond our expectations. What is more, it came with no strings attached. Recalling how the entire scenario unfolded brings tears to my eyes; tears of gratitude and appreciation for the wonderful human being that is Tony Elumelu. May God's blessings continue to flow to you, my brother.

The Tony Elumelu Foundation has the impressive idea of raising young African entrepreneurs who can transform the continent with innovative ideas and startups. I am proud of their achievements in such a short period. Mr Elumelu is bent on transforming Africa, one entrepreneur after the other.

In this book, it came to my awareness that UBA and I seem to have an intertwining history. It was at a UBA Branch in Port Harcourt that my sister Zoe, while looking for employment, met Ms Estelle, the American lady who facilitated her movement to the United States in 1966. She in turn, made possible my education there in 1971. The gentleman who inspired my return to Nigeria from the US was the Chairman of UBA at the time, and I continue to enjoy a cordial and productive relationship with the bank, under Mr Kennedy Uzoka.

Dele Momodu

Back in the days of the hostile press, when negative articles, distortion of events, outright lies and concoctions about Onyeka Onwenu were prevalent in Lagos-based newspapers, one journalist/social commentator who stood up for me was Mr Dele Momodu. I like to think of him as an honest brother with a genuine simplicity in his ways. In his journalism, he did not target individuals; he did not identify with negative stories about people; rather, he loved to be on the side of truth and preferred to elevate others, not tear them down.

When he was critical of something, he did so objectively and constructively. Mr Momodu remains the burgeoning publisher of the iconic Ovation Magazine and a politician in his own right.

I always recall that after the release of my album *Onyeka* in 1992, I received some of the most dubious and unmerited criticisms for what was an important body of work. The album contained songs like '*Iyogogo*', 'The Peace Song', 'In The Morning Light' and others. These unwarranted criticisms were from the usual motley crew of misfits and jealous underachievers who paraded themselves as journalists but who could only be rightly called pen-pushers and collectors of brown envelopes. It was in the thick of this period that Mr Dele Momodu stood up in defence of my work and called for a stop to the attacks.

That was an unusual stance as many would rather sit back and enjoy the bashing of a female artiste who is presumed to be uppity. But not Dele Momodu. He stood up for me when it was inconvenient to do so. He has always treated me with respect and consideration, all of which is reciprocal.

Kofi Annan – The Perfect Gentleman

I had written quite a bit about Mr Kofi Annan, the former UN Secretary-General, in connection with my UN experience. However, I find it necessary here to thank him posthumously for all the support he gave me whilst there and for epitomising in that position, the quintessential African spirit of which I am proud.

Kofi Annan was, without a doubt, one of the finest diplomats of his generation. To have encountered him was to encounter a good man whose worldview was ruled by deep empathy. He carried himself with dignity, as an African who was very much assured of his place in the dynamics of world affairs. As the UN Secretary-General, he is remembered for his unwavering stand against US-UK unilateral action in Afghanistan and Iraq. A decision that came to have disastrous and destabilising consequences for those states and the region. He is also remembered for the UN not taking up the threats of genocide in Rwanda, under his watch as head of the UN Peace-keeping Unit, until it was too late. This he regretted and apologized for, quite profusely.

On one occasion, while watching television, I recall seeing the Secretary-General ask that an overbearing white reporter stops acting like a 'spoilt schoolboy'. I let out a chuckle, thinking that he had not changed from the person I knew; a kind-hearted fellow, perhaps even gentle to a fault, but who never broke a sweat calling to order anyone who crossed the line.

I had hoped to share this book with a retired Kofi Annan as soon as it was finished. But I had dithered on it for too long, and God called him back before we could have one more encounter. All the same, it was a rare privilege and honour to have known such a man. May his noble soul continue to rest in peace.

Charity Agbakuru – Acid Attack Survivor

One day in early 1996, a young journalist, Okechukwu Nwobu, came to my house with the horrific pictures of a young, female university undergraduate. She had been disfigured by a vicious acid bath. The perpetrator of this crime was a former boyfriend from whom she was recently separated. A classic case of 'If I can't have her, no one will'.

The victim was Ms Charity Agbakuru, an indigene of Rivers State. For the next two years, a group of professionals, artistes and journalists met every week to organise several fundraising events. We needed enough money to send Ms Agbakuru to the United States of America for reconstructive surgery on her face, eyes, ears and the neck area. Some of these people were Mr Sunny Allison, who was a top executive at DHL, Chizoba Omeokachie, a dynamic administrator and lawyer who provided us with a meeting place in Ikoyi at the Onwuka Kalu Organisation where she worked. There was Tony Ogbu, Akachi Umeh, Nelly Onwuchekwa, myself and others. We were the nucleus of the Save Charity Agbakuru Fund which another member, Ikechukwu Nwobu, had brought to our attention.

My manager, Mr Femi Jarett, threw himself into the effort, and so did my husband who halfway through our campaign had been cleared to return to Nigeria. He gave us strategic fundraising ideas and financial support. Ms Agbakuru was successfully treated by the world renowned plastic surgeon, Dr Ferdinand Ofodile.

Charity Agbakuru was the first national acid victim that we were aware of. It was the beginning of this novel crime wave. I was disturbed by the indifference of the police towards such a premeditated act of violence. The perpetrator was left to roam the streets unperturbed, while the victim was treated as though she had no rights. Her only offence had been the termination of a relationship she was no longer interested in.

Charity Agbakuru's fundraising campaign engaged everyone – the rich, poor, company executives, market women, and everyday people. Sadly, there was no justice for her, except the healing at the hands of Dr Ofodile, who rendered his services free of charge. He made it possible for a badly disfigured Charity to have a new lease of life, and not be defined by the horrendously wicked act done to her.

After the successful send-off of Ms Agbakuru to the US, I gave birth to my second son, Abraham. Other members of our team got fantastic job offers. Spectacularly, one of us was able to raise enough capital to launch an international courier company, Red Star. I had been impressed with Sunny Allison's conduct and dedication to duty, both at DHL where he worked and at our two- year effort to help Ms Agbakuru. When he approached me with the idea of setting up a courier company, I had every confidence in recommending him to my husband, who in turn introduced him to a partner. Together they built the Red Star Courier Company from scratch. Such were the blessings that the Lord visited on all of us.

I remain grateful to all who worked so hard and gave their widow's mite to Charity Agbakuru's fundraising effort.

Professor Uche Amazigo

During my one-year stint as a television journalist at Anambra Television (ATV) in Enugu, I met a young woman, Dr Uche Amazigo, who taught at the University of Nigeria Nsukka (UNN). She had reached out to me for some humanitarian programme she was running, and from day one, she was quite an impressive individual. She was a quiet and dedicated researcher. Therefore, it was not surprising when the World Health Organisation recognised her groundbreaking work that linked the different manifestations of Onchocerciasis (river blindness) and the debilitating skin disease found in the southeast of Nigeria.

Both are caused by the Black Fly which breeds in fast-flowing rivers and streams and can be eradicated by the yearly intake of Ivermectin. This medication, formulated by Merck and Company for use as an ectoparasiticidal agent in animals, was found to be effective as a parasitosis in humans. It was provided free of charge by the company.

WHO took on Uche Amazigo as the Director of the World Health Organisation Programme for Onchocerciasis Control (WHO-APOC) in Ouagadougou, Burkina Faso. Dr Amazigo again involved me in advocacy work, all done pro bono, to spread awareness about the medication. Together we toured the back streets and village hamlets of Plateau, Taraba and Adamawa States, sleeping in dirty hotel rooms with filthy bathrooms. But we counted it all joy. At every stop, we sang and danced and shared information with welcoming villagers.

Out of the advocacy tours came a song on river blindness, 'Have You Heard', which I recorded with Ameria Amity, a Burkinabe artiste. Together we launched it with performances in Ouagadougou.

The multiple award-winning Dr Amazigo now retired, runs a very effective NGO, Pan-African Initiative on Education and Health (PACIEH), for a community-based approach to school feeding. The NGO has a vision to act as a 'driving force' that promotes social safety nets for children living in resource-constrained communities.

Ms Tyna Adora Onwudiwe,

aka 'African Oyinbo' (White African)

Tyna Onwudiwe was born of an Igbo father from Ogbunike, Anambra State, and an English mother. She was, therefore, of mixed race. However, she was more African than me. She was proudly Nigerian too. That should explain why she was very critical of her country's missteps, as exhibited in our exchanges, in the documentary: *Nigeria, A Squandering of Riches.*

This friendship of two stubborn Igbo women began in 1982 when I met her while recording at Tabansi Studios, Onitsha. I had known Tyna in Lagos when she was a staff of Times Communications, a music promotion company. She moved to Onitsha but was not happy there. After work on my album, I invited her back to Lagos, to share my flat in Surulere. My brother, with whom I lived had been posted by his organisation to Casablanca, Morocco. We came back to Lagos together after my recordings in Onitsha.

In line with our growing Nigerian/African consciousness, Tyna and I set up a clothing outfit called African Konnection. It was a novel idea to use our locally favoured materials *ankara, aso oke, akwa george, akwa nmiri* and *akwete* to produce Western styles or modernised Nigerian fashion. For example, instead of the two-step 'up and down' wrapper, we would make a single skirt, long or short and a top, with a combination of other materials – lace, plain cotton or another *ankara* altogether. It caught on.

We also derived a certain amount of enjoyment in 'shocking' society. We did not care what people thought, as long as we believed we were on the right track. Tyna and I were comfortable in our jeans and *ankara* tops when the occasion called for something more sombre or traditional. My mother understood that it was a phase I had to pass through and left me to my stubbornness. I appreciated the fact that she gave me the space to make my own mistakes, so to speak. I have done the same for my children.

My relationship with Tyna was not without the usual patches of misunderstanding. Both of us were budding artistes with tall ambitions; socially aware and engaged. At some point, we disagreed and went our separate ways; our lives were headed in different directions anyway.

Before Tyna's move to South Africa with her children in 2000, we had reconciled and publicly too. At an event at Ken Olumese's Niteshift Club in Ikeja, my husband walked up to me on stage with Tyna, and said to both of us: 'You people should make up.' He then walked away, leaving us to follow through.

It was a great relief to reconnect and catch up after almost eight years of non-communication.

We lost touch again after she moved to South Africa, until sometime in 2004 when word came that my friend was gravely ill. Tyna needed help to pay her mounting medical bills and, of course, for the upkeep of her children. She was a single mother of three.

The campaign to raise funds for Tyna Onwudiwe's medical needs was spearheaded by the music impresario, Charles Oputa aka 'Charly Boy' and me. Charles and Tyna had been close friends as well. His wife, Diane joined us. Nigerians are very generous people and responded to this appeal. I cannot forget to mention the tremendous help rendered by the Lagos State Government of Senator Bola

Ahmed Tinubu. He made a significant donation towards her medical bills and also made it possible for Charly Boy, his wife Diane, Tyna's father and I to travel to Johannesburg to see her.

Our last get together was Tyna's birthday celebration, just weeks before her death. It was poignant and painful at the same time. We got to say goodbye without really saying goodbye.

I had to leave after one week, to get my children ready for school resumption but Tyna would not let go. She asked if I could move to South Africa with my family. I guess she was trying to tell me that she may not survive the illness. I had contractual obligations in Nigeria and had to honour them, but I promised to be back in two weeks. Sadly, she passed away before my return.

Tyna Adora Onwudiwe died in September 2004 at the age of 51.

I admired two things about my friend: her sense of self-worth and identity, and her stubbornness, which could cut both ways. Raising her third child, Negeste, Tyna would often lament in a way mothers do when they are confronted with children who take after them. In dealing with Negeste's stubbornness, my friend began to appreciate what her parents went through raising her. You could not get Tyna to do something unless she wanted to. Sometimes she would dig in her heels, even in the face of superior argument. However, when she was on the right track, you were lucky to have her on your side.

A few months after starting our fashion business, we bought a small petrol power generating set to counteract the incessant disruption of the power supply from the national grid. It is not possible to run even a small business in Nigeria without owning one. Late one evening, as one of our tailors prepared to fuel the generator, I happened to walk by with a kerosene lantern. I watched in horror as the rising vapours from the generator's fuel tank drew the naked light from the holes at the top of my lantern and set the flat on fire.

The power generating set was at the veranda and I was 20 metres away.

I panicked. I could not save anything. I could not even think, as smoke filled everywhere. My strength failed me and my courage was nowhere to be found either. I suddenly heard a voice from behind me scream: 'NO!'

In a flash, Tyna ran downstairs, quickly shoved sand into a bucket, ran back up and began pouring it on the burning generator, all the while calling out to neighbours for help. And they rallied around. In the meantime, I became unfrozen from fear and threw myself into the rescue effort.

We saved the day, or should I say, Tyna did. Our flat did not burn down, just the generator and a portion of the patio on which it stood. The rest of the rooms were covered with soot and stank of smoke for weeks. We repaired the damages, even before the landlady heard about the incident. All in all, I gained a deeper appreciation of my friend's sense of resolve and thanked God for it.

The fire incident which happened in 1983 was not our only brush with death. The following year, Tyna suffered the rupture of an ovarian cyst, just weeks after having her second baby, my godchild, Kamara. We were alone in the flat and did not own a car with which to rush her to the hospital. I carried her downstairs to the street, flagged down a taxi and rushed her to Dr Ohieri's First Consultants Hospital in Ikoyi. We nearly lost her.

In mourning Tyna Onwudiwe, I had said that her life's story could not be written without a mention of me. The same applies here. We were meant to be in each other's lives and for me, it was an honour. Tyna was an artiste through and through. Her creativity came across in her songs, videos, clothes and designs. In South Africa, she became a successful events planner and manager. She made me proud.

Bashorun MKO Abiola

When MKO Abiola's name is mentioned, one of the first things that comes to mind is his larger than life image. He was a businessman, patriot, kingmaker, a towering social and political figure, a philanthropist and a purveyor of colourful proverbs. Chief Abiola had a great sense of humour, but he was much more than that in the life of our country Nigeria. In 1993, he won the freest and fairest presidential elections in the country's history. He became the hope of a nation and generations yet unborn.

Chief Abiola was first and foremost, an *agidigbo* musician (*agidigbo* is a Yoruba form of social music). He made a living playing at weddings and naming ceremonies. As he told audiences very often, his earnings sometimes amounted to no more than a meal. He sang for his meals. He had been born into abject poverty: humble beginnings which he never despised. Chief Abiola was proud to be a musician and he identified with the rest of us. On many occasions, he spent his time, money and effort to settle disagreements among musicians, especially PMAN, the most serious musicians' union in Nigeria.

It was in the process of these interventions that we were exposed to Chief Abiola's wise sayings, such as: 'If you stay too long in the toilet, you will be visited by all manner of colourful flies,' he advised Tony Okoroji, as President of a beleaguered PMAN. This he said to encourage Okoroji not to prolong his tenure, but to allow others a chance to make their own contributions.

There was another one; 'You cannot shave a man's head in his absence.' MKO said this to those who tried to negotiate away his win at the presidential elections. If only we had listened to him, it might have been possible to salvage PMAN; it may have been possible to save Nigeria as well.

Among MKO's closest friends were musicians such as Sonny Okosuns and Chief Ebenezer Obey.

Before I met Chief Abiola in person, his reputation had preceded him and it was not all good. One heard about how he hated Christians, how he burnt Bibles and churches. As it turned out, MKO had the largest philanthropic heart imaginable. He helped countless people in various ways. A lot of his generosity was outside public glare. I was surprised to learn that he was responsible for one of my close relatives attending graduate school abroad. He neither previously knew her nor her husband before footing her graduate school bill. He certainly was unaware that the beneficiary was related to me.

My relationship with Chief Abiola was based on mutual admiration. He called himself my 'big brother', and I was honoured. At the launch of my album *Onyeka* in 1992, he declared to the world that he considered me his favourite African singer. He stormed the event with his eldest son, Kola. I was not expecting him because just a week earlier, his wife and my friend, Dr Doyin Abiola, had launched the same album to the press. That on its own was sufficient honour for me. But MKO chose to double my joy, and it was a day never to be forgotten.

Some of my contributions to Chief Abiola's presidential campaign effort were known to people very close to him. I remember catching up with him at the National Theatre, Iganmu, Lagos. He was attending an event organised by Christy Essien- Igbokwe, another supporter of his and my colleague. I insisted that he gave me an audience right away. I had a piece of advice for him. Chief Abiola took me seriously enough to ride home with Tyna Onwudiwe and I, and we went straight into his room. Kudirat, his senior wife, who sadly was felled by an assassin's bullet years later, was with us. She excused herself to allow us to talk in private. I am not at liberty to disclose the conversation, but it may have led to Chief Abiola making up his mind to choose Alhaji Babagana Kingibe as his running mate. It was a Muslim/Muslim ticket, that ordinarily, Nigerians would have kicked against. But they did not. This was the level of trust Nigerians had in Chief Abiola.

I saw MKO last at a petrol station in Maryland, Ikeja, just a few months before he was arrested and held by the government. I got out of my vehicle when I spotted him there talking to a group of people who had gathered around him. As soon as he saw me, he rushed out and picked me up as a big brother would a little sister. He spun me around before setting me down. The gesture was both delightful and sad at the same time. I did not know why. The agitation to reclaim his mandate had heated up and no one could predict how it would all end.

It ended badly for Nigeria with the death under mysterious circumstances of Chief MKO Abiola on 7 July 1998.

Abiola was the man with a booming voice, born poor but with a million dreams. He came with a philanthropic vision and a thousand proverbs. Alhaji Moshood Abiola died for Nigeria, and he will never be forgotten.

General Sani Abacha
(Former Head of State of Nigeria)

Y ou underestimate him at your peril and Nigerians did, until it was too late. General Sani Abacha was an autocrat who ruled Nigeria from 1995 until his death in 1999.

I have had the privilege of relating well with most Nigerian Heads of State. General Abacha and the First Lady, Hajiya Maryam Abacha, treated me with respect.

I have also prided myself with the ability to speak truth to power, sometimes out of naivety but I have never regretted it. I believe that was part of why I have enjoyed tremendous goodwill and accommodation from those in power. General Sani Abacha certainly saw that side of me, when he asked me for a favour I could not grant.

Amid his disagreement with Nelson Mandela in 1996, when Madiba publicly and openly criticised Nigeria for its relapse into military rule, General Abacha asked me to write a song that would express his anger and disappointment with Madiba's chastisements. I refused. I said, 'No!'

I could understand his rage. Madiba expressed his disappointment with Nigeria in a no holds barred manner. I never saw a normally calm Abacha any angrier. He felt that it could have been delivered more respectfully, especially given the role Nigeria played in the emancipation of South Africa. But I still was not going to write a song in the diminution of a man who had spoken his mind and told

435

the truth about my county, not even when a Head of State had so requested.

I dared to look the Head of State in the eye and let him know that not only was I not going to write such a song, but that he should have his revenge on Mandela by being the best Head of State he could be. He should deliver on all the promises he had made to Nigerians. General Abacha was shocked at the audacity of my response, but I thank God that he took my words in good faith. I could have been in deep trouble if that was not the case.

At a national event, the launching of the second War Against Indiscipline (WAI) – the first one was launched by the Buhari/Idiagbon regime in 1984 – inspired by the images of bad national behaviour in the documentary *Nigeria, A Squandering of Riches*, I had mounted the stage to sing my song, 'God Bless Nigeria' when rain threatened to fall. I declared in the name of Jesus that the rain would not fall until I had finished my performance. The rain that had started drizzling ceased. As soon as I sang the last note, everyone had to scamper and leave the open-air venue in a hurry. The heavens opened up with showers of blessing, as I called the rain. General Sani Abacha mentioned to me years later that on that day, he marvelled at the authority I wielded. I told him that it was simply the grace of God.

President Felix and Madame Thérèse Houphouët Boigny of Côte d'Ivoire

One of the funniest photographs I ever saw of my husband was one taken of him in 1992, with his mouth agape whilst he looked at the incredible treasures on display at President Houphouët Boigny's living quarters in Yamoussoukro, Côte d'Ivoire. My husband and I, as well as my brother Richard, who was fluent in French, were special guests of the President at his 88th birthday celebrations.

Unknown to me, my song 'Ekwe' embedded in the album, 'In The Morning Light' and released in 1984 was a massive hit in Côte d'Ivoire. The problem was that they were convinced that the singer was either Cameroonian or Congolese. They found out who I was by chance.

Coming back from a musical tour of India in 1985, I was forced by scheduling conflicts to reroute my return trip with a stopover in Abidjan, Côte d'Ivoire. Richard had been posted there as Regional Accountant by African Re-Insurance Company. Passing through customs, it was found out that I was an artiste. When jokingly asked to sing a song by one of the officers, I opened up with 'Ekwe' and the whole airport went wild. Ivorian customs men and women gave me an incredible welcome, and from there began my relationship with this most welcoming nation.

If Ivorians loved 'Ekwe' they were completely blown away by

the 'Peace Song' in the album in *Onyeka* in 1992. They fell in love with it. My concerts in the country were usually sold out. Still, if the promoters did not hire a big enough hall, people had to be turned away at the gate. This was the state of affairs when an invitation came from the Presidency for me to perform at his birthday celebration, in 1993. Both the President and the First Lady were great fans of mine. They loved my music and can be seen in a photograph taken at the occasion, waving the traditional white handkerchief at the performance of the song 'Iyogogo'.

Our visit started with a mass at the incredibly beautiful Basilica of Our Lady of Peace, the world's largest church, in Yamoussoukro. It is adorned with exquisite stained-glass windows, some of which depicted President Felix, in the company of saints. The Basilica was a rather controversial project because of its cost in a poverty-stricken environment.

At the President's country home, we were given a tour of a crocodile-filled moat and shown a pair of tortoises rumoured to be over 200 years old. There was a grand mausoleum, hosting the bodies of members of the Houphouët Boigny family. We were free to move around and take in the various collections of art objects from around the world. Even our waiting room had what appeared to be gold plated doorknobs.

Madam Thérèse, I must add, was an admirer of Nigerian fashion and I was able to have some things made for her by top Nigerian designers, as I did for Mrs Winnie Mandela. They both wore them proudly. She and her husband were excellent hosts and we thoroughly enjoyed the day with them.

Justice Eugene Ubezonu

U ncle Eugene Ubezonu is my mother's cousin. His own mum came from Obosi but was married in the nearby town of Nnewi. Like me, he lost his father early in life and his mother was subjected to the usual maltreatment that widows often experienced in Igboland. Uncle Eugene would always recall Papa Nnukwu's intervention, trekking by foot from Obosi to Nnewi to settle matters and protect his niece, Uncle Eugene's mother, from an oppressive brother-in-law. The recollections were made with love and gratitude.

When you walk into Uncle Eugene's house in Enugu, you would immediately notice an enlarged photograph of Papa Nnukwu with his trophy of a slain leopard. That was why he was called '*Ogbuagu*', one who slays a leopard. Papa Nnukwu was a hero to Uncle Eugene.

Ndigbo believe that it is possible to reincarnate, even while the person is alive. Uncle told me that my mother and his mum were so much alike that it was possible that this may indeed have happened. He loved Sister fiercely for that reason, and that love was extended to Sister's children, myself included.

Uncle Eugene was one person I could share a bottle of red wine with. He would regale me with stories about the old people and discuss issues of law, politics and philosophy in one stretch. He was always interested in family and how everyone was doing.

Justice Ubezonu was outspoken but could scarcely confront nor blame his cousin, my mum for anything when I complained about her harshness with me. He would rather make excuses and urge patience and understanding. Indeed, he understood Sister. However, on the rare occasions that he interceded, he managed to ask her to ease up on heaping every family obligation and responsibility on me, just because I was loath to resist. On those occasions, I felt I had an ally who my mother was forced to listen to.

Uncle Eugene is the junior brother to Dr Alex Ubezonu, the Fourah Bay College trained educationist who along with his family sheltered with us in Arondizuogu during the Biafran war.

Mrs Cecilia KO Mbadiwe

(Omekadiya – One who behaves like her husband)

Long before I learned that my family, the Onwenus, actually came from Ndimoko village in Arondizuogu, I knew a woman, a distant cousin, who sought in a most unique way to tell me about my background. My paternal grandfather had settled in Ndianiche, a story that was told earlier in the book. During the civil war, when we all returned to the relative safety of Arondizuogu, Mrs Cecilia Mbadiwe, wife of Dr KO Mbadiwe, a notable and colourful politician, would often send a car to pick up the Big Three to spend the weekend at the Peoples' Palace. That was the Mbadiwe family house. We spent time with some of the children who were in our age group, and entertained the Mbadiwes and their guests with our unique song and dance routine.

I had a special relationship with Omekadiya. She would spend time telling me stories about Papa – her cousin – whom she was very proud of.

Mrs Mbadiwe would often ask me where I thought my family came from and I would reply, 'Ndianiche, Obinetiti of course.' She would laugh and without explanation, postpone the conversation for another day. I was intrigued. I knew that there was some weighty information that she wanted to pass on. I also knew that only she would determine when. I had to be patient. This went on for two years, until sometime in 1970.

My grandfather, Mazi Onwenu, came from the Onu/ Okereke/ Alisa family in Ndimoko, so did Mrs Mbadiwe's father. I knew that she and her sister, Mrs Grace Kanu, had both enjoyed a close relationship with my parents. However, it was only after the revelation of our connectedness that I understood why. From then on, I began to inquire about Mazi Onwenu and the circumstances under which he moved from Ndimoko to Ndianiche.

I noted that no ceremony or *nme-nme* could take place in my family without the presence of a representative from Ndimoko, and vice versa. A few decades later, it was Mazi Okereke, father of Mr Gil Okereke, a notable Lagos-based architect, who stood in for my father on the day of my 'wine carrying' (traditional wedding). From my findings, I gained a better understanding of the often-repeated demand by some unfriendly elements in Obinetiti, that the Onwenus go back to where they came from (meaning Ndimoko). This is so that all the land belonging to them could be taken away. They conveniently forgot that no one sprung from the ground. We all came from somewhere.

Interestingly, after my re-entry into Nigerian society in 1980 and my becoming a 'celebrity' in the country, there was a tug of war between the young people of Obinetiti and Ndimoko, as to who 'owned' Onyeka Onwenu. Success, indeed, has many parents!

Omekadiya was a tall, stately woman, a stunning dresser with an unrivaled sense of style. She had a reserved and composed disposition and commanded respect with her intimidating presence. Yet she was the epitome of humility and kindness.

What Mrs Mbadiwe did for me by simply caring, my mother, Mrs Hope Onwenu did for her daughter Betty Mbadiwe-Ijeomah. One particular encounter explains this special relationship. Betty was the only girl among five boys. After her parents passed away, my mum took to praying for her on a regular basis. At a gathering of Arondizuogu people in Lagos, Sister spotted Betty trying her best to look happy. But my mother was not fooled. She gently pulled her aside and without much explanation, taught her a memorable song. The song was actually a prayer for times of distress. And it worked. Betty's spirits were lifted immediately and she has never forgotten it. She plays it forward by sharing and teaching others.

Chineke nke igwe
Igbaputawo m
Mgbe nmuo mu no na nsogbu
A gam enye g'ekele
Ekele oma ka m g'enye gi
Otugo oma k'am buru bia
Abu Ndi Nso k'amgabu
I di ngozi na I di ukwu
Ma I di Ukwu
K'am Keta oke n'ime gi.
Okwa gi si n'iga eburu m ibua
Okwa gi s'ina I g'abu nke muo
A n'om n'iru gi
K'am keta oke n'ime gi.

Israel Anyanele

The cross parenting that my mum and Omekadiya established became the foundation of my friendship with Betty Mbadiwe. She is her father's daughter like me. I have seen her make great sacrifices for the unity and progress of the KO Mbadiwe family. For that, she has my admiration, respect and support. She is my 'sister' indeed. We both have an understanding of who we are and perhaps our role in our wider family circles.

443

Their Father's Daughters All

I know them when I encounter them. They have confidence in themselves and make no apologies for their strength. They have nothing to prove to anyone, except to themselves, for the high expectations they have. These are women who possess the innate ability and mental conditioning, right from childhood, to succeed. They are not afraid of the world; rather, they take it head-on.

Their fathers had told them that they could do anything they put their minds and hearts to and they believed so. Some of them are: Ambassador Tokunbo Dosumu (nee Awolowo), Ngozi Okonjo-Iweala, Denderin Adeniran Ogunsanya, Senator Kariat Gwadabe (nee Abdulrahman Abdulrazak), Oby Ezekwesili, Margaret Onyema Orakwusi, Chimamanda Ngozi Adichie and Mrs Olajumoke (nee Ajasin).

To hear these women talk about their beloved fathers, the enablement, empowerment, and validation they received from them is a study in the virtues of a parent's loving relationship. I salute them all for making their fathers proud.

Great Igbo Men

There are some people whom I feel compelled to thank and appreciate each time I see them. I give posthumous honour to Dim Chukwuemeka Odumegwu-Ojukwu, former Head of State of Biafra and Senator Uche Chukwumerije. They served the best interest of the Igbo race. Others are: Senator Enyinnaya Abaribe, Professor ABC Nwosu, Ochudo Agbaso and Professor Eleazu, amongst many others.

I feel obliged to mention in small details the attributes of some of them.

Commodore Okoh Ebitu Ukiwe
One-time Chief of General Staff (Second-in-Command to General Babangida in the Armed Forces Ruling Council of 1985- 86)

Chief Emeka Anyaoku
Ichie Adazie of Obosi. Former Secretary of the Commonwealth 1990-2000.

Prof. Anya O Anya
Described as a man with an interdisciplinary mind. He is a former Chairman of Nigeria Economic Summit Group, as well as of Ndigbo Lagos.

Rear Admiral Ndubuisi Kanu

Former Governor of Lagos State and Imo State.

Prof. Joe Irukwu

Renowned insurance guru, lawyer and Senior Advocate of Nigeria, lecturer and author.

Rear Admiral Alison Madueke

Former Governor of Anambra State and Imo State, as well as a member of the Provisional Ruling Council of the Abacha regime.

The list is much longer but suffice it to say that these are great Igbo men who can be relied upon not to let down the nation for personal benefit as some others have done. Men who have shown remarkable consistency in leadership and are veritable role models for the rest of us.

They remind me of my father, Hon. DK Onwenu (*Ogbufo* – One who clears the path) I hold them all in high esteem.

Interviewing Gani Fawehinmi

Having a discussion with Madame Thérèse.

Receiving my National Award, MFR from
President Obasanjo in 2004

With my friend Tyna Onwudiwe - aka
African Oyibo

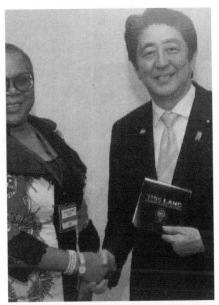

With Abe Shinzo, Japans longest serving
Prime Minister at a Womens Conference
in Japan 2015

With EC Clark at the National Awards

With Margaret Ekpo. Renowned female politician of Pre and Post Independent Nigeria

With MT Mbu and Prof Anya. O. Anya at an event in Lagos.

With my mentor Alhaji Maitama Sule Dan Masani Kano

PART IX

Whose Life Is It Anyway?

Whose Life Is It Anyway?

Every Boxing Day, December 26, my maternal grandmother would prepare us for a special church service – *Uka ndi amunye n'uka* – a service for those born into the church.

Only people whose parents were Christians and who wedded in the church were allowed in. It was a service my grandmother could not attend herself. She would see us off to the gate, and watch, a little forlornly, but proudly, as her grandchildren marched up the steps of St Andrews Church.

I have never failed to appreciate being born into a strong

Christian family, one that was passionate about the faith and tried to live by what it taught. Mama Nnukwu had run away from home at the age of fifteen to live with the missionaries who had converted her. That passion was passed down in the family.

Growing up a Christian, however, never made anyone a born-again. I had a corporate relationship, and not a personal one, with the Lord. There comes a time when circumstances beyond your control may conspire to draw you closer into a deeper relationship with the One you worship.

For me, it came in 1996 when for the second time, I gave my life to Jesus Christ at the Fountain of Life Church, Ilupeju, Lagos. Three months earlier, I was at an event where Evangelist Ebenezer Obey, the former Juju music maestro turned pastor preached. My friend, Mrs Taiwo Obasanjo hosted it, and I could not say no to the invitation. When the altar call was made, I responded and said the sinners' prayer so that I could quickly get out of there. But the emptiness I was feeling at the time did not go away.

I sank back into my depression and self-pity. I had just enough strength to continue functioning as if all was well.

When it all came to a head, it did so spectacularly. The combination of a serious illness in the family and the downgrading of our financial standing left me reeling. The clincher was an armed robbery attack days after dropping my children off in the US for a vacation. I came back to Nigeria, needing rest and time alone to heal emotionally. I was exhausted.

My friend, Funke Adefowope, came around in the evening of the day before the attack. She warned me that there were gangs of armed robbers operating quite regularly in the Opebi, Ikeja, area where we lived. They had been in her house the night before and had managed to enter the kitchen through the back door. They were rattled by her presence and left in a hurry. I thanked her for the warning but thought nothing more of it, after praising God for the safety of her family.

At about 1 a.m the following day, in between sleep and awareness, I heard the smashing of bottles outside. My brother Richard was in the guest room downstairs. I wondered what kind of party he was having without telling me. It turned out that someone was smashing all the light fixtures around the house. Two armed men had jumped over the fence from a neighbour's house. Our neighbour's fiancée who was alone and whom they had threatened to rape, directed the robbers to me. She told them who I was and that I had just returned from the US. They quickly left her and made their way to my house.

'What's going on there?' I asked. I got a gruff reply.

'Common get back up there.'

I had come down at the side of the building where they were and which had a side window, the only one in the whole house that was unprotected with anti-burglary metal grills. It was precisely at that point that they noticed it. They simply broke the glass window and came in. While the robbers ransacked the rooms downstairs, I ran back up to try and hide some valuables.

My brother would later make a joke out of his encounter with the two armed robbers. Richard tried to hide, but could not find a suitable corner apart from the one where the steward had chosen for his safety. When my brother tried to hide in the same room, James politely asked him to look for another spot as he got there first. In other words, it was a case of every man for himself. Even in danger, there is humour to be found. This part of the story always made my brother and I laugh.

When the robbers caught up with me upstairs, the first man gently removed the gold necklace and cross pendant I had on. He did not yank it off; he carefully unhooked it. The second man went straight to my underwear drawer and pulled out an envelope with money that I had reserved for my return to the US to pick up my children. They seemed to know all the places in my room where I had hidden valuables and cash. They took them away without threatening or manhandling me. But I sensed that they would not have hesitated to use violence if I had resisted.

On their way out of my house, the robbers were cornered by a group of neighbourhood security guards. One was captured and handed over to the police, the other, the one who took my necklace, escaped with the loot. He was killed months later in another operation in Badagry, the police told us.

An armed robbery attack in someone's home is an invasion of privacy that leaves the victim vulnerable and fearful. I was grateful that my husband and children were not around to witness it. Perhaps my husband may not have taken it well and would have endangered us all, I thought.

But I was shaken by the experience and recovery took some time. I developed insomnia and was unable to sleep between the hours of midnight and 5 a.m, till I could hear sounds of people rising with the day. Only then could I rest for a few hours. Everything made me jittery; I was living in fear of the next mishap or disappointment in my life.

My relationship with the church had grown cold. Right from my time in the United States, I had stopped attending church service. No one was around to make me go, not Mama Nnukwu and not Sister. I was free to do as I pleased and Sunday mornings were for lay-ins, sleeping late, having Sunday brunches, hanging out with friends, reading the Sunday papers and catching up with television. I continued this practice when I got back to Nigeria in 1980 until I had children and began feeling bad that I was not giving them the foundation of Christian education and worship that I had been privileged to have.

Brother Richard to The Rescue

I n 1995, my brother Richard became a born-again Christian and began taking the children to The Fountain of Life Church, Ilupeju, where he worshipped. All of us had resisted attending our mother's Anglican church because we did not find it exciting and we felt our mother's influence was overbearing. We wanted to worship God on our own terms. Sister understood and put no pressure on us, except on Harvest days and special services which she insisted her grandchildren must attend.

By the end of 1996, I ended up at the Fountain of Life Church by happenstance. With God, however, there is no such thing. This is how it unfolded.

Funke Adefowope, my friend who had warned me about the armed robbers, invited me to a programme at the Latter Rain Church in Ikeja. Pastor Bakare, a firebrand preacher, was ministering. I was to meet up with her at home, and we would then go together. I got on very well with Funke's parents, General and Mrs Adefowope. Funke's mum, a beautiful and godly woman, liked me a lot and the feeling was mutual. It was always a pleasure to see her. When I stepped into the Adefowope living room, my friend's mum was in deep conversation with a younger woman. She was Pastor Bimbo Odukoya of the Fountain of Life Church.

I was introduced to her and she asked one question only: 'Onyeka, how is your Christian life?'

I fell apart. All the fear, anxiety, depression and insecurities came tumbling out. I could no longer contain the heartache. The tears came tumbling down. I was broken and could not hide it any longer. I needed to join a fellowship for corporate worship, but one of the things that kept me away was the loss of privacy at worship when people recognised me. I wanted a place where I could sit in a corner and not be recognised, noticed or distracted. Pastor Bimbo asked me to pray and ask God to guide me to a place of worship. This happened on a Friday. On Sunday, I decided to go to church with my brother and children. I ended up at the Fountain of Life Church and was pleasantly shocked to see Pastor Bimbo there. I gave my life to Christ and thus, began the best of the rest of my life.

There has been no looking back as a born-again follower of Christ. At the Fountain of Life Church, I lost my fear and dread of life and I found my courage again. That heavy dampening fear of everyday calamities, the uncertainty about other people in my life, the overwhelming weight of expectations and let downs, all began to melt away. I regained vision and the purpose of service. I began to learn about the benefits of forgiving others, even when they did not ask for it. It was for my own relief and growth. My life was in my hands and God's, if I let Him, if I had just a little bit of faith, He would work with whatever I had. The choice was mine, and I chose Jesus.

The fact that I gave my life to Jesus Christ did not put an end to my challenges in my life. In fact, they intensified. It was as if the devil got angry and unleashed a ton of additional problems for me to deal with, to test my faith. But I had learned something very important: the issue was not whether troubles will come, but that I would overcome them; not whether I would fall sometimes, but that I would always get up and rise higher every time.

With regards to corporate worship, I began to see its benefit again. Hearing other people's testimonies and triumphs over challenges, as is the case in pentecostal churches, was particularly encouraging. Worship was both intense and exuberant, as the Holy Spirit moved.

My relationship with God is one that continues to deepen every day. It is intimate, and it is one-on-one. The first thing I learned from my pastors at the Fountain of Life Church was that I had a direct link to God. I had the power and the ability to pray and relate directly with Him. Being prayed for and laid hands on was a good thing. But you can also do those things for yourself. Your walk with God is a personal thing, a journey of discovery, as God reveals Himself in inexhaustible ways. I am privileged, indeed.

In every twist and turn, I see God's grace, and I am overwhelmed with gratitude. I shall continue to strive and to thrive, knowing that the journey is part of my destination. I have resolved to enjoy life's experiences, while I try to do as much good as possible.

Whose life is it anyway? It is His and to Him I give it back, to be used in whatever way the Lord pleases.

GREATEST LOVE

I woke up one-morning
Feeling life had passed me
I knew I was hungry
For a love I could not find
All you lonely people
All you sinners lost out there
Let me tell you about the greatest
Love of all

I know that He loves me
Even when I go astray
He gives me much courage
When trouble comes my way
Even though I may fall
He wipes away my tears
Yes, I know I found
The greatest love of all

Greatest love
I found in Him
Greatest love
He gives to me
He is the living waters
He quenches oh my thirst
Yes, I know I've found
The greatest love of all.

Onyeka Onwenu 1996

(The lyrics of my first song after I gave my life to Christ)

And We All Ate From The Same Bowl: A Lesson In Humility
After giving my life to Christ in 1996, I became a full member of
the Fountain of Life Church, Ilupeju, Lagos. I managed to extract a
promise from Pastor Taiwo Odukoya and Pastor Bimbo, his late wife
and Associate Pastor at the time, that I would be allowed to stay in
the background as a new member. I wanted to be able to melt into
the congregation and not be singled out for special mention or role.
That agreement lasted for just three weeks.

On my third Sunday Service, Pastor Bimbo asked to see me after church. What for? I asked myself as I made my way to her. There, I met a young woman whose passion for Christian missionary work was immediately infectious. Pastor Blessing Awosika, then Billy Awosika, is a carpenter and the owner of the Chair Centre, as well as other businesses. She is now the chairman of First Bank Nigeria. She had set her mind on creating a Christian Missionary Fund to help evangelise Nigeria and my purpose was to give her full support.

In that meeting that Pastor Bimbo called, we came up with the idea of a compilation of gospel songs by various artistes and a joint Christmas medley. The artistes, some of them recording for the first time were Pastor Bimbo Odukoya; the very special Ms Esse Agese, a powerful singer; Pastor Kingsley Ike, then a rising gospel artiste; Beatrice Oletue, a beautiful choir leader and singer; James Munor, an upcoming artiste and myself.

While Pastor Bimbo and Pastor Blessing were the Executive Producers, I was the coordinator. The idea was novel; it had not been done before and it was well executed. The endeavour provided a rallying point for what it was designed – the fundraising for missionary work in Nigeria.

We threw ourselves into the project of recording and promoting the album, *A Sacrifice of Love*, through concerts and media interviews. It was an exhilarating time for us all.

During the recording, when we would all gather for rehearsals at my studios on Oregun Road Ikeja, we would order what my children called 'office rice', meaning rice bought and eaten at mummy's office. It was a very tasty kind of jollof rice prepared with fried meat, which was washed down with a soft drink. The recording team was soon introduced to this instant crowd pleaser whenever we needed some grub. The rice was bought in a huge dish which we all ate from. For me, it was a lesson in humility, never to be forgotten. It felt like one big family.

The importance of this work was aptly demonstrated by the discovery, not long before then, of a previously unknown indigenous group discovered in the Koma Hills of Adamawa. The group lived as if in the Stone Age. However, the Gospel reached them, and then development and education followed. Part of the proceeds from the album was sent to the missionaries there.

The Unity Centre

I t is fitting that this chapter comes up here, right after the one on being born-again. One could not have happened without the other.

As a Christian of the Anglican persuasion, I was not taught about seedtime and harvest, except that the Bible exhorts us to do good and love our neighbours as ourselves. As a born-again Christian, I decided to give God a gift – the proceeds of my first gospel album, which I donated to a church building fund. No sooner had I done that, than the Lord began to bless me in diverse ways. It was not as if one was not generous in the past, but God opened my eyes to the value of sowing.

In 1996, The Fountain of Life Church Ilupeju embarked on a fundraising appeal for a new building. I also embarked on the recording of my first gospel album, *Greatest Love*. The Lord put it in my heart to donate to the Church Building Fund, the proceeds of the album sales. I was perplexed. It was self-funded and had cost a lot of money to produce; I began to haggle with God, the terms of the donation. I asked if I could give the church 60% and keep 40% to cover my expenses. But I knew no peace until I stood up on the podium and announced my gift to a grateful church. 100% of the proceeds would go to the Building Fund.

Greatest Love turned out to be a hugely successful album and the church raised millions from its launching. To God be the glory. I did not expect anything in return; I had only done what I thought was put in my heart to do.

Months later, as I looked through The Guardian newspaper's property section, I spotted an interesting advert. I had contemplated moving my office from Oregun Road, Ikeja, where I had been running a music rehearsal studio for six years to a more central location. The new property was a section of the Sea Gardens on Isaac John Street GRA Ikeja, right in the middle of town.

It turned out to be a rundown building, rotting away due to years of neglect. It had no roof and no discernible partitioning inside. It looked like a jungle with a few disused cages here and there. There were a few monkeys and birds, as well as an alligator in a pond on a makeshift driveway. At the back of the roofless warehouse, there were banana plants flourishing.

Initially, I was overwhelmed by the dilapidated state of the property and decided to walk away. It would take an awful lot of money to rehabilitate and I did not have a huge amount at my disposal. But God had another plan.

It turned out that the gentleman who ran the place was a member of my church. Apart from wanting to lease the property, he was looking for an artiste to take up monthly performances in the open court that formed part of the premises. Lágbájá, the masked artiste who had been using the spot for years, moved into his own venue on Opebi Road called Motherland.

I went back to the property a second time, at the invitation of the church member. He convinced me that I could make something great out of it. With an initial lease of nine years and an option to renew for an additional ten years at least, you should be able to recoup your investment, and then some, he assured.

I decided that with a dearth of event centres in Ikeja, there were only Onyx Plaza, Sheraton Hotel and Etiebet's Place (which was under construction). I would be meeting a need people had – to stop holding events in their homes. Armed robbery was a real menace at the time, and hosting parties at home meant exposure to such dangers.

To show seriousness, I was required to make an initial deposit of N1m. However, I had only N200,000 in all of my accounts put together. From the period I registered an interest in the property, I felt convinced that having found myself there a second time, I should give it serious consideration. Nothing convinced me more than how I raised the N1m I needed for a deposit.

Somehow, my father, DK Onwenu, with his far-reaching legacy as a generous man, would come to have a huge bearing on my fate. It is a true testimony to his calling as a teacher that despite his punishing schedule, he found time to guide his wards to academic excellence.

One such student was Mr Chidi Offong. His parents, who were close family friends, handed him over to my dad at Baptist High School where he was the first African vice-principal. Mr Offong turned out to be a successful administrator of a government agency and an astute businessman.

I had taken a decision that leasing The Unity Centre would depend on my ability to secure a loan for the initial payment. Mr Offong was my only viable option. If he were unable to assist, I would abandon the idea altogether. To my greatest surprise, Mr Offong quickly wrote a cheque for the amount, even as I was still making the request. God and destiny were on my side. I cannot thank him enough for that gesture.

Securing the lease of the Unity Center was one thing, financing its renovation was another. Despite spirited efforts, I could not secure a bank loan. I realised then that all the years of negative press that artistes like me were subjected to, may have made it more difficult for us to be taken seriously by banks and lending institutions. I had to build on my own. I was the sole investor.

In the entertainment industry, an artiste may go for months without work. There could be a lot of barren spells; dry periods where it would seem as though the world had forgotten the artiste. Throughout the five years of building, I had to shoulder other obligations, such as raising my two boys and nephew. I also had the responsibility of taking care of my aged mother, her siblings and the extended family of cousins and uncle's wives in Arondizuogu. I do not know how I survived. Everyone was well taken care of but myself. Apart from the inevitable costumes I had to put on for my shows, there were no luxuries in my life. None whatsoever.

There is an Igbo proverb that says '*Aguu nwe nchekwube a da agugbu*' which means 'Hunger does not kill someone who is hopeful of a hearty meal.' I had my eyes fully fixed on the ball; to run an outstanding professional outfit for events, rehearsals and meetings. The Unity Centre was an insurance policy of sorts, a secure source of revenue for my boys' college education.

The Centre hosted its first event, a wedding, on 4 March 2002, as one of only four such outfits in the Ikeja area. It was a proud moment for me. My office, the administrative centre, was the first building to be completed in 1998, on the banana patch. It afforded me a vantage position from which to personally supervise work on the main auditorium. Typical of an organisation with lean resources, everything was done through direct labour.

Predictably, the fact that an artiste had built an events centre elicited all manner of reactions from people. There was admiration, but also jealousy from both the usual and unexpected quarters. The Sea Garden outfit from which I leased the property initially had folded up and the Managing Director was relieved of his duties. Before he left, he had for no reason at all, grown belligerent towards me, blaming me for his loss. At some point, he was physically aggressive, calling me *ole* – a thief – in the presence of my workers.

With the disintegration of Sea Gardens and the possibility that their lease may not be renewed, I decided to contact the owner of the place and establish a direct relationship with her for continued business. I had made a huge investment there, which needed protection. After signing an initial four-year lease agreement with the owner in 1998, she was forced to back out of it as soon as the Sea Garden partners protested. Apparently, she had equally agreed to continue their lease arrangement. She, however, was not able to return the money I paid her. She asked me to continue dealing with the Sea Garden people until she is able to retrieve her property from them.

The greatest opposition I had about the successful completion of the Unity Centre came from within my family.

I am mostly a loner, not deliberately but by a natural and subconscious pull. I enjoy my own company. If an appreciable length of time passed without my having some 'me-time', I would feel out of sorts. There are few times in my life that I have felt lonely.

On this particular night in 2006, I felt lonely and alone. I was on my way to Area F Police Station to see the Area Commander. Trouble was brewing at The Unity Centre and not for the first time. It was a rare situation for me, this bewildering loneliness.

I had rented the place out to my first cousin, the daughter of Aunt Dorothy, while I pursued my political ambition in Imo State.

However, it turned out that she and her powerful lawyer friend were working underground to have my lease terminated and the property sold to them. In the meantime, I had the privilege of first refusal in the lease which I had signed. I was fighting some very powerful forces all by myself.

I drove to the Police Station late that night to lodge a security complaint. Someone, on behalf of my cousin – her younger brother to be exact – had threatened to shoot me. He was capable of it and he owned a gun. He also lived on the premises of the Unity Centre, in a section of the property that had been converted to an apartment for him. This threat was coming from home. It was too close for comfort.

My relationship with Aunt Dorothy and my cousins was a close one. I loved my aunt and considered her a second mother. I never gave my mum a gift without giving one to her as well. It was usual for me to take them both out to restaurants and on trips or vacations abroad. I spoilt them with presents and attention. I did anything they requested me to, well almost anything. I took care of anyone they asked me to and contributed to their favourite charities, even with free musical performances.

Whenever I travelled to Cross River, Akwa Ibom or Adamawa States, I would bring back loads of dry and fresh fish, dried shrimp – *oporo* and crayfish, *okazi* leaves, and other local delicacies for my mother and my aunt to share with relatives and friends. They were givers, both of them; it brought them great fulfilment.

Whilst in Lagos between 1996 and 2001, I cooked for them every Sunday, a lunch of marinated guinea fowl fried to perfection, with fried rice and salad. They called it their 'Sunday-Sunday Medicine'. Such was my relationship with these two sisters that on the rare occasions when they quarrelled, I was the one they trusted to settle the matter fairly.

Emboldened by the authority of the lease and offer letter I gave my cousin, she and her powerful lawyer approached the owner of the property and convinced her to sell the property to them instead. They accused me of attempting to sell her property to them. How could that be, when I had no papers to back up my ownership of it? It was a blatant lie, of course, but the owner bought it. Let me tell you why.

My relationship with the landlady started out on a good note. She visited the Unity Centre regularly and got to know my brother, Richard, and my husband as well. She got on well with both of them. At some point, she became sufficiently close to my brother that they talked about dating. That was when she began to complain about me. She was uncomfortable with my closeness to Richard. She began criticising my music and even attempted to 'teach' me how to sing better. I patiently listened for two unbearable hours as she 'tutored' me on precious little about show business.

From that moment, our relationship changed and she became an adversary of sorts. Each time I put a new tenant on the property, they were threatened until they began to pay her and not me.

For the five years that my cousin was a tenant on the property, she only paid me for the first year. The rest she paid to the property owner.

My cousin and her co-conspirators wanted me out of the property by all means and they worked very hard to do that. However, with each effort, they made me more determined to hold on to the truth. They went to court and the case was decided in my favour. The battle was fought with threats and belligerence. It was also fought within the family.

By the year 2006, when the trouble with my cousin started, my aunt had gained sufficient control over her sister, my mother. In turn, she had become very dependent on their relationship that she was willing to give up anything to please Aunt Dorothy. It was bewildering for my siblings and I to watch this process happen, gradually but surely. We all suffered for it, from Azunna and Richard to Zoe, Ijeoma and myself, and paid the price as well. But our mother's happiness was also important to us and if Aunt Dorothy made her happy, we were ready to put up with the inconvenience of her meddling in our private affairs.

My aunt and her daughter wanted the Unity Centre, and the Unity Centre they had to have. My mum was warned, right in my presence, that my refusal to give it up could sunder the family and affect her relationship with her sister. My mother appealed to me to let go of the property, so that peace would reign.

I would have done so in the past; I always walked away from any contentious matter involving my aunt and her children, and be the loser for it. But not this time. The jealousy and covetousness exhibited by her was too obvious and quite disturbing.

Sister finally realised and admitted to Azunna and I that she had been wrong about her sister's intentions all along. She died knowing that her children had been at the receiving end of unrelenting jealousy and obstruction by her sister. This was most satisfying for me.

Throughout the five year ordeal with my cousin, the property owner remained hidden from us, while collecting rent from my tenant. In 2010, long after the former Sea Garden partners had lost interest in the place, we were able to locate her through her new lawyers. We went back into negotiations, to continue the direct relationship she had suspended after collecting money from me.

The new rent was outrageously high. The landlady forgot that I was a sitting tenant; I was being treated as a new prospect who must start negotiations from ground zero, my N50m investment notwithstanding. Her lawyers ordered a new survey and property assessment of the Unity Centre, then served it to me who had built parts of it and renovated others. The property owner even denied ever knowing who I was, let alone signing a contract with me. This outrage was until she was reminded that there were scientific ways of authenticating a signature. She then claimed that she was intimidated by my fame and thus signed the contract. But it was one which her lawyer had drafted; an unlikely scenario.

Several court cases were filed and are ongoing on the Unity Centre. As we were going back and forth, we began experiencing harassment and abuse of my person written on the walls of the property, part of which served as my office. My life was also being threatened by lawyers representing the owner. In their words, 'You will leave here, dead or alive, you choose.' Several reports were made to the police.

On three occasions, judgments of doubtful legality were obtained in a Magistrate Courts against Sea Gardens Ltd, the company from which I first leased the property and which no longer existed. One such dubious judgment was used to seize valuable items in my office. Some of these items were immediately returned on the affirmation that the judgment had nothing to do with me and on the Chief Justice of Lagos State's orders.

Six months later, 20 armed thugs descended on the property and began to dismantle the roof over my office, carting away more valuable equipment. The Police intervened and stopped them. The landlady was asked to maintain the status quo in respect of the court order given to all concerned. All this happened in 2013. On Thursday 4

July 2019, the property owner and her lawyers, once again convinced the Police and court bailiffs that they had an authentic court ruling. It was the same one that had been disavowed. Before we could reach the Acting Chief Judge of Lagos State, they had destroyed my office and personal effects (awards, picture collection, documents and precious mementoes.)

Again, electronics, musical equipment and office furniture worth over N100m were taken away.

The court cases continue, including an appeal to have the Magistrate Court ruling which was not directed at me but which was illegally used against me, to be sanctioned. I will continue to seek justice on the matter. Nigeria is not a banana republic and our laws ought to be fairly administered.

Lessons Learned

A pastor whose church had rented the Unity Centre after my cousin had left was again threatened by the Landlady's agents while she was still in hiding, and he began paying rent to her instead of me. He admitted as much in a letter. Yet, he was in court to swear on the Bible, that I had claimed the property as my own. It was a bare-faced lie, and I felt sorry that he found the need to do that, in spite of his calling as a man of God. This same Pastor had advised my cousin to withdraw her lies and pay me what was due to me. He knew the details about the ownership of the property and the lease agreement he signed with me said so.

I have come to understand that being a man or woman of God does not a robe of innocence confer. If anything, the church is a spiritual hospital to which all are welcome. I felt very let down by the lies and the false swearing on the Bible. I lost respect for the gentleman.

My ordeal at the Unity Centre was the catalyst in my having a closer walk with God. I was stretched to the limit in every way, through it all; from finding the property, building it and defending my right to enjoy my investment. The opposition I encountered was huge, but I sought and found strength in my faith. The Lord had brought me to the Unity Centre for a reason, and as a result of the seed I sowed, the proceeds of my first gospel album. He let me know that He had a bigger Unity Centre waiting for me. I believe Him!

The Unity Centre – An Ode

It was a covenant place
Into every cement block
Every woodwork
Is my blood, sweat and tears
Patience and sacrifice,
hours of fervent prayers
Sometimes hunger
Sometimes deprivation
But always hope
In quiet meditation
I trusted in the Lord
I held on to my faith
He is a covenant God
Five years of careful planning
Ten more of labour - building
I was financier, fundraiser
Foreman and landscape designer
Through trials, betrayals and self-denial
Setbacks, push backs and nightmares.
My dream was born.
I had what I wanted.
I did not know it would take this long.
I did not know it would cost this much.
Fifty million bucks
Before it stopped.
The Centre for Unity
That brought me nothing but...
Maybe I should have had it named
A Covenant Place

For I gave God something small
An Album called Greatest Love
But He turned around

And gave me Real Estate
Yes, into every window
pane In every door frame
Is that faithful name
The One Who makes a way.

Onyeka Onwenu, August 2007

PART X

By Serendipity –
A Love Story

SERENDIPITY: Finding something good,
without looking for it, a chance occurrence.

There are things in life that one is not able to explain.
They happen, seemingly by chance but, if you examine
them carefully, you may just find that there are no coincidences,
only happenstances that make sense in the end.

To All The Men I've Loved

I f my mother, the indomitable Ochie Dike were alive, she would with feigned consternation ask, on reading the subtitle above, 'So how many men have you loved?' I would look her straight in the eye and with a poker face, give her a one-word answer: 'Many!' She would then roll her eyes, twist her mouth to one side and walk away to mind her own business, aware that her leg had just been pulled.

As you may have noticed, this book is not a kiss-and-tell. However, it is a book of very significant stories. Without question, it is an autobiography. Still, there are aspects of my story that cannot but remain private.

The writing of a book such as mine inevitably throws up emotions that had been carefully laid aside, but which demand revisiting. At some points during the writing process, it became so difficult and painful to carry on, having to remember things that for far too long had been put away. I abandoned the project for months on end. I had to give myself time to regain some strength. I had to accept, all over again, the things I could not change. I had let go and yes, let God. The Serenity Prayer comes to mind here.

This particular memory came back to me at the tail end of the writing of **My Father's Daughter**. It had been so well tucked away that I did not consider writing about it at all. The entire period of 37 yrs – from 1982 to 2019 – save for a brief encounter at a Nigerian airport, was suppressed in my mind. I forgot them. That may have been a coping mechanism and it worked. I had too much going on in my life and I was in survival mode for the whole period. That was until it jumped right back at me – by serendipity.

I fell in love for the first time at the age of 13, in 1965 and two years before the outbreak of the Nigerian civil war. Looking back, I realise that I was indeed too young to know what love was. What does a 13-year-old know about love, anyway?

I am not sure, however, that in my case love was something conceptualised as much as it was intensively felt. I was struck by a bolt of lightning from out of the blues. My heart skipped a beat each time the object of my attraction entered my space, and I wanted to be in his presence for as long as possible. The attraction was not physical at this point. It was a meeting of two souls that effortlessly understood each other. This strong connection was felt from day one, as I saw myself in his eyes and he thought that I was beautiful. The sound of his voice was like something I had heard before; there was a sense of familiarity in it. The attraction between us was so powerful that I said to God, not long after meeting Prince Charming, that I had met the man I was meant to marry. If the person in question was not the one, then God Himself, should just forget it, because I would not marry another. It was an ultimatum.

I was so sure of what I felt that my heart's conviction came out in such a steely, matter of fact way and with so much determination, firmness and finality. It was almost frightening that a girl of 13 would know her mind and express it so fearlessly. What a pugnacious little girl I must have been. I had no idea of the meaning of the words I was uttering; they just came tumbling out from the very depth of my soul.

I did learn a huge lesson afterwards: be careful what you say, what you ask for and what you wish for because you may just get it.

At 13, I was in my second year of secondary school. It was a time when, if you fancied a guy, you stayed far away from him. You were too shy to even admit that he was your love interest. If you saw him on one side of the road, you quickly moved to the other. There would be no contact, only an inner excitement that you had just sighted him. It was the age of innocence.

My prince was a friend of my brother's, and the whole family knew and liked him. They were probably aware of my attraction to him, I think. Later events would bear me out.

During the school holidays, our house was filled with a lot of people, friends, schoolmates and acquaintances.

If you had friends, even of the opposite sex, you brought them home, and they became friends with the whole family. There was no 'corner-corner' love, as we say in pidgin English. Everything was out in the open and devoid of physical contact, of course. My mum was liberal that way. Many times, she would join our debates and interactions. Her looming presence and the training she gave by example let us know that should we betray this trust; we would be 'skinned alive', quite literally. It allowed us to grow up in an atmosphere of trust and responsibility, while enjoying a vibrant circle of friends and the learning opportunities tied to it. I have raised my sons the same way. Today, some of their closest friends are women, intelligent and capable people who they respect and honour.

As the youngest child in the family, I had the opportunity to learn from older minds, both from within and outside. This was because my siblings brought their friends home. My sister, Zoe, however, went the extra mile by taking it upon herself to tutor me in the arts and in comportment – poetry, music, debating, carriage and self-confidence. She was my 'finishing school'. My brother,

Richard, would correct my tenses. In fact, the biggest faux pas to commit in the Onwenu family was to speak grammatically wrong English. However, the corrections were made with humour and met with laughter. We welcomed the exercise as a learning tool. Growing up in this lively and vibrant environment, I was not your regular 13/14-year-old.

My Prince Charming really fit the bill. He was a tall, dark and handsome young man. A versatile, artistic, Shakespeare- quoting kindred spirit who lit up the room for me. There was something very special about him, an uncommon civility that made him interesting to engage. I am not sure that he was fully aware of my feelings for him. I do know that he was fascinated and was always attentive. He was interested in whatever I had to say and never talked down at me. I was treated with a great deal of respect, almost as an equal.

For sure this young man was the romantic focus of a girl's active imagination, one made vivid by fairytales and romantic novels of the cheap kind, like the ones exchanged among friends, worn out, frayed and slightly torn, from use. In those gushing stories, the Princess always got her Prince Charming in the end and they lived happily ever after.

Could this love story, deep and intense as it felt, and hardly understood, be the product of the imagination of a 13-year-old with a creative mind? What were the chances that this strapping, good looking man, fancied by more beautiful and sophisticated women would fall for little, ole me, in a city like Port Harcourt, where he had by far better choices? But he did and hopelessly so.

By the close of 1966, when the echoes of war were heard in Biafra, the 'love of my young life' had left Nigeria for further studies in

Europe. I was trying to survive the war with the rest of my family. My brother, Richard, and sister, Zoe, were also outside the country. My love and I lost contact, and I had no idea whether I would ever see him again.

I remained in love with him all this period. In fact, throughout the Nigeria/Biafra conflict, I was known as Miss 'No Man's land' – the area or piece of land between two sides of a conflict. It belonged to no one. There were a few token and peripheral friendships, for sure, but they were all just that. I wanted to be by myself mostly, alone with my fantasies and my dreams. I constantly thought about the man who had captured my heart.

In 1971, after the war had ended and just months before I was to leave for school in the United States, I ran into Prince Charming on the streets of Lagos. It was quite simply by serendipity.

From then on, and in full view of my family, we began a friendship. I was 19 years old. He was 26. We talked for hours, went out for meals and danced at a family gathering. My love worried in a letter later that my mum may not have approved the obvious relationship.

'Tell me,' he wrote, 'what comments did your mum make regarding our obvious interest in each other that night at the party? I have a feeling she does not approve.'

He needn't have worried; he was like a son to her and at 19, I had matured into a sensible young woman who could take care of herself. I had my mother's trust. In the short period of our reconnection, my love had fallen hopelessly in love with me. For the next three years and with my family's knowledge and acceptance, we began a truly romantic relationship, one which we both expected would end up in marriage. Yet my darling was sensitive and respectful. It was not a physical relationship.

485

I was still a little green behind the ears, having just survived a brutal war and still trying to catch up with a world that had moved ahead of me by four years. Yet my love considered me 'beautiful and extraordinary'. He would write a few weeks after I arrived in the United States, 'Thank you for those photographs you gave me. You are beautiful and you photograph fabulously. Did I give you photographs of Florence? I mean the city of Florence in Italy. I meant to give you some of the shots I took of it. Florence is a city that reminds me of you.'

He Wrote Beautiful Letters

My love and I were from a time when letter writing was how you communicated with people. There were no mobile phones, no email and no Internet. With him in Europe and me in the United States, we wrote regularly, even as we spoke occasionally on the phone. Those letters, I now realise, were instrumental in helping me survive my first two years in a foreign country. Having a friend and a mentor who understood me, who in fact, saw the potential in me before most others did, was the deciding factor in my ability to thrive intellectually and emotionally. His love and attention gave me confidence in myself and my abilities.

As a young woman, being told that you are beautiful, special and unique is an elixir for success. Knowing that there were people who had invested so much faith in you and who would be greatly disappointed if you were to take a wrong turn, meant that you didn't. You had to respect the very confidence they reposed in you. I kept every letter. I read them over and over again. They were a great source of encouragement and support for me.

But for 37 years, I put them away and forgot about them. On the occasions that I did sight them, I had no interest in opening them up. They would have been too painful to read.

But what did I do for Prince Charming? Well, I wrote him letters as well.

I sent him cassette tapes of songs and poetry. I can only tell from his responses that they meant the world to him.

In 1972, he wrote:

As a result of the past few weeks' hectic burst of activities, I got a little fatigued and lost all composure. It was playing your cassette recording while I drove to the office this morning that stroked me back to my natural cool and completely rejuvenated me, especially the string of poems. I love them and I wish I were there to encourage you to do more.

Let me share more excerpts from some of those letters that tell the story of this relationship.

At Baldwin School/Wellesley College – 1971-73

I'm sorry for having not found time in Lagos to talk to you about the changes you were going to encounter in the US. I shall write to you a lot more...you have never been much of a talker but you have got to go out now and make friends. I hate to hear that you were by any measure feeling lonely. I love you and can't sit and watch anything or situation make you unhappy. Try and do a lot of reading and write to me as often as possible about all that you read and observe about America and its society. You will be communicating with me as soon as you sit down to write. Besides, I have already fallen for the way you write.

In another letter, he wrote:

I adore you Onyeka! And one of the facets of you that makes me hold you very high in my books is that you do have great promise and future. I want to be by your side, while you develop. Don't misunderstand the use of the word develop. You have developed far beyond my expectation and you are a beautiful woman. But life itself, in my opinion, is a continuous process of development and we should both share in its excitement.

My sweetheart was a bright and intelligent guy who thought the world of me. He wanted to design clothes for me and take photos to show the world.

Hear him:

> I like the photograph enclosed in your letter. Someday, I shall have you model for me and I can treat the world to photographs of you, taken and printed by me.

In another letter, he wrote:

> Darling, you are indeed a very wonderful lady and someday I shall help you prove it to the world. When you telephone your sisters and Chukwudum (Richard), tell them I love you.

There was no point in keeping quiet about the tremendous connection we both shared. I believe that if it were possible to consummate the relationship with a marriage proposal, my love would have done so. But he was not ready and neither was I, to take on the responsibility of marriage. What he did, however, in the interim, was to serve notice to my family that he was coming for my hand.

At school, in small-town Bryn Mawr, Pennsylvania, alone in a strange land, these letters from the love of my life were a source of emotional sustenance for me. I told my sister, Zoe, about them and she approved, commenting that it would be nice to have him in the family. My love and I talked about everything, from Russian literature to my visits to the Theater and Art Exhibitions.

We discussed the latest books we were reading. He critiqued my school papers and grades, giving praise, encouragement where deserved and advice, where needed. He even commented on my figure; if I were starting to put on weight, he would admonish, ever so gently, but firmly. He was my mentor, motivator, teacher and Svengali. Hear him again:

> Many and sincere congratulations on the results of your last exam. They were remarkable and you must keep up that standard. If I were there, though, you would certainly be forced to improve on every subject.

He went on:

> All your letters are rich sources of joy and rejuvenation to me, so you must continue to write. I love your easy style and the depth of your thoughts. Your earlier letters and the latest, accompanied by your school papers have arrived. I am indeed very proud of the 'Open Letter'. It was brilliant for a newly arrived. You certainly have untold talents which I must see you develop.

On my difficulty with making friends, my love had this to say:

> Don't worry your sweet self about not being able to make friends easily. I love you and you do not have a single fault. Making friends may seem easy when you judge by me but making good friends, real friends, in fact, is by no means easy. Enjoy yourself at your own

pace and in your own style. You are unique.

On mathematics, my most unpopular subject, he offered:

Mathematics is often a pain in the neck for most people. I wish I were around you to help you through with some calculations. On second thought, that may not be such a good idea as I'm too much in love with you now to concentrate on my maths... you are my special person.

On an even more romantic note, my darling wrote:

Spread in front of me now are three of the photographs you gave me during our fateful meeting in Lagos. I could pay anything now to relieve my time with you. In the absence of your very person, I am left with images of you to stave my passions. I love you.

The letters grew even more romantic:

I have according to my watch been sitting here for 3 1/2 hours by this fire. In all that period you have occupied my mind. The setting in this room is just right for dreams. The room is a small front room of a friend's cottage in a small village of ———— . My friend is out and all I can hear is the soft washing sound of River ———, flowing only 30 yards away, past the back garden of this cottage. In this quiet setting, I have let my mind roam all around and over you. I have pictured both of us alone in this room, reading aloud to each other or you playing

Bach to me on a piano. I pictured us waking to a bright but frosty morning and having to walk five miles in the fields before returning to breakfast. Before my friend comes back in to disturb this peace, I must reach you, touch you and tell you that I love you.

It is so beautiful here that I could settle to play out my life's romance, here with you. Your grace, dignity and beautiful love will just add the crowning touch to the whole setting. I have never missed anyone more than I am missing you tonight. When I get to London, I will look for remembrances of you and I will try and get word to your mum. I badly need your presence to sort my whole life out. Much love!

You must be wondering by now why I did not marry my Prince Charming who had fallen head over heels in love with me. I wonder too. Looking back at the time we drifted apart in 1973; I realise that our timing was off.

We were both not ready to marry and settle down; I was a sophomore at Wellesley, with a whole life of learning ahead of me. The intensity of the emotions was overwhelming sometimes. We were still oceans apart and the long-distance romance was tasking. My one visit to Europe at the time, with my sister, Ijeoma, was not a huge success. Family rules demanded a protocol. We had to stay with a first cousin in town and Ijeoma went everywhere with me. She was the unofficial chaperone and she excelled. We had no time together, my love and I, not even to talk. Later on, he had plans to come over to study and live in the United States, but they did not pan out. We lost touch and we both moved on. On my part, I did so, with much sadness. But move on, I did.

My love and I found each other again in 1980, just as I prepared to return to Nigeria for good. It was a momentous reunion, an indescribably exquisite time together. We explored my city, New York, walking on the streets of Manhattan and talking about everything under the sun. We listened to free classical music with the New York Philharmonic Orchestra, together with thousands of others in Central Park. It was my thing to do during the Summer and my love absolutely enjoyed it. Alone together for the first time in eight years, we had a wonderful time rebuilding an almost forgotten friendship. Again, my darling was a sounding board for my ideas about coming home.

The trip to my base in New York had come up on its own and for an entirely different purpose. My darling, however, obtained my number from my brother and got in touch, once he was in town. At the end of this reunion, he declared: 'Being with you is like being with myself.'

I knew exactly what he meant. The feeling was mutual. It always has been that way with us. It came quite naturally. Our time together was always filled with joy and laughter; we could laugh at everything, even ourselves. Sometimes, it was filled with silence, very eloquent silence.

Again, my Prince Charming had found his way back into my life, at a time of great change and transition. Moving back to Nigeria, a rather traumatic venture, was made easier by his friendship, support and counsel. He was even at the airport in Lagos to welcome me back, together with my whole family. He insisted on refunding the money for my ticket back home. He gave it to his friend, my brother, which is why it never got to me.

My acclimatisation to Nigeria complete, my friend and I went our separate ways again. The intensity of our feelings made being just friends very difficult. We lost contact for twenty-seven years until we bumped into each other at a local airport in Nigeria in 2009 and yet again it was by serendipity. He had moved back to Europe and was just visiting. It was a difficult meeting this time. We were like two ships passing each other in the night. We greeted briefly and talked about family, mainly. We did not exchange contacts. I was out of the Airport in a flash, leaving him at the first opportunity I got, almost in mid-conversation. I ran away. Looking back, I understand why. I was going through a lot of emotional upheavals in my on-again, off-again marriage. The worst thing I could have done would have been to add another emotional dimension to the muddle. I fled. After this uneventful chance meeting, I was sure that I could now put this friendship in a box and store it away from view, forever, perhaps.

I thought I had succeeded in doing just that, until serendipity threw up another meeting, one which reconnected us, once again, at a time of great transition in my life.

I was pleasantly surprised to meet my friend again. After the airport sighting in 2009, this meeting had taken 10 years. But then, we had known each other for 55 years. I have tried in all this time to define the relationship I had with this very special person in my life and the continued strong connection we feel as if we were meant to help one another along life's way. I am, however, unable to. I will just draw lessons from it.

The timing of this most recent meeting has provided me with the opportunity to write about someone who had played a major role in my life, even when he was not physically around me. The story of my life would be incomplete without this sometimes sad but always inspiring love story.

My friend and I may be in contact, or we may not. But no matter how many oceans are between us, I remain grateful for this friendship and all that it taught me.

My friend had written in 1980, thus:

> You write so easily and so beautifully. Reading you is like reading one's own mind – in a clearer perspective. One never replies to one's thoughts – they call it talking to one's self and from thereon, it is madness. Please write whenever you can – often!

To the love of my life, I owe a huge debt of gratitude. Thank you for your kindness, for treating me with care, respect and appreciation. Thank you for believing in me. It gave me confidence. You saw my potential, even before I did and you convinced me that I was made for great things. I learned so much from you; even when you were not around, your compassion was palpable. Even now, I feel your encouragement. I hope I have not disappointed you. Thank you for being my brother and mentor, my friend and encourager – for not being afraid to love me for myself, even as a pugnacious 13-year-old. Your friendship has enriched my life and I am glad that I finally have the opportunity to say: Thank you.

May the reader find comfort in the knowledge that God will always put in your path people who are meant to help you along life's journey. But ultimately, my God, my Jesus is my first and last love. Every aspect of love that we are privileged to experience is a gift from Him, a revelation of all that He embodies. He is the Flame that ignites the fire which lights us up to His greater glory. I had written this poem and never really understood it until now.

The Flame

And so must we all come
To the call
The test of faith
Of life
This is the point of reckoning
It beckons
It called us in the past now it's back
Compelling recognition
It's now or never
For it was never this strong

The fire has flared
We see it
Like testy children
It pains us
As would an exposure
So fierce
We pull away
Hurt in the examination
We ponder it
We learn
So it is with all who feel
With all who dare to touch

We will come back to the fire
If we do not
We live not
The fire is the heart of life
The why - the essence
It draws us to itself
We cannot resist it
Yet we cannot abide it.
For we are what we are
What we can modify
But cannot change
The Essence never changes

Onyeka Onwenu, March 15, 1978

PART XI

Sister Goes Home

The Last Time I Saw Her

This is a weighty subject for me, one that I remember with tears and a heavy heart. That is probably why it is surfacing here, at the end of this book of memories. My mother, Mrs Hope Onwenu, passed away on 22 October 2011.

She was two months shy of her 93rd birthday.

Sister had lived with me for ten years in Lagos before her death. You would think that I would be prepared for the eventuality of her passing. She warned me on several occasions that it would be a huge event. But I lived in denial, in the face of her obviously failing health. My mother had the best medical care all of her life, in the country and abroad. I had taken her to Harley Street, London for the treatment of her heart condition and Greaves disease in 1985 when she was in her 60s.

In 2009, we had a major health scare. My mum suffered a stroke and fell in the bathroom. She, however, recovered completely. In my estimation, it was a remarkable comeback. Many people of her age would never have survived it. But this was classic Ochie Dike, solid as a rock, standing *gidigba* as we say in Pidgin English. In actuality the remainder of her time was short, but I still lived in stubborn denial.

One of the major challenges I had been a caregiver to my mum was my inability to spend enough time with her. I was the breadwinner; I had to work very hard to take care of everyone and scarcely had any free time. But I had no social life either, so when I was not working, I was at home and she had my full attention.

Twice every week, I gave up my car so she could be driven around to visit her friends, or go to the market to buy fabrics and gifts for the women in the village, one of her core constituencies. I would take her to church every Sunday and hand her over to her church members, while I attended mine. We would then go home together to a sumptuous lunch prepared by me.

It was a big surprise to my mum that my sister Ijeoma and I turned out to be good cooks. We did not pay much attention to the kitchen while growing up, but somehow, we were watching and learning all the while. Sister particularly loved my *onugbu* (bitter leaf) soup with fresh fish and pounded yam. She is from Obosi in Anambra State, where they make the best. Therefore, it was hugely flattering for me that she was impressed by my version of that revered dish. Sister also loved my Sunday meals. She would have on offer chicken, guinea fowl or prawns, marinated in garlic and ginger and steamed to perfection. There was jollof or fried rice and the inevitable salad as well.

My mum's vegetable salad was the best I ever tasted. It was a culinary masterstroke, one of the skills she acquired in Freetown, Sierra Leone when she accompanied my father to Fourah Bay College. Thankfully though, I could match her culinary abilities as I had watched her do it since I was a child. The vegetable salad consisted of lettuce, parsley, beetroot, peas, baked beans, potatoes, sardine, white onions, eggs and cabbage. It was topped with a salad cream dressing. If you lived at 1 Degema Street, our compound in Port Harcourt, you got this every Sunday and during the holidays. You also got a share of a whole goat that was slaughtered for special occasions.

The Jolting Truths

Much as we had the 'Jolting Lies' earlier in the book which tended to confuse and disappoint, there was also the flip side. I call it the 'Jolting Truths'.

I recall vividly the unforgettable moment in 2008 when my mother declared: '*Ebe a kam mu onwe m*' – 'This is where I gave birth to myself '. I had always suspected that most times when I butted heads with Sister, it was because we were very much alike. I was not just an independent-minded person, but stubborn too. My mother's statement would appear to have come out of left-field, but she was right. We were alike in more ways than one. I had Sister's discipline and ability to take shocks and keep going. My mother had her own swagger and charismatic presence. I got a bit of that too. But all the while, I thought I was so much like my father and only him.

Once in 1975, my mum came visiting at Wellesley College in Massachusetts. On our way back from shopping in Boston, we got into an argument and I told her, offhandedly, that I did not see the reason why my father married her. My mother exploded on me: 'Your father was not exactly perfect; he had faults, you know.' For the first time, I came off my high horse regarding my father and began to see him as a human being, not just an angel.

I classified this as really the first 'Jolting Truth', the second being that I was also very much my mother's daughter.

The third 'Jolting Truth' came in 2009, two years before her death.

'*Gi ka m na rapulu ezi na uno a*', meaning 'I am leaving the family in your hands'. With those words, Sister sentenced me to a lifetime of receivership for the Onwenu family and she told no one else. How do I make decisions when my brother and one sister are working at crossroads with me? My mother was again dumping all the family problems on me because she knew that she could. She was not asking me to do anything she had not done herself. Even if she had not 'handed it over to me', she knew that I would have taken care of business. I loved my father too much to let his family go under. That had been our shared goal, my mum and I.

My dilemma, however, was how to explain it to my siblings. In the end, I did not have to. Events and happenstances, conveniences and inconveniences all conspired to put me in the position of caretaker for the Onwenu family. Sister was right all along. She saw far into the future. Ochie Dike, I salute your foresight.

My mother, Mrs Hope Onwenu, held keenly to the mantra of 'life must go on, so get on with it.' If God gave everyone a special battery to endure life's hard times, He gave my mother three. Sister never lost sight of the fact that life was greater than the sum total of the hard knocks one had to endure. It was worth living because it had a purpose. For her, the joy of serving the Lord was more than sufficient, no matter what one had to go through.

From the day my mother made that declaration 'This is where I gave birth to myself ', I gained a better understanding of my strengths. One of the things I remember my mother for was her faith in God, much like her own mother. God was not just her Heavenly Father but also her husband. She was widowed for the second time at age 37. She did not marry a third time; instead, she remained committed solely to raising a house full of children.

After her treatment in London for Greaves disease, Sister was placed on a special medication for the rest of her life. The prescription was difficult to find in Nigeria and very expensive too. But my sister Ijeoma and I ensured that it was always available. Three years later, my mum took herself off the medication and gave God an ultimatum. Heal me or take me home. God healed her. She never took that medication again. She lived for an additional 26 years.

My mother had an effortless elegance to her. She was not only good looking but fashionable as well, with her own style. Indeed, she was a trendsetter, even in her old age. Sister's colours were always well-coordinated and she liked gold trinkets. Her father, Papa Nnukwu, once joked that when the time came to go, as it would for all mortals, the only way to tell whether Sister was dead or not would be to dangle a piece of gold trinket in front of her eyes. If she did not get up, then surely, she was gone.

Living with me, my mum lacked nothing, but she was lonely for someone her age and orientation. There was so much she could talk about to the two housekeepers we had, or to any of her nieces or nephews who came around. My mother's closeness to her only sister, Aunt Dorothy, meant that any time they were separated for long, my mum would miss her dearly. It was, therefore, a relief when Sister announced that she was relocating to Obosi to spend time with her brother Ernest and sister, Aunt Dorothy, who had just returned from visiting her children in the United States.

We prepared her for the trip, putting in place all the required funds and appurtenances that would make her stay comfortable. My mum was in Obosi for eight months before she indicated interest to come back to Lagos. However, she had fallen ill with malaria and had to be admitted into Iyienu Hospital in nearby Ogidi. The intent was to get her stabilised before flying her back to Lagos.

My brother had been in Obosi with our mum and gave me the impression that she was getting better when she was not. Sister repeatedly asked for me, as she slipped in and out of coma. I was advised to just send the funds for her treatment. Speaking with my son TC, who was in school in San Francisco, about his grandmother's illness, he advised me to drop everything and go see her for myself. The very next day and just five days before her death, I flew into Asaba Airport and drove straight to Iyienu Hospital. On seeing her condition, I decided to move her back to Lagos with me, but the doctors advised against it.

As I walked into Sister's hospital room, something interesting happened. My mother, who was seated on a chair with her back to the door, made a half-turn and asked:

'O onye?'

'Who is it?' Her question carried all the certainty of one who already knew the identity of who was walking into the room. Sister had sensed my presence.

Now in the room and facing her, I answered, 'O mu.' This means 'It is me.'

My mother's face crinkled in a cry as if to say, 'I am going.' I quickly took charge of the situation and comforted her.

There was no reason to cry, I assured her. I told her I was fully in control and would keep all the promises I had made to her. I asked if I had ever broken a promise to her and she shook her head, suggesting her faith in my steadfastness.

'I have never broken my promises to you, and I am not about to start now,' I confirmed.

I watched her face come alive with a bold smile shining through the wrinkles. She was now more relaxed; it seemed. I had brought with me her favourite drink, Irish Cream, which I poured into glass cups and we both drank.

My mother and I had talked a lot about death and dying after her stroke in 2009. I took the time to prepare her for what we both knew was coming. That was when she shared with me her pact with God for an easy death. I shared with her all I knew about near death experiences, and how some people who had to come back to life did not want to because it was so much better on the other side. This was very comforting for her, I sensed. She gave her life to Christ then, even though previously she had not been so accepting of the Pentecostal style of worship, but she gave her life all the same.

I found my mother's comb and plaited her hair. While I was doing so, I raised choruses of 'Ochie Dike', 'Alleluya', 'Bia Nulu' and other songs. We sang to our hearts' content, together with my sister, Azunna. We had a good time. I could not believe that my mum, who was not so openly demonstrative of affection, had allowed me to cuddle and kiss her. I could not remember the last time I did that, as an adult. But on that occasion, she was absolutely happy to let me.

Soon though, Ochie Dike began to tire from all the excitement of seeing me, from all the singing, hugging and teasing, and the Irish Cream. She asked to be helped back to bed. We made her comfortable and she quickly fell asleep. That was our last encounter, our last party, our last performance together. But I still had no idea of what was to come. I went back to Lagos to put my affairs in order and return to Obosi to stay with my mum until she was strong enough to travel back with me.

Before I left her, I said a prayer at her feet. It was a prayer confirming the covenant she had with God. My mum had told her God that she did not want a long hospital stay. She did not want the sort of death that was preceded by a protracted illness, a situation where her family and children were drained before her passing. When it was time for her to go, she wanted the journey to be short and full of ease. I simply reminded God of their agreement and asked Him to either heal her or make her well enough for me to take her to her doctors in Lagos. If not, He should call her to glory in the manner she had wished.

Perhaps I should have known that my intercession would bring a quick response. I had said the prayer but surely, God knew that I still needed my mum around. I fully expected to take her back to Lagos with me.

I visited Sister on Wednesday. I planned to return on Sunday. On Friday, she seemed well on her way to recovery and was upbeat. I spoke with her and prayed over her, while she muttered 'Amen.' (My sister, Ijeoma, was doing the same from the US). Azunna was with her during the day, and my brother Richard had just returned to Lagos to refresh, after spending a week with her.

That Friday, she ate breakfast and dinner very well and sat up quite a bit. She even engaged the nurses in conversation, but it had all been a smokescreen; a veil of comfort that masked an ending whose time had come. My mother's time had come, and that was it.

At 6 a.m on Saturday, I got a call from Sister's caregiver who always spent the night with her. I immediately knew what it was about. The young lady was in tears and spoke through muffled gasps. She said that my mother was not responsive and was not breathing normally. I sent for the nurses who, shortly afterwards, confirmed that my mother, Ochie Dike, Hope Onwenu had passed away. I exhaled with a deep howling sound that came from an unknown place within. The unthinkable had happened.

Nothing prepares anyone for the death of a parent, no matter how old they are. I felt instantly that something great had been severed from me. My mother had left the earthly realm, and I was at once overcome by a deep sense of loss and emptiness. It dawned on me in the intervening days that a special emotional tissue that held us together, that bond that made her show me the discipline of a mother and the supportive shoulder of a sister was no more.

I would cast my mind back on how my mum repeatedly asked about me. It appeared as though she needed my permission to die, with reassurances coming from my own lips of all I would do for her memory and the family when she was gone. Sister needed to know that I would do everything I said I would do. She secured that promise once more and died peacefully.

While Sister and Papa now rest with God and the angels, I still live, day to day, patently mindful of preserving their good name, for I am the sum total of them both. Papa had the charisma and vision that I embodied and which saw me rise to stardom with ease, yet none of it would have lasted for long were it not for the discipline I inherited from my mother. I also inherited my mother's showmanship. She had her own charisma. It was powerful, resilient, elegant and sublime, all at once. Sister was someone you could rely on to get things done and she would do so with aplomb, no matter the difficulties. She was never off-footed and if she were, you wouldn't know it.

Hope Onwenu was never afraid to speak her mind; she spoke her truth, and you could either take it or leave. Sister attended events by herself, representing the man and the family she loved so much. She did not have a husband beside her - she was a widow – but when she walked into a room, there was grace and dignity all around her. That made me proud.

Ochie Dike taught me to avoid conflict by all means.

'Bend over backwards or walk away, if need be,' she admonished. 'But if you are pushed to the wall and there is nowhere else to go, then fight like your father.'

'How did my father fight?' I asked, the first time.

'Like a wounded lion,' she replied. I suspect that she had the same trait herself.

So, for all the discipline I needed to preserve the gifts that God gave me to share with the world, I have my mother, Ochie Dike, Hope Onwenu to thank.

Daalu Ochie Dike, Ogbueshi nwanyi, Nwunye dim okpanpkulu ito. Nwunye DK Onwenu, Ogalanya nwanyi, Onye obi oma, Omenanwata, Daalu ezigbo nwanyi! Nwoke Iri akaro gi!

Warrior of old
One who slaughtered cows
My mate with three toes (a joke we shared)
The wife of DK Onwenu
A woman of great wealth
A kindhearted woman
One who did great things even in her youth
Good woman.
A woman greater than 10 men put together.

Sister Goes Home in A Blaze of Glory

Most families thrive even with the occasional disenchantment among members, and mine is no exception. Indeed, most families are dysfunctional and it is on occasions such as burials that emotions tend to become heightened. Conflicts of who pays for what and who inherits what escalates into unhealthy dimensions. My mother's burial provided such a scenario.

On the night of 11 January 2012, which was the day before Sister's burial, it became obvious to me that someone with a powerful influence over my siblings was determined to ruin the day for the DK Onwenu family. Our family was fractured right down the middle with Richard and Ijeoma on one side, and Azunna and I on the other. This was despite the fact that we all saw it coming and had vowed, holding hands in prayer, that we would not allow anyone to spoil the day for Ochie Dike, no matter the provocation.

Amidst the looming imbroglio, I got down on my knees and prayed a tearful prayer. I asked my mother and father if this was how they wanted it to go down. I said that if they were in heaven, they needed to intercede on behalf of the family they left in my care. I was emotionally exhausted, physically too, but I had to give my mum a befitting burial. I challenged God to keep His promise and step into the matter as the Father He is and had always been to me.

My prayers were answered, but it was not obvious until we got to the church for the funeral service. With me in this early morning heart cry to God were my sister Azunna and cousins Izunwanne, Esther and Gladys – all Uncle Charles's daughters. We slept in one big room, some on the bed and others on mattresses on the floor. It was my room, the only one that had been left open while Richard and Ijeoma were still in Obosi for a ceremony that Azunna and I had not been invited to.

My eldest sister had, in the meantime, surprised me with her preparations for the post-interment entertainment of guests. I had brought a caterer for the occasion, and so had Azunna. I bought a big cow for meat, Azunna did likewise and Ijeoma as well. Slaughtering a cow at the funeral of a parent is an Igbo tradition and we made sure that we were not found wanting in that department. There was so much to eat and drink – just the way Sister wanted it.

The people of Arondizuogu, particularly Obinetiti where she held sway as benefactor extraordinaire, were agog with excitement though tinged with sadness. They knew that there would never be another Ochie Dike.

I had been refused permission to set up a tent to receive and entertain my friends and political associates after the burial. Having contested for Local Government Chairmanship eight years in a row, I had quite a few. My cousin, Goddy Onwenu and my brother Richard, bluntly ordered that my political associates were not welcome. I had repainted the family house and had the surroundings cleared and ready. I refurbished my father's grave, repaired the water cistern and generator set, all which I had provided myself.

Ochie Dike's coffin was very special. We knew what she wanted and I ensured that she got it. But someone was unhappy that the money was not handed over to him to spend. He wanted to control the funds but found it condescending when asked to render an account.

I had to be careful that whatever money was being spent was properly deployed. There was no room for misplaced expenditures or work half done.

Sometime in 1990, my mum in her wisdom decided to sell to me a piece of land adjacent to the Onwenu compound. She had purchased it from Mazi Owette, a distant relation. Since it belonged to her and not my father, she had the right to dispose of it any way she wanted. Sister called a meeting that involved Richard and Mama Goddy as witnesses. She sold the property to me for a considerable sum. According to her, she would have preferred to give me the land as a gift for all I had done for the family, but she did not want to be accused of showing favouritism. She, therefore, sold it for profit.

Sister wanted to keep me close to the family home, should I decide to build my own house in the village. It was on this piece of land that I decided to set up a tent, whether brother Richard and cousin Goddy wanted it or not. It was my land, not theirs.

According to Igbo tradition, Richard stood to inherit all that belonged to my father, being the only male child. Sister's clothes, trinkets and any movable properties belonged to her daughters. But as far as Richard was concerned, everything of value left behind by our deceased mother belonged to him and he would dispose of them any way he wanted.

Before the burial, he ordered Azunna and I out of the family home. We moved into a cousin's house. His widow, Mrs Lizzy Nwokocha, gave us full reign of their huge compound for our use. After the burial, brother Richard took over all my landed property in Arondizuogu. It did not matter that I bought them all myself. In this, he was fully supported by our cousin, Goddy, who maintained that as a woman, I had no right to own any landed property.

But I would not be dragged into any quarrels about funds and inheritance. I paid for Sister's burial as I had promised; my sisters Azunna and Ijeoma made their own contributions. Sister was buried in the manner that she had wanted. I probably surpassed her expectations. I hoped so, anyway.

Azunna and I were deprived of sharing in our mother's personal property, her clothes and her gold. But we were not bothered about that. All that mattered was ensuring that we kept our promise to our mother that her burial would be special.

Just a year after Sister passed, Aunt Dorothy sold off two landed properties; my mum had purchased in Obosi. The papers had been altered to favour Aunt Dorothy, whose properties were close to Sister's. We did not raise a whisper, except to let her and other relatives know that we were aware of what she had done. We did exactly what Sister would have wanted us to do under the circumstances – walk away.

My mother's funeral service was beautiful and moving. It was quite long because it was difficult to break away. I rendered the song 'Ochie Dike Nnem', with everyone singing along.

When the presiding pastor got on the pulpit, his admonitions and the response of the audience blew me away. I thought people did not know about the oppressive conduct of some members of my family. I did not think they knew the role Aunt Dorothy was playing to ruin the ceremony. When she walked up to the altar to make negative comments about Azunna and I, the Bishop, ignored her and no one would allow her to speak a second time. Then came the clincher, a no holds barred sermon which not only underlined the exemplary life of sacrifice my mum lived but also indicted Aunt Dorothy Ejindu for dividing, instead of uniting, the family of her sister.

In the words of the man of God, 'Onyeka is who she is and you cannot put her in a bottle. She must be allowed to shine.'

To make matters worse, my siblings were chided for not taking any interest in supporting the church and I was praised for doing the very opposite. Of a truth, that was one praise I probably did not need. Certainly not at that moment. It put me more in jeopardy within the family as I could not convince them that I had not arranged for such a sermon to be preached. At any rate, I was in trouble.

My mother's burial was a very successful one and we put the devil to shame. After she was interred, a carnival of sorts sprang up. My musical group, Kabassa, was on the bandstand and all manner of dancing groups came from far and near, even from Amichi, the town that loved my father and where he is still revered. I have Pastor Amaka Maduneme and her husband, Mr. Maduneme, to thank for that.

Every so often, during the last five years of her life, my mum would ask me, '*I g'emenwukwia? Aburokwam obele nmadu*', which means 'Are you equal to the task? I'm not a small person, you know?'

But that, I already knew. Yet, I did not appreciate the enormity of what was to come, until the day was upon me.

Sometimes when my stubborn mother could not have her way, she would threaten to go back to Obinetiti, Arondizuogu. I used to think it was an empty threat because I would have to be the one to make all the arrangements and provision anytime she wanted to spend time at the country home. But she was really talking about her death, as that was where she would be buried. It only hit me as we prepared to lower her in the grave.

Goodness me! I wish that I understood on time.

Six months after Sister's burial, my brother passed away in his sleep of an apparent heart attack. We should have suspected that he would have a harder time coping with our mother's death. They were very close. Richard's death was a shocking blow to the family. It was devastating for me. I thought of what I could have done to avert it, but I am not God. It still hurts.

After his burial in August 2012, Ijeoma was soon back to her station in the United States and Azunna was back in Obosi with her husband. The job of caretaker for the DK Onwenu family fell on me again. Pretending to defer my responsibilities to the Onwenu family was akin to running from one's shadow. My mother had been right all along.

One image of my mother remains in my mind. It best captures her character, attitude and stance in general. This story was told to me by my dear friend, Justice Pearl Amobi-Enejere. Our grandfathers had been bosom friends, from childhood to old age. Pearl's father and my mum, both of the same age group, were friends as well. They teased each other to no end, with jokes and jabs that were well humoured. Once when my mother was ill and Pearl's father came to visit, he left my mum with these words.

'I see that at the rate you are going, you are likely to see the old departed before me,' he said. 'Please tell them that they should not be impatient, I am not ready to come home yet. You can greet them for me.'

My mother defiantly got well, I suspect, just so she could prove him wrong.

In the story that Pearl told, she was in the church in Obosi with her dad when my mum, well dressed in a very beautiful outfit, walked in. Pearl complimented her.

'Ochie Dike, this dress is really something else,' Pearl said.

My mum turned, playfully raised an eyebrow, then swung back around and declared — '*Ana m anu ife?*' *It was a rhetorical* question, one which acknowledged the compliment; In other words - 'Do I give a damn?'

That was my mother – Hope Onwenu.

THE END.

Lady Onyeka Owenu was born 1952 and grew up in the city of Port Harcourt. After receiving her education in Nigeria and the US, she returned in 1980 and took the country by storm as a broadcaster, singer/songwriter, actress, social critic and politician. Ms Onwenu has won many national and international awards in recognition of her inspirational work in many fields, she is a mother, role model and motivator.

Made in the USA
Middletown, DE
04 August 2024